D0811976

The Catholic Subjects of Elizabeth I

The Catholic Subjects of Elizabeth I

ADRIAN MOREY

ROWMAN AND LITTLEFIELD
TOTOWA, NEW JERSEY

© George Allen & Unwin (Publishers) Ltd., 1978

First published in the United States 1978 by
Rowman and Littlefield, Totowa, N.J.

Library of Congress Cataloging in Publication Data

Morey, Adrian, 1904—
  The Catholic subjects of Elizabeth I.

  Bibliography: p.
  Includes index.
  1. Catholics in England—History. 2. Elizabeth,
  Queen of England, 1533–1603. 3. Persecution—
  England. I. Title.
BX1492.M57   282'.0942   77–2231
ISBN 0–87471–970–4

Printed in Great Britain

Contents

Acknowledgements

The story of lost causes will always retain its interest, and the survival of a minority, whether religious, national or political, will always retain its significance. The Elizabethan Catholics have therefore received considerable attention from historians, and this brief outline is based on the published source material, specialist monographs and articles that have been published in recent years. I have endeavoured to place the emphasis of the story on the Elizabethan Catholics themselves and on the way of life possible for them, with less stress on the familiar background of the plots.

The late Professor David Knowles read a first draft of this book, and Professor G. R. Elton very kindly allowed me to discuss some of the questions with him. I am especially grateful to Dr David Rogers of the Bodleian Library, whose specialist knowledge and hospitality have always been available. I was also able to discuss the work of Cardinal Pole with Dr R. Pogson and to draw on his unpublished thesis, 'Cardinal Pole: Papal Legate to England' in Mary Tudor's reign. Lastly my thanks are due to the staff of the University Library, Cambridge and to Dom Mark Pontifex, Librarian of Downside Abbey, Bath.

The language of quotations from source material has been modernised, and the term 'recusant' is used in the limited sense of 'Catholic' recusant.

1 Queen and Cardinal: The Restoration of Catholicism 1553-8

That accursed school, and that apostate household, of
the Cardinal of England.

Paul IV

The task of restoring Catholicism in England after the death
of the young King Edward VI in 1553 fell to two idealists,
neither of whom was gifted with political judgement. If
Queen Mary and her cousin Cardinal Pole came unprepared
to the opportunity that the accident of death provided, they
shared a common background of past suffering at the hands
of Henry VIII. Mary's formative years had been over-
shadowed by the tragedy of her mother and by her opposition to the religious changes of her father; the Cardinal had
lived out his youth in exile and had lost a mother, brother
and cousin by execution at Henry's command. The story that
the new Queen had her father's embalmed corpse disinterred
from its grave at Windsor and burnt may have had some
foundation: it was related by the Jesuit Robert Persons in
Elizabeth's reign, but he had heard it from Sir Francis
Englefield, one of Mary's councillors who claimed to have
been present. If the Queen was thus revenged on an unloved
father, the Cardinal regarded himself almost as a martyr at
that father's hands, an attitude that did not commend him
to colleagues in the English episcopate who had lived through
the dangers and uncertainties of two reigns instead of the

safety of exile. The two principals in the Catholic restoration were not then forward-looking : they could neither forget nor forgive the past.

Twenty years had passed since Henry VIII had cast off papal authority and devised his own form of Catholicism, and during those years religion had suffered a series of changes with a generation reaching maturity unused to stability in religious affairs. If Protestantism was now to show its vitality by its martyrs and exiles, there is evidence of disillusion and cynicism, especially among the governing class. Protestantism tended to flourish in London and the south-east where foreign influence was strong, and secret Protestant congregations were to survive under Mary.[1] However, in the rest of the country, wherever Catholicism had a hold at all it was a Catholicism that for twenty years had been cut off from European influence and had missed the rekindling of the Counter Reformation.

The new Queen's plans for a fresh settlement of religion could not be completed until the arrival of a papal legate, and this was delayed for more than a year. During this initial period Parliament, in spite of a substantial and hostile minority, withdrew authorisation of the *Book of Common Prayer* and the prohibition of the Mass. Hence, from December 1553 the permitted liturgy was that of the last years of Henry VIII. But the government failed to secure the repeal of all laws concerning religion passed since 1529, and the Commons also refused to repeal the royal supremacy.

Foreign envoys at this time saw no enthusiasm in London for the restoration of Catholic worship, although it was effected without marked opposition. The Queen's determination to restore papal authority was another matter. It is doubtful if the ordinary people held any opinions on this question, while the younger generation had never known a papal England. On the other hand, members of the governing class, all those implicated in earlier religious changes or who had profited by them, could not be otherwise than strongly opposed. Yet there were limits to the opposition of Tudor Parliaments, and the third, and most compliant, Parliament of the reign passed the necessary legislation and also lifted the attainder placed on Cardinal Pole eighteen years earlier. Significantly, it exacted an assurance that there would be no compulsory restitution of church lands.

The choice of Reginald Cardinal Pole as papal legate by Rome was almost inevitable and in many ways suitable. Of royal descent through his mother, who was a niece of Edward IV and Richard III, he was a man of personal distinction untainted by past compromise, a humanist and an early church reformer. As Governor of the Patrimony of St Peter in the Papal States he had befriended at Viterbo some distinguished scholars who had been suspected of heresy. In 1550 he had narrowly missed election to the papacy. He was still regarded as *papabile*, so that his nomination as legate by Pope Julius III in August 1553 aroused interest and expectation. When the Cardinal reached the Netherlands the English ambassador in Brussels reported favourably : Pole was free of ambition 'for his living is already so honourable . . . he looks for no more neither honour or estimation', and his aim was 'the established wealth of his native country'. Arrived in England, he declined appointment as Chancellor, and his personal holiness won respect. Even the Protestant Nicholas Ridley, who refused to remove his hat out of respect for the legate's office, was prepared to do so out of respect for the man.[2]

The appointment also had its disadvantages. The legate had lived away from England for more than twenty years, and although he now returned eagerly to his native land he was in fact more at home in Italy and brought with him a largely Italian household. He does not seem to have appreciated the full significance of the recent past or of the extent to which the ruling class had a strong vested interest in material profit derived from the Reformation. Even as a young man at the head of a princely household in Padua, Pole had been a somewhat withdrawn and reticent figure, although he attracted a wide circle of friends and the members of his own household were devoted to him. Some contemporaries in England were now to find him lacking in warmth and inspiration, and the troubled times through which he had lived had left their mark. He was not a priest and had little experience of pastoral work, seeming unable to appreciate the great need in England of a missionary clergy. His royal background, and his mother's devotion to Catharine of Aragon and her daughter, made him a natural confidant of the Queen. However, Cardinal Granvelle, who was himself a polished diplomat and administrator, had formed no great opinion of Pole as a man of affairs during the latter's enforced stay in the Netherlands.

For fifteen frustrating months the legate's arrival had been delayed by the Emperor, who was anxious not only to prevent the possibility that Pole might oppose Mary's marriage to Philip of Spain but also to obtain Pole's acceptance of the need to abandon hope of securing restoration of the lost church lands. Towards the end of November 1554 Pole at last reached London. Four months earlier the Queen had made her disastrous marriage to Philip, and her earlier popularity was lost amid much discontent, which the pomp and circumstance of the legate's reception could not disguise. Armed with full powers of absolution for the holders of former church property Pole was able, albeit unwillingly, to grant the request of Parliament, supported by that of Convocation, that owners of church lands might 'without scruple of conscience enjoy them . . . clear from all dangers of censures of the Church'. On 30 November 1554 the formal reconciliation of England with Rome took place, in a joint session of both Houses of Parliament attended by the Queen and her husband. The actors in this historic scene could not foresee that in less than five years the two royal cousins, Queen and Cardinal, would both be dead and their work would be undone.

It was now the legate's task to purge the Church of Protestant elements and stimulate a renewal of Catholic life, clearly no easy matter. The years of religious change had left a plundered church served by a clergy of poor education and low morale. The priesthood had ceased to attract either as a vocation or as a career, and there had been a steep decline in the number and quality of those ordained. The findings of the Protestant Bishop Hooper of Gloucester are well known: of 311 clergy in the diocese, 39 did not know where the Lord's

Prayer was to be found in the Bible and 34 did not know who was its author. Such was the clergy on which a Catholic renewal had largely to depend. In spite of the enormous confiscation of Church property that had been such a feature of the English Reformation, nothing had been done to improve the economic status of the parochial clergy or to remove inequalities of income. In turn, this affected the quality of recruitment. Many parishes had no resident priest, and the steady dilapidation of church buildings had continued unchecked; a laity that had seen its parish churches stripped of their treasures no longer showed the generosity of past generations. A reform of the whole parochial system was long overdue. These complex problems needed sound administration, finance, and above all time for their solution, and in fact they were still largely unsolved by the end of Elizabeth's reign.

A good beginning was made with the appointment of new bishops. Of those who survived of Henry VIII's appointment seven had suffered imprisonment or deprivation under Edward VI; these were restored to their sees. No new appointments were made as a reward for secular services to the Crown, and the background of the new bishops was mainly theological and pastoral. Led by Archbishop Heath of York this was substantially the hierarchy that was later to refuse all compromise with the Elizabethan church settlement. The ministration of married clergy was soon forbidden, and steps were taken to discipline those clergy who had taken advantage of the permission to marry given by the 1547 Convocation and the 1549 Act. These offending clerics were ordered to put away their wives, to perform an act of public penance, and to be deprived of benefice, although in most cases the latter merely involved removal to another parish. It has been estimated that one-sixth of all parishes were affected overall, but the number of married clergy varied in different parts of the country : from nearly one in three in the London diocese to one in ten in the York diocese. One conservative contemporary, Robert Parkyn, saw the rout of his married brethren with satisfaction : 'How it was joy to hear and see how these carnal priests . . . did lower and look down, when they were commanded to leave and forsake their concubines and harlots and to do open penance'.[3]

As papal legate Pole was given the widest powers, and from time to time he was urged by his Roman authorities to use his own judgement and not to refer back for confirmation. In March 1556 he succeeded Cranmer as Archbishop of Canterbury and so retained his position as primate when his authority as papal legate was revoked in 1557. The most important use made of his powers was to summon a national synod in December 1555, uniting the two provinces of Canterbury and York in one assembly. This gave the legate an opportunity to meet his leading clergy and to learn from them what was needed for a programme of renewal. He was well pleased with the result. In its first session the synod discussed doctrine and the scriptures. It also made plans for a translation of the New Testament and for the establishment of seminaries in cathedral towns for the training of new clergy. Great emphasis was laid on the duty of preaching, as urged by the Council of Trent, the Pope and the Queen, and as an interim measure homilies were to be prepared for the use of unskilled clergy. Two of the Cardinal's foreign correspondents, the Archbishop of Toledo and Ignatius Loyola, were critical of him for a certain lack of initiative in this field, but although Pole was diffident of his own powers as a preacher he took his share of this duty in the dioceses of both Canterbury and London.

The scrutiny of candidates for the priesthood and their training were matters of prime importance. It was Pole's intention that the new cathedral seminaries should be open to the sons of both rich and poor alike, whether or not they were destined to the priesthood. The cost of the seminaries was to be covered by a levy on the bishops and higher clergy. Cranmer's school at Canterbury already provided an example, and the legate had first-hand knowledge of the Acolytes' school that his friend Giberti had revived in the diocese of Verona. Pole's decree on this subject was issued in 1556, was printed at Rome six years later, and influenced the decrees of the

Council of Trent in 1563. In view of his concern for the
education of future priests it is surprising that he rejected the
offer of Ignatius Loyola to train young Englishmen at Rome.[4]

The legate also encouraged the restoration of monasticism,
and in the short time available seven foundations were made.
The most notable of these was the refoundation of Westminster Abbey, which resulted from a petition to the Queen
by a group of the dispossessed monks. Two other historic
communities were restored : the Carthusians of Sheen and
the Bridgettine nuns of Syon, a community founded by Henry
V in 1415.[5]

The synod also reviewed the financial state of the Church,
a complex task that it was unable to complete. In the autumn
of 1555 the Queen renounced by statute the income from
first fruits and tenths : the first being a tax annexed by Henry
VIII from the Pope, and the second being a new tax that he
had imposed on the clergy. The Church now became responsible for the payment of pensions to the former monks and
nuns, an additional administrative burden to the legate's heavy
load. Part of the income made available by the Crown was
to be used for education and for the relief of poor clergy. In
normal times the first fruits or first year's income on a new
bishop's appointment would have gone to the Pope, but Pope
Paul IV had genuine concern for the poverty of the English
Church at this moment and in July 1555 gave the legate
authority to retain in England all money due as papal taxes.[6]

After passing twelve decrees the synod was prorogued so
that bishops and clergy could spend Lent with their people.
It was destined not to meet again, for with the loss of his
legatine office in April 1557 Pole lost this legal power to
summon a synod of the whole English Church. The work
accomplished was therefore incomplete, but within its limits
it was constructive and, given time, might have done much
to inspire both clergy and people.

One problem that could not easily be solved resulted from
the condition and furnishing of the churches on which the
right ordering of services depended. Throughout the reign
royal commissioners were investigating what had happened

to the church plate and valuables that, confiscated during the reign of Edward VI, had failed to reach the Court of Augmentations and had disappeared into private hands. When such property was found it proved difficult to induce the new owners to part with it. Visits to the dioceses of Canterbury and Lincoln revealed a depressing picture : 90 out of 146 churches visited by the legate were in urgent need of structural repair, while priests and parishioners were often unable to pay for the new service books and vestments.

While this inevitably slow work of restoration was proceeding there was, as in the previous reign, much unrest in the country, breaking at times into open rebellion. The most dangerous moment for the Queen came with the Kentish rising of Sir Thomas Wyatt in 1554, which was primarily political and largely inspired by opposition to the Spanish marriage.[7] Mary and some of her advisers, however, believed that the uprising originated in opposition to the government's religious policy, and it convinced her of the need to stamp out heresy at all costs. Thus began a grim process of persecution. Protestants who wished to leave the kingdom were not hindered, so about 800 went into exile, mostly members of the gentry, clergy and professional classes. Many of these were to have great influence when they returned after the Queen's death;[8] In exile too were trained nearly 100 future ministers. The burning of heretics began in February 1555 after Parliament had revived the old heresy laws. Most of them occurred in London and the south-east, only one being recorded in the diocese of York. By Mary's death in November 1558 some 273 people, chiefly of humble status and including women, had been executed.

The burning of heretics was not something new. Cranmer himself had condemned heretics to this death, a few were to suffer in Elizabeth's reign and the last burning of a heretic occurred in 1612. Both Catholics and Protestants shared the conviction that heresy deserved death, but it was the scale of the Marian burnings that made such an impression. Moreover, it could be argued that most of the Protestant martyrs of Mary's reign had had legal approval of their views under the previous government. In a supplication to the Queen and Parliament in January 1555, the London preachers declared that they had acted 'as the laws of God at all times and the statutes of the realm did then allow'. In Elizabeth's reign the publication of Foxe's *Book of Martyrs* was to make powerful and lasting propaganda against the Catholic cause and, by equating the burnt heretics' sufferings with those of the martyrs of the primitive church, was to help foster the idea of the English as a chosen people.[9] Queen Mary was undoubtedly the driving force behind these burnings, urging on bishops and officials to a duty some certainly found uncongenial. It was all the more tragic since Mary was in other respects a merciful ruler compared with her father; when 600 men were brought before her after Wyatt's rebellion, 'coupled together two and three, a rope running between them', she pardoned and released them all. Cardinal Pole cannot escape his share of the censure that must also fall on members of the governing class, prominent in the next reign, who did not strongly oppose revival of the heresy laws.

Pole's work as legate has not escaped criticism, but he was throughout working under grave disadvantages and an excessively heavy administrative burden. In addition, for part of the time he was unable to concentrate on his work in England. Pope Julius III appointed him to mediate in the conflict of Habsburg and Valois, which involved a journey to the French Court in April 1555, and in July of the same year his legatine commission was extended to Ireland. Also in that year Julius III and his successor Marcellus II both died. On each occasion Pole was regarded as a favourite for the papal succession, and although he was entirely free of ambition the prospect must have been unsettling. The election of Paul IV at the age of 79, an old critic, was a disaster for Pole, who now found himself fighting a rearguard action at Rome where his close friend and confidant Cardinal Morone was being questioned under suspicion of heresy. It was now difficult to transact business in the Roman Curia or to secure papal approval of appointments to vacant bishoprics, and this delay, which was so opportune for the promoters of the Elizabethan

Church settlement, has often unfairly been blamed on Pole. Then in 1557 came the arrest of Morone and the revocation of Pole's commission as legate with Paul IV's hostility made clear. Pole was recalled to Rome, where the Inquisition was moving against his friends and the Pope was denouncing them as members of 'that accursed school and apostate household of the Cardinal of England'. The Queen refused to allow his departure, and Pole was by now a very sick man. Cardinal Morone survived these stormy days to play a leading part in the final sessions of the Council of Trent; Pole died in disgrace in November 1558, within a few hours of the death of the Queen. A recent study of Pole and his friends has remarked that he was uneasy in office, at home with individuals and most at peace in monastic circles where he had many friends.[10] He was essentially a man of prayer.

What then on balance can be said of the Catholic restoration? It was not a success, if only because little more than three years were allowed for a task that needed thirty. The lost years could not be made good. Nearly forty years later Robert Persons blamed the men of this time in his *Memorial for the Reformation of England* and contrasted their vested interests and spirit of compromise with the zeal of the Catholic clergy and laity of his own day. Queen Mary had managed to associate Catholicism with the burning of heretics and the influence of Spain; increasingly the Catholic faith would be identified with the foreigner. Yet there was some gain, for the government of Elizabeth was to discover that Catholicism could not be stamped out in England and that it was to survive as a minority religion. Considerable success had been achieved in Lancashire under two energetic Marian bishops, marked by the restoration of churches, the foundation of schools, and a notable increase in the number of vocations to the priesthood.[11] It was in this county also that the old religion was to retain its hold during the next reign. Moreover, there developed a new appreciation of papal authority that had been unknown in medieval England. In 1570 a member of the Council of the North, Sir Thomas Gargrave, noticed how different the attitude of convinced Catholics to the papal primacy was compared with the attitude that had obtained in the reign of Henry VIII.[12] In 1569 the Venetian envoy in France had reached a similar opinion. Before the religious wars he reported: 'His Holiness was regarded rather as a great Italian political power than as Head of the Church and universal pastor. But as soon as the Huguenots appeared the Catholics began to have a new respect for the pontiff and to recognise him as the true Vicar of Christ.'[13] The Roman pontiff might be gravely mistaken in his attitude to English affairs, his political policies might prove unwelcome and cause much suffering to his English followers, but in 1580 Robert Persons noted the esteem in which they held the distant head of their church.[14]

2 An Alternative to Catholicism: Elizabeth's Church

All this people . . . were in one day, with a blast of Queen Elizabeth's trumpet, of ignorant papists and gross idolators made faithful Christians and true professors.

Henry Barrow

It seems unlikely that the dead Cardinal Pole had been deceived as to the sincerity of Elizabeth's professions of Catholicism during her sister's reign, yet no plans had been made against the possibility of religious change. The Church was without leadership, and by the end of 1558 nine dioceses were vacant in addition to that of Canterbury. The Protestant exiles now began to return. They were to supply much of the leadership and most of the fervour of Elizabeth's Church and were to prove the driving force that would carry through a fourth change in official religion. Governing circles adapted without difficulty, and although the mass of the people were probably Catholic the views of the majority were unimportant. In the early months of the new reign a foreign observer noted that Mass was still said 'in all the London churches before numerous congregations who show much devotion. So it is evident that religion is not on such a sorry footing as was supposed, for everyone is at liberty now to go or stay away.'[1] Tudor habits of obedience to the Crown were strong, however, and it was the ruling class alone that counted: A Venetian diplomat had earlier reported to his government that Englishmen would turn Mahommedan or Jew if the sovereign so willed![2]

Of Elizabeth's own religious beliefs we cannot be certain. Her Protestant upbringing led to ignorance of Catholic teaching, but she had some liking for the externals of Catholic worship, if not for its theology, and was to fight an amusing battle for the cross and candlesticks of her own chapel against puritan divines. She detested religious 'enthusiasm' and had little appreciation of the value of theological speculation. As the daughter of Anne Boleyn she might have been predisposed to discard the Pope, but to retain England within the fold the Papacy would accept her and that she would hold the support of Philip II of Spain so long as the claims of Mary Stuart were maintained by France. Politics certainly influenced her decision; the strong anti-Spanish feeling that was a legacy from the previous régime and the treaty of Cateau-Cambrésis of April 1559 that ended war with Spain and gave her freedom of manoeuvre. From the beginning she was under strong pressure from the returned Protestant exiles, yet her decision in favour of yet another religious upheaval was not an easy one and, in the view of some historians, not inevitable. Elizabeth's own preference would have been for a religious settlement resembling her father's rather than for the one that ultimately emerged.

Indications of the wind of change were soon apparent, and by the day of the coronation the bishops had no doubt of the Queen's intentions. They refused to assist at a coronation oath that must have no meaning, and although the Bishop of Carlisle was persuaded to perform the actual coronation all left the church before Mass was sung by one of the reforming clergy.[3] It had already been noted that a proclamation that forbade all preaching favoured Protestants. Richard Hilles wrote to Bullinger at Zurich: 'silence has been imposed upon the Catholic preachers . . . and sufficient liberty is allowed to the gospellers to preach three times a week before the Queen herself'. But the Lenten sermons at Court were abruptly stopped, and it seems that the Queen felt that extremists were getting out of hand. The returned exiles were not united in their views, and in January 1559 Jewel mentioned in a letter to Peter Martyr that there were already disputes about ceremonies, 'some declaring for Geneva and some for Frankfurt'.[4] Meanwhile, Protestant divines and laymen were hard at work devising a new form of church service, and when Parliament met in February a Bill was introduced for 'the alteration of religion'.

Professor Neale has commented that 'the Elizabethan religious settlement is shrouded in mystery', and he has shown that what finally emerged was far more Protestant than what the Queen had desired yet more moderate than what later Parliaments would have accepted.[5] A Supremacy Bill that would have retained the ancient services with minor changes was drastically amended by a House of Commons committee to include a Protestant service and to legalise clerical marriage; it probably revived the Second Act of Uniformity of Edward VI and the *Prayer Book* of 1552. This Bill in turn was amended by the House of Lords to restore its original form, with the bishops and two lay peers opposing the transfer of supremacy from the Pope to the Queen. The Commons was then faced with the alternatives of accepting the Lords' changes and losing the *Prayer Book* or of rejecting them and retaining papal supremacy for the time being. They voted therefore for a Supremacy Bill in much the form desired by the government, and by 22 March it was ready for the royal assent.

Had Elizabeth signed this Bill there would have been no Protestant *Prayer Book*, but she changed her mind. The steadfast opposition of the bishops to religious change had created an unexpected problem : if they refused to play their part, who were to be leaders of the new state Church? Convocation and both universities had affirmed their adherence to the traditional Catholic doctrine, and the government could not therefore count on the higher clergy below the bishops to fill key church offices. On the other hand, some of the returned exiles had strong political influence: twelve or more now sat in the House of Commons, and perhaps a quarter of its membership shared their views. This influence had already been shown in the attempt to change the

Supremacy Bill, but it seems likely that the opposition of the bishops and Convocation convinced the Queen, reluctantly, that she must rely on Protestant divines for much of the leadership of her Church.

A fresh start was made and the government brought in two Bills, one of supremacy and one of uniformity, and these passed both Houses. Thus the Queen was given the title of Supreme Governor of the Church but not that of Supreme Head. This implied some limitation of her powers compared with those of Henry VIII, but within these limits Elizabeth was able to exercise a strong influence over the Church throughout her reign. A supremacy oath must now be taken by all ecclesiastics, judges, mayors and officers of state, and by men taking clerical Orders or university degrees. Refusal of the oath was to be punished by loss of benefice or office, and penalties for maintaining papal jurisdiction included : loss of benefice or property for the first offence; premunire, loss of property and imprisonment at pleasure, for the second; and the penalties of high treason for the third. The Act of Uniformity passed the Lords by a majority of three, nine lay peers joining the nine bishops in opposition. The Lords had also in committee mitigated the penalties attached to the Supremacy Bill; if all the vacant episcopal sees had been filled the Act of Uniformity might have had a different history. The *Prayer Book* of 1552 was now reinstated, but some details offensive to Catholics were removed, including the litany petition against the enormities of the Bishop of Rome, and the 'Black Rubric', which declared that no adoration of the Real Presence was intended by kneeling at the communion. The addition of a traditional sentence from the 1549 *Prayer Book* to the Zwinglian formula at the ministration of communion also made possible some latitude of belief as to what exactly that service signified. Here was perhaps a step on the path of compromise that was to be a distinguishing feature of the Elizabethan Church, but if so such comfort for Catholics was later removed by publication of the *Book of Homilies* and the Thirty-Nine Articles, which contained much that was offensive to them.

The Penalties attached to the Act of Uniformity were milder than those of Henry VIII but more severe than those of Edward VI. Beneficed clergy who refused to use the *Prayer Book* or spoke against it were to forfeit a year's income and suffer six months' imprisonment; a second offence merited loss of benefice and a year's imprisonment; the third offence merited imprisonment for life. Laymen speaking or writing against the *Prayer Book*, influencing the clergy to use another form of service, or interrupting or hindering the service, were fined 100 marks for the first offence, 400 marks for the second, but suffered life imprisonment and loss of goods for a third. Attendance at church was now compulsory on Sundays and holydays and it was a legal offence to assist at Mass, punishable by imprisonment : six months for a first offence, one year for a second, and life for a third. With the two Acts of Supremacy and Uniformity the foundations of the Elizabethan Church were laid.

This Church now established by Parliament was not, as at one time supposed, a half-way house between Rome and Geneva. It was a compromise between the moderate position desired by the Queen and the Calvinism desired by extreme Protestants, and in future Elizabeth was to be hard pressed to alter the settlement to one more extreme. Contemporaries, as Elton has commented, agreeing with Neale, thought that Elizabeth's Church was a Protestant one : 'The Elizabethan settlement created a church, protestant in doctrine, traditional in organisation, and subject not to a lay pope but to the Queen governor in Parliament.'[6] Bishop Jewel wrote at this time to Peter Martyr at Zurich : 'We have pared everything away to the very quick and do not differ from your doctrine by a nail's breadth.'[7] However, two Acts of Parliament were not sufficient to create a national Church. A new hierarchy had to be found to replace the Catholic bishops, relationship to the lay control established by Parliament had to be worked out, while the lower clergy had to be sifted and won over from passive acceptance to genuine conviction. Above all, a theology had to be found to suit a Church that was neither Catholic nor Calvinist. Few expected the settlement to endure.

The Catholic bishops had maintained a consistent and dignified opposition during the parliamentary debates, arguing that religious faith could not depend on an Act of Parliament, but even so the government had hoped to secure acceptance of the settlement from at least eight of them, especially from the much respected Archbishop of York, Nicholas Heath. All refused the supremacy oath. First to be deprived of office was Bishop Bonner of London, but proceedings against the archbishop and some others were not begun until July 1559. As late as September of that year the Queen issued a mandate to Bishops Tunstall of Durham, Bourne of Bath and Wells, and Pole of Peterborough for consecration of her newly appointed Archbishop of Canterbury. The bishops refused to obey. One Welsh bishop, Kitchin of Llandaff, recovered his see after deprivation. Writing in July 1559 the Spanish ambassador reported to Philip II: 'I understand that the bishop of Llandaff who is a greedy old man of little learning is wavering, and it is feared that he may take the oath as he is wearing a bishop's garb again.' Kitchin was then in his 80s and seems to have signed a declaration instead of taking the oath. He retained his see until his death in 1563.[8]

By November 1559 all the bishops of English sees had been deprived, and the most notable of their replacements was the new Archbishop of Canterbury, Matthew Parker. He was reluctant to take the office but was an excellent choice, being a distinguished Cambridge scholar and a man of moderate views. Parker was wholly loyal to the Queen and somewhat in awe of her, and was fearful of exceeding the legal limits of his jurisdiction. He had never joined the Protestant exiles and was dismayed by the extremists, while the Queen sometimes compelled him to enforce unpopular policies for which she would not accept public responsibility. It is not surprising that he was inclined to pessimism.

It was important that these new bishops should be validly installed, but here the government was in a quandary. By law, episcopal elections needed confirmation by the archbishop and two bishops, or by four diocesan bishops, but none could now be found who were willing to confirm those newly appointed. Cecil made vain attempts to persuade some of the Marian bishops to consecrate Parker, and finally four non-diocesan bishops were commissioned : Barlow, formerly Henry VIII's Bishop of St David's; Hodgkin, once suffragan of Bedford; and two bishops of Edward VI, Coverdale and Scory. The legal difficulty was surmounted by a clause added to their mandate in which the Queen declared that 'by our supreme authority royal we nevertheless supply whatever is or shall be lacking of those things which, by the statutes of this realm or by the laws of the Church are required'. This procedure led to trouble later on. In April 1563 the Elizabethan Bishop of Winchester tendered the supremacy oath to the deprived Bishop of London, Bonner, who was then a prisoner in the Marshalsea. He had already refused it once and would now by a recent Act be liable to the death penalty for a second refusal. Bonner was a canonist and an able lawyer, and he claimed that Winchester had no power to tender the oath as he was not a true bishop : his consecrator, Archbishop Parker, had not been confirmed and consecrated according to the law. The judges decided that a trial of the case might prove embarrassing, Bonner was left unmolested, and a special Act was passed to legalise the consecrations, the Elizabethan bishops having to petition in 1566 for a declaration that they were lawful bishops.[9]

As hardworking officials Elizabeth's bishops have won some praise. Rowse has judged the majority to be 'conscientious hardworking men struggling in difficult circumstances with a heavy burden of administrative toil'; Trevor-Roper has stressed their services to charity and education : 'especially the bishops deserve remembrance, those hardworking harassed Protestant bishops whom Papists and Puseyites have so long conspired to dishonour'.[10] Academically, most were well qualified, six having held major university posts, and Parker wrote to Cecil of the first appointments that 'the Queen's Majesty may have good cause to be well contented with her choice of most of them, few excepted'. Many of the important sees were given to returned Protestant exiles, to what Bishop

Sandys termed 'Germanical natures', and it has been claimed that this gave the Church an emigré government out of tune with the Queen's own conservative views.[11] Not all the former exiles who were offered bishoprics were willing to accept them for they did not believe in episcopal government; seventy received Crown benefices. These were all men of conviction and ability, but they were probably not the equal of their religious opponents.

Some individuals, including two Archbishops of York, have been singled out for criticism. Edwin Sandys was appointed to Worcester in 1559 and has been described as 'a spoliator, who robbed the Church for self enrichment, impoverishing his successors by leasing out the estates of the see to his own family and dependents'. As Archbishop of York Sandys was discovered in bed at an inn in Doncaster with the innkeeper's wife, a former maidservant of Mrs Sandys. He was the victim of a plot by Sir Robert Stapleton, the innkeeper and his wife, and he tried to avoid scandal by handing over an episcopal manor to Stapleton and a large sum of money to the innkeeper. An attempt at further blackmail forced Sandys to inform the Privy Council : Stapleton was prosecuted in the Star Chamber, and his accomplices were severely punished. Ordered to make a public apology to Sandys at the York assizes Stapleton enraged him by making a mockery of the ceremony, while the innkeeper wrote to Sandys asking him to admit that he had led his wife on. Stapleton eventually went to prison, and the archbishop wrote bitterly : 'I see now that while I live here I shall . . . labour unprofitably, hurling pearls before swine.' Sir Walter Mildmay deplored the scandal given to the papists – 'acceptable news to Rome and Reims and other seminaries of popery'.[12]

Bishop Curteys of Chichester, to some extent a victim of his own tactlessness, remained an outsider after ten years in his diocese, 'spurned by the greater part of the gentry and scoffed at by all but a handful of the citizens of Chichester'. Nevertheless, he was diligent in preaching and did his best, with some success, to raise the standard of his diocesan clergy.[13] Archbishop Young of York has been described as 'vain, stupid, idle and greedy', and William Overton, Bishop of Coventry and Lichfield, as 'a thorough scoundrel'. Bishop Watson of Chichester, whose predecessor was appointed at the age of 77, has been judged as 'an inept timeserver and pluralist', and Bishop Chadderton of Chester as 'a thoroughly self-seeking and money grubbing prelate'.[14] More unfortunate was Bishop Middleton of St David's, whose unpopularity embroiled an archdeacon in a plot to kill him. Middleton was found guilty of embezzlement by the Court of High Commission and of forging a will by the Star Chamber. He was deprived and degraded.[15] Not all the Elizabethan bishops were men like these, however. Most of them were conscientious in the discharge of their duties, hardworking men but on the whole unloved : Catholics regarded them as intruders, and puritans saw no necessity for an episcopate.

The social status of Elizabeth's bishops was much diminished compared with that of their Catholic predecessors, although Archbishop Parker lived in considerable state at Lambeth and his colleagues ranked among the major gentry. To a German visitor it seemed that Bishop Jewel lived in considerable splendour at Salisbury.[16] The Queen showed no great respect for their office, and besides making public comments on their preaching she threatened at times to depose them if they incurred her displeasure. If the size of their families did not equal the twenty children of Archbishop Loftus of Dublin, they still needed provision. Clerical marriage, though not yet legal and much disliked by the Queen, had come to stay. Catholic controversialists were not polite on this subject either, and Stapleton aimed a shot at Bishop Horne : 'Ye keep now your said Madge in the face of all the world without shame, which in king Henry's days ye kept in hucker mucker and lusky lanes.' The question of clerical marriage was regulated by Injunctions of 1559, by which clergy who proposed to marry were required to present the lady for examination before a bishop and two justices while bishops in their turn were to be regulated by the archbishop or the Queen's Commissioners. In 1561 Elizabeth issued an order without consulting the bishops : 'no head or member of any college or cathedral church . . . to have his wife or other women haunting his cathedral or collegiate lodging'. After a difficult interview with her, Archbishop Parker, himself a married man, wrote to Cecil of his horror at 'such words . . . as she [the Queen] spake concerning God's holy ordinance of matrimony . . . in so much as the Queen's highness expressed to me a repentance that we were thus appointed in office, wishing it had been otherwise. Which inclination being known at large to Queen Mary's clergy they laugh prettily to see how the clergy of our time is handled.' Bishop Cox of Ely protested that only one prebendary was resident there with his family : 'Turn him out and doves and owls may dwell therein for any continual housekeeping.'[17] The Queen's attitude to a married episcopate was shown in the case of Richard Fletcher, a favourite pro- moted successively to the sees of Bristol, Worcester and London : when he took a young widow of doubtful reputation as his second wife he was banished from Court and suspended.

This married episcopate had its family troubles. Bishop Cooper of Lincoln suffered from his wife's adultery with his brother, and a son of Bishop Scory of Hereford became a Catholic; when the son of Bishop Woolton of Exeter followed the same path, the bishop had him gaoled and he conformed. It was not uncommon for the bishops to present members of their families to benefices and bestow episcopal manors on wives, children and other relatives. This practice has been excused by the need to build up some support in their dioceses to counter the frequent hostility of the local gentry. Bishop Godwin was a case in point. In 1584 he came to Bath and Wells at the age of 67, after a seventeen-year (and not entirely uneventful) tenure of the deanery of Canterbury, where an angry canon had threatened to nail him to a wall with his sword. Understandably, Godwin wanted peace, so he seldom descended on his cathedral town, living instead on one of the episcopal manors with a staff of twenty-two lesser servants. A family of five sons and three daughters were happy to relieve him of the more tiresome burdens of administration. All five sons obtained ecclesiastical preferment and with the sons-in-law obtained control of diocesan finance. When the bishop died his family seized his property and emptied his houses of furniture; the Privy Council had to appoint a commission to secure the return of their loot. Harington had ground for his comment that Godwin was 'used like a conduit pipe to convey water to others'.[18]

More serious perhaps was the steady spoliation of church property that the bishops had to endure at the hands of the Queen and her Court. Elizabeth has indeed been termed 'the supreme plunderer of the Church'.[19] Sees were kept vacant for long periods to the profit of the Crown : Oxford for forty-one years, Ely for nineteen and Bristol for fourteen. By an Act of 1559 that defined the Queen's right to the temporalities during a vacancy, she could take over any episcopal estate and exchange it for impropriate tithes of equal value, an unfavourable exchange that was made a condition of appointment. Five of the first bishops elect protested against this condition, but they were forced to accept it. Hill has given instances of payments in cash or leases that new bishops were compelled to make to the Crown or to courtiers. The patronage of bishops was also limited, and in 1604 it was alleged that five-sixths of all benefices were controlled by laymen, including the Crown. It has been estimated that Thomas Bentham, Bishop of Coventry, presented to only five out of the 147 benefices that fell vacant during his ten years in the see.[20] The puritan movement was to be greatly strengthened by the use of this lay patronage to secure the appointment of clergy of acceptable doctrine.

One of the many problems facing the bishops arose from the shortage of clergy. For many years there had been a decline in the number of men ordained, and many clergy had died during the severe influenza epidemic at the beginning of the reign. Also, as Bishop Jewel complained, clerical incomes were so low that 'all shun and flee the ministry'. In these circumstances the Lambeth Articles of 1561 required even clergy who had refused the supremacy oath to minister in parishes if called upon : 'priests deprived and other private chaplains to administer cures at bishops' orders in this great necessity or face excommunication'. When controversy broke out because Dean Whittingham of Durham had not been ordained in the State Church, Huntingdon wrote to Cecil: 'Your worship can judge what flame this spark is likely to breed . . . for it cannot but be evil taken . . . that we should allow of the popish massing priests in our ministry and disallow of the minister made in a church reformed.'[21]

For much of the reign the quality of those ordained was not high. The puritan Marprelate's attack on the bishops included a charge that Bishop Aylmer of London had given his porter the living of Paddington; in defence it was urged that other bishops had made similar presentations and that the porter in question was a God-fearing man. In 1585 Lord Burghley asserted that one bishop had 'made 70 ministers in one day, for money: some tailors, some shoemakers and others crafts-men, I am sure the greatest part of them are not worthy to keep horse.'[22] The Catholic exile Stapleton had earlier made a similar charge: 'And wherein, I pray you, resteth a great part of your new clergy but in butchers, cooks, catchpoles and cobblers, dyers and daubers, fishermen, gunners, harpers, inn-keepers, merchants and mariners, potters, pothecaries, and porters of Billingsgate, pinners, pedlars, ruffling ruffians.'[23]

The decline of standards contrasts with the improvement noticeable in the years before Henry VIII's break with Rome. During Archbishop Warham's tenure of the Canterbury diocese some 39 per cent of institutions to benefices had been of university graduates, and at Lincoln, during the quarter-century ending in 1520, the proportion of graduates presented for ordination rose from over 3 per cent to over 11 per cent, all with Master's degrees.[24] More than fifty years later at Lincoln nearly one in three of those accepted for ordination had 'insufficient knowledge', and of 396 diocesan clergy only fifty-one were licensed to preach. To their credit, the Elizabethan bishops made strenuous efforts to raise the educational standards of their clergy and a notable increase in the number of university graduates resulted. Nevertheless, in 1598 Hooker regarded the problem of securing well-qualified ministers as almost insoluble and implied that some of them were 'the scum and refuse of the whole land', while James I, justifying his own appointment of bishops, has been reported as saying that 'no good men will take the office on them'.[25]

The parochial clergy as a whole had accepted the religious settlement without difficulty, and only a small number were deprived as a result of the early visitations. However, many absented themselves from attending on the commissioners, and in the Northern provinces 314 incumbents of 968 parishes stayed away. It seems likely that absentee parish priests and curates faced no test before 1561, but although the great majority of beneficed clergy made no difficulty in accepting the settlement not many gave it a welcome. Criticism came not only from the Catholic side but also from many of the returned Protestant exiles, who regarded the settlement as an unsatisfactory beginning that fell far short of their hopes. In exile there had been much theological dissension, especially among the congregation at Frankfurt, where both sides appealed to Calvin, and John Knox had led his own followers to Geneva. Calvinist theology had influenced both sides, but the more moderate held by the 1552 *Prayer Book* and episcopacy against those who wished to follow the Genevan models. Elizabeth's Church was therefore from the beginning affected by two schools of thought. The more moderate accepted the settlement but excused themselves for its shortcomings to their continental friends: 'Our Queen', wrote Bishop Horne to Bullinger at Zurich in 1571, 'holds the helm and directs it hitherto according to her pleasure.'[26] The more extreme wing objected both to the 'dregs of popery' remaining in the *Prayer Book* and to the very idea of a lay settlement of religion; many would eventually be driven out of the State Church. The influence of this Calvinist element was reinforced by the popularity of the Geneva Bible published in 1560, a popularity far greater than that of the official Bishops' Bible of 1568: sixteen editions were published within five years. The more extreme view was notable in the Convocation of 1563, when its more Protestant programme, which would have carried further the changes authorised in 1559, was defeated in the Lower House by a single vote. From then on the puritan element tended to carry to Parliament its struggle for further reform. The 1563 Convocation revised Cranmer's Forty-Two Articles, which were published as the Thirty-Nine Articles. To these articles all clergy not ordained according to the *Prayer Book* had now to subscribe, as did all future holders of benefices. The Articles expressly repudiated the Catholic doctrine of the sacraments, and the differences between Elizabeth's Church and the old religion were reinforced by a *Book of Homilies* issued in 1562 to be read at services throughout the year if no sermon was preached. This work attacked the Mass as a horrible blasphemy and aimed many shafts at the papacy : 'We boldly and with safe conscience pronounce of the Bishops of Rome, namely that they have forsaken, and do daily forsake, the commandments of God.' As the years went by such propaganda – aided by the vivid pages of Foxe's *Book of Martyrs*, first published in English in 1563 – was to make a great impression on simple congregations. In 1571 schoolmasters were ordered to use Dean Nowell's *Catechism*, which drew much of its inspiration from Calvinist sources, but by then Bishop Jewel's *Apology*, issued in 1564, had provided the classic defence of the Elizabethan settlement.[27] Jewel appealed to the Bible and the primitive Church : 'We have planted no new religion but have only renewed the old.' He also attacked in some detail the practices of contemporary Catholicism, and it was the negative side of his apologetic that Catholic opponents stressed in the long-drawn-out controversy that ensued with the writers of Louvain. 'What is all your preaching but down down,' wrote Stapleton. The former Dean of St Paul's, Cole, raised the same objection: 'One thing . . . I long much to be answered in, why ye offer . . . to dispute in these points than in the chief matters that lie in question betwixt the Church of Rome and the Protestants.'[28]

In the early years of the reign an infinite variety obtained in the conduct of services and the furnishing of churches. The vicar of Weaverthorpe in Yorkshire was still administering communion in 1565 in one kind; and in sixty-four Norfolk and Suffolk churches the surplice was not worn. The vestments worn by the consecrators of Parker in 1559 had foreshadowed the confusion : Barlow wore a cope, Scory and Hodgkin surplices, and Coverdale a black gown. A document of 1565 entitled *Varieties in the Services and Administration* revealed a chaotic state of affairs. In January of that year the Queen intervened and complained to Archbishop Parker of the 'diversity, variety, contention and vain love of singularity' present in the Church and required him by 'the authority you hold under us' to take instant action to secure 'one manner of uniformity throughout our realm'.[29] In the next year Parker issued his *Advertisements,* but in spite of the Queen's request it did not secure her official support. Rather it led to public disorder in London and opened up a bitter controversy. The *Advertisements* regulated the dress and vestments of the clergy, baptism and marriage, Sunday observance, and the training of candidates for Holy Orders. In future all admitted to ordination were to accept uniformity in these matters, but in the event these regulations were not widely imposed outside the London diocese and met with great opposition. In 1573 Bishop Pilkington wrote to a foreign correspondent : 'mourn over this our church at this time so miserably divided, not to say wholly rent in pieces'.[30]

Two years later Parker was succeeded by Edmund Grindal, 'an archbishop for thoroughgoing protestants'. A sincere reformer, Grindal was anxious to deal with recognised abuses, but his views soon clashed with those of the Queen. The puritan element had developed a practice of regular meetings for Bible study and moral improvement, but the Queen saw these 'exercises' or 'prophesyings' as an attempt to secure further church reform. Consequently she ordered the archbishop to suppress them. His refusal to obey and his request that she should leave matters 'which touch the doctrine and discipline of the Church' to the bishops led to his suspension from office. A more congenial successor was found in 1583 with the appointment of Whitgift, in the view of Neale one of the decisive events of the reign. The new archbishop demanded a complete acceptance of the *Prayer Book,* something that few of the clergy could wholeheartedly give, and he made great use of the Court of High Commission with its

procedure unlimited by the common law. By 1590 considerable success had been achieved.

In their task of enforcing the new religious settlement the
leaders of the Elizabethan Church made use both of new
administrative machinery and of the old church courts. A
remarkable number of matters still came within the jurisdiction
of canon law : probate of wills, matrimonial cases and sexual
offences. Schoolmasters needed a bishop's licence to teach
and after 1563 could be required to take the supremacy oath.
The educated class might be affected by a strict censorship
of books. It was hoped that with the assistance of the churchwardens the bishop's officials could superintend the conduct
of incumbents as well as that of their parishioners : churchwardens were required to fine absentees and make a round
of the alehouses during services to round up defaulters. At
three-year intervals the bishop or his officials were to make a
visitation, when offenders would be presented for trial and,
if necessary, excommunication. The efficient use of this
machinery varied, but in strong puritan centres, such as
Northampton in the 1590s, churchwardens joined with
ministers to visit every household before the quarterly communion and to decide if its members were fit to participate.[31]
It is not surprising if there was a good deal of sullen resistance
to this supervision, and not only from convinced Catholics.
Indeed it has been claimed that many of the poorest classes
never became regular churchgoers, while, if the puritan clergy
can be believed, their religious knowledge was slight. In 1600
the Bishop of Exeter declared that scepticism was rife in his
diocese and that the existence of God was a matter of common
dispute.[32] It has also been claimed that the tone of many
Elizabethan congregations resembled that of a tiresome class
of schoolboys, and no doubt also the country folk were like
those with whom George Herbert was later familiar : 'thick,
heavy, and hard to raise to a point of zeal and fervency, and
need a mountain of fire to kindle them'.

Gradually, however, Elizabethan religion began to take
root, and in the face of exaggerated puritan complaints the
labours of the bishops secured a remarkable improvement.

Saintliness was not a mark of Elizabeth's Church, and in that respect it compares ill with the attractive saints of the Counter Reformation. However, not all Elizabethans lingered in the outer courts, and there were many godly pastors. Such a one was Richard Greenham, rector of Dry Drayton from 1571 to 1591, who felt deeply about the pastoral abuses of his time and whose masterpiece, in Thomas Fuller's words, 'was in comforting wounded consciences'.[33] Greenham was a puritan who remained within the State Church, but, lacking the gaiety that his contemporary, Teresa of Avila, brought to her religious life he ended despondent about his ministry. Yet he was a more attractive figure than John Carter, who prayed for five or six hours a day in his study, 'very loud' and mostly 'very long', for the edification of his children. He would have provided a target for the unruly Eures of Yorkshire, whose comic imitation of the Hoby family's puritan psalmsinging has been reported as reducing Sir Robert Cecil to tears of laughter.

In the final decade of the reign Elizabeth's Church did not lack men of real distinction, such as Archbishop Hutton of York and the energetic Richard Bancroft of London, later Archbishop of Canterbury. It also gained the most important contribution to its apologetic literature with the publication of the first four books of Richard Hooker's great work, *Of the Law of Ecclesiastical Polity*, in 1593. This to some extent marked the development of a new anglican tradition. Yet the future of Elizabeth's Church could not be foreseen. The Queen had been remarkably successful in holding together its discordant elements and had resisted to the end all attempts of the extreme Protestant wing to revise the settlement of 1559. The first two Stuarts lacked her skill and wary detachment, and the death of Archbishop Bancroft in 1610 has been seen as marking a turning point.[34] The appointment of unsuitable men as bishops by James I increased Protestant questioning of the institution of episcopacy, and the Laudian bishops of Charles I intensified division by their attitude to doctrine and discipline. The historian of Charles I has drawn a depressing picture of the Anglican Church eighty years after the settlement of 1559: 'young and insecure, doctrinally divided, imperfectly organised, open to criticism, and but feebly rooted in the affection of the people'.[35]

3 A Flock Without a Shepherd: 1559-70

How can that flower but fade and soon decay
That always is with dark clouds over run.

Thomas, Lord Vaux

If the majority of the English people had no great desire for further religious change in 1558, theirs was a Catholicism still untouched by Counter Reformation fervour, depending largely on the traditional relationship of country squire, parish priest and people, unintellectual and unprepared for martyrdom.[1] Leadership was notably absent, and although the formal deprivation of Archbishop Heath did not occur until July 1559 the freedom of the bishops to exercise their functions was soon restricted. By February 1560, of the nine bishops then in England only Bishop Poole of Peterborough, an invalid, was not in prison, although he was under a form of house arrest. By the summer of that year six were in the Tower, one was in the Fleet prison, and Bonner of London was in the Marshalsea where he remained until his death in 1569. Thereafter most of the Marian bishops were to alternate between prison and the custody of the men who had supplanted them. The conditions of their confinement varied and were always subject to uncertainty, but Archbishop Heath, always much respected, was eventually permitted to retire to his Surrey estate.

The firm stand of the bishops gained them little sympathy from their supplanters, and in August 1559 Bishop Jewel wrote to Peter Martyr at Zurich: 'The bishops, rather than abandon the Pope . . . are willing to submit to everything not however that they do so for the sake of religion, of which they have none. But for the sake of consistency which the miserable knaves choose to call their conscience.'[2]

From time to time the Elizabethan bishops called for greater severity to be used towards their predecessors, several of whom had already experienced imprisonment during the reign of Edward VI. The last surviving Marian bishop in England, Watson of Lincoln, died in confinement in 1584. No doubt this refusal of the Marian bishops to accept the new religious settlement was later to be an inspiration to many English Catholics, but at the outset it had little influence on the decisions of the ordinary parochial clergy. Moreover, no guidance came from Rome, where, without any sense of urgency, reliance was placed on diplomacy. If Catholicism was to survive at all some sort of organisation was needed, and above all a priesthood. No attempt to fill these gaps was made until an Englishman, William Allen, had the foresight to found a college overseas in 1568. The Roman authorities more tardily grouped Allen's secular clergy under an Archpriest in 1598. It was precisely on the lack of priests that the government built its hopes that Catholicism would quietly die and that, as the years passed, its attrition would be aided by the continued silence of Rome.

One essential was lacking in England for the successful struggle of a proscribed religion : leadership from a member of the royal family, such as was given to the Huguenots in France. In England there was no royal family, and the ruling class had an exaggerated veneration for Tudor kingship. A change occurred when a strong claimant to the succession appeared with the arrival of Mary, Queen of Scots, in the North during 1567. The English nobility was not notably interested in religion, and peers were exempt from the supremacy oath unless they held an office. Also, the government accepted the implicit right of the nobility and gentry to regulate the religious life of their households, with private chapels and chaplains. In the event, as Stone has pointed out in his *Crisis of the Aristocracy*, this licence proved of immense importance for the survival of both Catholicism and Puritanism.[3] With freedom in the private exercise of their religion the Catholic peers had therefore little inclination to revolt against the Elizabethan settlement, and below them, sometimes sheltering under noble patronage, a large number of country gentry favoured the old religion without aspiring to challenge the existence of the new State Church.

It was the convinced Catholic below these classes who felt most the change of religion : The central act of worship of his faith, the Mass, was forbidden under penalty; recognition of the Pope as head of his religion was a legal offence that might involve high treason; and access to the sacraments and religious instruction for his children were rarely possible. Although he was free to hold his religious convictions provided they were not given public expression, he was not permitted to worship as his convictions required. He had to conform to the new worship of the State Church in which he did not believe, attending its church services on Sundays and holydays and accepting the ministrations of its clergy. Under legal and social pressure a steady decline in the numbers of Catholics resulted, until a certain stability was reached in the 1580s. Naturally enough, this process was more noticeable in the humbler classes. For them the 12-penny fine for absence from church was perhaps equivalent to twice a labouring man's wage, but it was not the main reason for their conformity (see also pp. 68 and 71). Enforcement of the fine proved to be a problem for the authorities and might lead to pauperdom and hence to a charge on the parish, something that officials were anxious to avoid.[4] More serious was the lack of Catholic priests and of instruction for their children; consequently, congregations of poor people normally only survived where they were in contact with a gentry household and its chaplain. By the end of the reign there was a marked disparity between the incidence of recusancy among the total population and that among the nobility and gentry. It has been estimated that the total Catholic population of the Yorkshire West Riding was under 3 per cent of the total in 1605 but that 25 per cent of the gentry class still held to the old religion.[5] At first, however, conformity to Elizabeth's Church was slow and superficial.

Writing in 1580, the Jesuit Robert Persons stated that almost all Catholics without distinction attended the religious services of the State Church during the first ten years. Attendance was eased by the probability that the familiar parish priest of Marian days was still the incumbent, and although the majority of the clergy had accepted the religious change without difficulty there is ample evidence of their dislike of it. Writing of his visitation of the western counties in 1559, Bishop Jewel mentioned that 'if inveterate hostility was found anywhere it was altogether among the priests, especially those who had once been on our side'. In 1561 the Bishop of Carlisle wrote of his clergy as 'wicked imps of Satan', Mass being celebrated openly in parts of his diocese. In 1562 the Bishop of Winchester complained to the Privy Council that some of his cathedral clergy daily encouraged the people in the doctrines of popery. At Hereford the cathedral chapter, Catholic in sympathy with one exception, was denounced by the bishop in October 1564 : some have Mass in their houses, 'come seldom or not at all to church, which never received the communion since the Queen's Majesty's reign . . . the communion was not ministered in the cathedral church since Easter'.[6] Things were as bad in the Chichester diocese, where Bishop Barlow complained in 1564 of the lack of reliable men among his clergy and cathedral staff and despaired of winning over the common people until more of the gentry had been persuaded to accept the new religion. At Battle, where the Catholic Lord Montague had his seat, seven beneficed clergy were described as hostile and one was sending money to the exile Thomas Stapleton at Louvain; Ten years after the Queen's accession the bishop reported of Battle : 'When a preacher doth come and speak anything against the Pope's doctrine, they will not abide, but get them out of the church . . . It is the most popish town in all Sussex.'[7] Another Sussex incumbent, William Weaye, was summoned before the Dean and chapter of Chichester in 1569 and affirmed his belief in Catholic doctrine : 'He believes as the Catholic Church does whereof he thinks the Pope the head.'

There were churches that kept the forbidden equipment for celebrating Mass, where everything was ready 'to set up Mass again within twenty hours' warning', where church-wardens concealed the Catholic furnishings but certified them as destroyed. Bishop Bentham of Coventry had no doubt that many were 'hoping and looking for a new day as may thereby be conjectured'. The continuance in benefices of priests who were often prepared to say Mass privately before conducting the new service made things easier for the Catholic who was willing to attend church. So late as 1582 the charge was brought that 'Sir Miles Yare, parson of Sturson near Skole in Suffolk, sayeth Mass commonly in his parlour chamber in his own house and also . . . that in the said chamber are all things necessary pertaining thereto'.[8] In the early years of the reign the bishops sometimes turned a blind eye to the superficial conformity of some of their clergy, and Bishop Downham of Chester allowed them great freedom. The vicar of Whalley was allowed to retain his benefice in spite of constant complaints, which included an allegation that he had told his congregation that they should treat the church communion as 'common bread and wine' and that each should 'in heart exempt himself from this service . . . and make his prayer by himself according to the doctrine of the Pope of Rome'.[9] Dobson was not an estimable character, and by the time that Downham's successor secured his resignation had also been charged with drunkenness, dancing with a full cup on his head 'when he cannot discern black from blue'. For some Catholics an underground ministry was provided by priests who had the courage of their convictions and had refused to accept the religious settlement: the 'popish and perverse priests' of whom the Bishop of Worcester complained to the Privy Council in 1564, who 'misliking religion have forsaken the ministry and yet live in corners, are kept in gentlemens' houses, and had in great estimation of the people'. How many of these priests, known later as Marian or 'old' priests, were at work in the country as a whole we do not know, but a considerable number were functioning in the North before 1570. Between

1568 and 1571 at least fifty-six were ministering in Lancashire, and at one time they outnumbered the official clergy in the south of that county; more than 150 have been noted as working in Yorkshire, and a group in the diocese of Hereford were protected by the local gentry and magistrates.[10] These underground priests did not usually condemn the attendance of Catholics at the official services, and the 'church papist' for his part drew the line at joining in the rarely held communion service. It was Archbishop Whitgift who emphasised to the puritans that 'not the simplest and most ignorant papist could mistake the communion service for the Mass'.

With passive resistance only from Catholics and their priests the government had no need to resort to active persecution, and it was during the first ten years of the reign that the Catholic cause was lost, largely due to lack of guidance from Rome. The absence of episcopal authority made it difficult for the English Catholics to follow a common policy, and the question of church attendance soon made this clear. Canon law forbade attendance at heretical services, and doubts soon arose as to the lawfulness of attendance at services of the State Church. The Catholic clergy were divided. Some – such as Alban Langdale, the deprived Archdeacon of Chichester, and Robert Pursglove, the deprived suffragan Bishop of Hull – held that attendance was no sin if done solely as an act of obedience to the Queen. Others held it to be a serious sin, and the future Cardinal William Allen, not at the time a priest, persuaded a number of Lancashire Catholics to withdraw. Early in 1562 the Spanish ambassador in London, Bishop de Quadra, forwarded a request for guidance to Rome, and at the same time some English Catholics asked for a ruling from the legates at Trent. The ambassador had already assisted by obtaining the consecrated oils from abroad for use in baptism and in anointing the sick, and he himself favoured attendance at the church services. Another difficulty referred to Rome was that arising from the lack of jurisdiction for priests to absolve heretics who wished to return to the old religion. Identical opinions were given by a committee of theologians at Trent and a similar body at Rome: attendance at the services of Elizabeth's Church was not lawful.

These opinions had the authority only of the theologians who gave them, and there is no evidence that they were officially promulgated. However, in 1566 the newly elected Pope Pius V spoke out strongly against attendance, and an attempt was made to publish his views in England. In November of that year Laurence Vaux, former warden of the collegiate church at Manchester and a priest well known in the North, wrote a letter for circulation in which he claimed to have been present when the Pope delivered his opinion :

> I must therefore without halting, colouring or dissembling let tell you that the Pope cannot dispense any of the laity to entangle themselves with the schism as is aforewritten concerning sacraments and service : that ye may not be present amongst them . . . There is not one of the old bishops nor godly priests of God that will be present at the schismatical service.[11]

To spread this papal condemnation among the English Catholics and prove that it was authentic was not an easy matter, and even twenty years later it was not entirely accepted.

Although the government attitude during the early years was relatively mild it maintained a steady pressure in religious matters. A list prepared for the Privy Council in 1561 included a number of prominent Catholics who were in prison, and others at liberty were restricted to particular districts to isolate them from places where they might have influence. Catholics who attempted to hear Mass in the London embassies were arrested, and periodic raids were made on houses where Mass was likely to be celebrated. In 1563 came a stiffening of the law, and Catholics were charged with having 'grown to marvellous outrage and licenteous boldness'. In his sermon for Parliament, Dean Nowell of St Paul's urged that 'maintainers of false religion ought to die by the sword'. By the new law a first refusal of the supremacy oath was to be punished by loss of lands and goods and imprisonment; a second refusal became treason for which the penalty was death. The obligation of taking the oath was now extended to cover a wider class of office holders and professional men, including Members of Parliament, so that Catholics in future would be excluded from membership of the House of Commons. In the lower House a lawyer, Robert Atkinson, spoke in opposition to the measure, arguing that the maintenance of papal jurisdiction had never been considered to be treasonable, and that Englishmen should note the example of Germany 'where after long contention and so great destruction of their country, at last they are come to this point that the Papist and Protestant can now talk quietly together . . . in this bill though a man intended to live under a law and keep his conscience to himself, yet by the oath we will grope him and see what lieth secretly in his breast'. In the House of Lords Viscount Montague claimed that the law was unnecessary: 'The Catholics of this realm disturb not, nor hinder the public affairs of this realm, neither spiritual nor temporal.'[12]

Armed with these new powers the government requested the bishops in the following year to report on their dioceses and on the religious opinions of the justices of the peace, who were to be classified as favourable, neutral or hostile to the State Church, the latter to be removed from the roll when suitable replacements could be found.[13] The bishops were also directed to consult leading laymen and to put forward suggestions for the further repression of Catholicism. The inquiry revealed that in some dioceses Catholic sympathies were especially strong, notably in those of Chichester, Winchester, Hereford and the North. In Lancashire it was found that while six justices were completely favourable to the religious settlement eighteen were opposed, and there only ten names were put forward of men likely to be suitable for appointment. In the North Riding of Yorkshire eleven justices were suspect of religion out of a total of eighteen. The Northern counties, where it has been claimed that 'a protestant party hardly existed as material for an alternative government', presented a special problem.[14] Archbishop Young of York took office in 1561, at the same time as the establishment of the York High

Commission to enforce religious change, but both the Commission and the Council of the North included Catholic members and sympathisers. Two members of the Council kept Marian priests in their households, and one of the officials – William Rastell, a son-in-law of Thomas More – was a devout Catholic who went into exile at Louvain in 1563. No thorough attempt was made to enforce the State religion until the appointment of the puritan Archbishop Grindal in 1570 and of the equally puritan Huntingdon as President of the Council of the North in 1572. Until then the York High Commission had been satisfied with any sort of conformity however superficial. Catholics had also profited by the laxity of Bishop Downham, whose diocese covered Lancashire, and by the apparent slackness of Edward, Earl of Derby, whose family connections were mostly Catholic and sometimes recusant. Typical perhaps of Lancashire was Ribblesdale, where the vicar of Blackburn and ten priests of the district had refused the oath of supremacy and Sir John Southworth and his cousin Mr Hoghton were able to protect priests and the celebration of Mass on estates that covered 30 000 acres. Some headway was, however, made under government pressure on Bishop Downham at Chester, and by a year after the inquiry of 1564 ten out of twenty-six Sussex justices had also been replaced.[15] As it was a matter of family prestige to hold the office the threat of its loss might drive the weaker Catholic gentry into complete conformity. The Catholic peers were still immune, and so in Sussex rather than give offence the government preferred to secure a balance of influence by promoting peers of differing religious views.

So far government action amounted to harassment rather than active persecution, the death penalty of the 1563 Act being held in reserve, *in terrorem*; the Queen herself had no desire to see the death penalty enforced. It has been argued that the deliberate moderation of the government shown by an absence of persecution was only possible because government religious policies were popular, but it may have been due to the inability of the authorities to secure enforcement of the law. At the outset the attitude of the foreign Catholic

Powers could not be disregarded, especially that of Spain, and there was the possibility of a censure from Rome. The weakness of Elizabeth's position was at this stage more apparent to her supporters than her strength : 'So insecure did the state of things appear that few expected the new régime to last, and many calculated on its speedy downfall.'[16] In this atmosphere the religious opposition had every inducement to temporise and the government to avoid overplaying its hand. The change in religion created considerable problems for the administrators of the State Church, and there were delays before the new bishops took full possession of their sees. Thus three years passed before Bishop Barlow of Chichester exercised full authority, and Archbishop Young of York, who took over in May 1561, did not begin his first visitation until the following September. Yet it was on the Church authorities that the government depended for enforcement of the religious changes. At ground level it was the duty of the churchwardens to give effect to the Act of Uniformity, but in many parishes these local officials were reluctant to present the squire and his family for absence from church services while in some places, as at Racton in Sussex, the squire prevented their election. Churchwardens also did not normally function in chapels of ease and the private chapels of the gentry. Neither was it possible to rely on the parish clergy : those of Catholic sympathies were unlikely to act against recusants while those of Protestant opinions might not care to offend the local gentry. Catholics still held the patronage of livings.[17] Before the hardening of attitudes on both sides that occurred after 1570 it was not to be expected that friends and relations would denounce each other. In 1568 Archbishop Parker ordered certain justices of the peace, including Sir Thomas Guildford, to arrest Sir Alexander Colepeper for recusancy, but the latter took refuge with his brother-in-law Lord Montague, having received warning : 'But Mr Gildford, like a loving kinsman and friend, secretly advertised me thereof, advising me speedily to depart, for that they were to apprehend me the next morning if I were not gone before their coming, and therefore willed me to signify unto him by what hour I would be gone, lest he should happen to come before, which he was loth to do.'[18] At this stage then the machinery of enforcement available to the government was quite inadequate to cope with the wealthy and influential.

If a Catholic decided to follow the path of recusancy and refuse to attend church he could be summoned to appear before the archdeacon's court. If he ignored the summons, as was most likely, he might then incur a sentence of excommunication, which carried penalties that also were difficult to enforce. It is generally agreed that there was widespread contempt for the sentence of excommunication, and it has been estimated that for much of the reign possibly 15 per cent of the population had incurred the ban.[19] In 1582 Bishop Overton complained that recusants welcomed excommunication since it relieved them of fines for not attending church. This inability of the church courts to enforce discipline has been judged by Hill to be 'a reflection of the ineffectiveness of all sixteenth century administrative and judicial processes'.[20]

The many problems of the government, both internal and external, combined therefore with the weakness of the administrative machinery to ease the lot of the convinced Catholic during the early years of the régime, while at the same time an absence of leadership provided little hope for the future. There was a steady drift to the State religion, and as the conservative clergy died off or were replaced the Catholic patron found it increasingly difficult to secure a conservative incumbent who had been ordained according to Catholic ritual. During the 1560s a sixth of the clergy of the Sussex diocese were removed on account of their Catholic sympathies, and many churches and chapels there remained unserved. By 1577 a majority of the benefices in the West Riding of Yorkshire had changed hands.[21] The family of Sir Thomas Lovell of East Harling in Norfolk exercised a strong religious influence in their district where a number of related families lived on neighbouring manors. All had appeared in the recusant lists by 1577, but the first blow to their influence was the deprivation of the parish priest of East Harling in 1568.[22] By that year the supply of Marian priests was failing, and some Catholic patrons of Livings, like Lord Mordaunt, gave up the attempt to present. It has been estimated that by 1569 most of the Sussex gentry had abandoned their parish churches for private worship in their own house chapels, and positions were thus hardening. Two years earlier the Earl of Northumberland had been reconciled to the old religion, influenced, as were others, by the writings of the Louvain exiles. As the confidence of the government increased so did its pressure for conformity, and it seems unlikely that the penal laws would not have been applied with greater severity once it was clear that a Catholic minority was irreconcilable. Yet these were not years of plots, and Lord Montague could claim in Parliament that 'Catholics of this realm disturb not nor hinder the public affairs of the realm'. Spain was not yet the enemy, the Bishop de Quadra's successor as ambassador was advising the English Catholics to obey the Queen: 'Let them treat matters which are not against their conscience with moderation and reserve, since respect for superiors is a duty they owe to God.'

For the convinced Catholic therefore the situation during the first ten years of Elizabeth's reign was one of deprivation rather than persecution, and although the death penalty for recusancy in the matter of the supremacy oath remained on the statute book it was never applied. As they looked back on this period during later years Catholics must have regarded it as something of a golden age, terminated by four events of great consequence: the arrival in England of Mary, Queen of Scots, in 1567, the foundation of the English College at Douai in 1568, followed by the rising of the Northern Earls in 1569 and the papal Bull of Excommunication in 1570. Three of these events were disastrous in their consequences, but the foundation of Allen's college, though it was unrealised at the time, was to ensure that Catholicism in England would not die.

On her arrival in England the Queen of Scots was at first freely visited by members of the Northern gentry, who thus met at first hand the woman who, until her execution twenty years later, was to be a source of hope for some of the Catholic minority. Neither in her private life nor in her policies had the Scottish Queen previously shown herself as a champion of Catholicism, and indeed after the Darnley murder and Bothwell marriage she was viewed with great suspicion by the papal Court and the Catholic Powers. However, she was a Queen Dowager of France and derived importance and revenues from that source, her restoration in Scotland was a possibility, and above all she was widely regarded as the heir to Elizabeth's throne, while the latter's illness of 1562 had emphasised the question of the succession. Now the Queen of Scots was to become in Elizabeth's own words 'the daughter of debate that eke discord doth sow' and an inevitable centre of plots for her release from imprisonment and for her acknowledgement as heir. It is probable that this would have been the case even if she had not been a Catholic, but so long as she lived she was to afford some Catholics the hope of better things to come.

During the year after her arrival in England relations with Spain worsened as a result of the seizure of Spanish treasure ships, and Elizabeth's Council became divided between the peers of the old nobility and the 'upstart' Cecil. One section was led by Lord Arundel – a Catholic – and his son-in-law, the Duke of Norfolk – a Protestant. They were in touch with the Spanish and French governments, and their objectives were the dismissal of Cecil, a change in the direction of foreign policy, and recognition of the succession rights of the Queen of Scots. They were opposed to Cecil's policy of provoking Spain, which was hardening King Philip's attitude, and they feared a Franco–Spanish *entente* directed against England. The Northern Earls made this last point in their proclamation before the rising : 'They persuade that their cause of seeking to reform religion is that other princes have determined to do it, and this entering of strangers should be troublesome to the realm.' The Spanish king was interested but gave no support, and in June 1569 de Spes, his ambassador in London, was writing of Norfolk and Arundel : 'I do not know them . . . they are not entirely Catholic.'

At the York Conference in October 1568 a plan developed for the marriage of Norfolk and the Queen of Scots, a matter in which the Duke of Alba forbad de Spes to meddle. The Duke's wife had died that year and proceedings had been begun at Rome to secure the annulment of Mary's marriage to Bothwell, which had been performed with Protestant rites. This plan became part of the anti-Cecil plot, and at one time the peers who were implicated included the Earls of Leicester, Northumberland, Westmorland, Arundel, Pembroke and others. Leicester betrayed the plot to the Queen and Cecil, and by October 1569 the Duke of Norfolk was in the Tower. Against the advice of the President of the Council of the North – the Earl of Sussex, of whose own loyalty she was in doubt – the Queen next summoned the Northern earls to Court, and it was probably this summons that precipitated rebellion.

In the Northern counties the conservative spirit of the people expressed itself in attachment to the old religion and in quasifeudal loyalty to the families of Percy, Neville and Dacre. It was a country in which the Lord President could obtain little response to his call to arms 'except it be a few protestants and some affected to me'. A rising was likely to be a desperate enterprise, but its leadership was singularly ineffective. Thomas Percy, seventh Earl of Northumberland, was at this time in his mid-40s, not long reconciled to the old religion, very popular throughout the North, and son of a father who had been attainted for his part in the Pilgrimage of Grace. His nickname, Simple Tom, gives a measure of the man. He was a reluctant rebel, driven on by others: his wife, the priest Dr Morton, and the aged Richard Norton who was a member of the Council of the North and sheriff of Yorkshire and in turn was influenced by memories of the Pilgrimage of Grace. Of the young Earl of Westmorland it suffices to recall the judgement passed on him in later years by the Archduke Albert, ruler of the Netherlands: 'He is a man of very little substance as far as his judgement and manner of life.'[23]

The rebellion was not primarily a Catholic rising, although

the earls stressed the religious issue in their proclamations as important propaganda to enlist the support of the common people. Both earls were in financial difficulties and impoverished by compulsory residence at Court, while Northumberland had suffered heavily in this respect from government policies in the North. They claimed to be taking action against 'evil disposed persons about the Queen' and against those 'who seek the destruction of the nobility', not against the Queen herself. In the event, in December 1569 the earls fled without giving battle, and a few weeks later the rising was suppressed. It had been an almost bloodless rebellion, but the Queen ordered the execution of 700 persons, 'wholly of the meanest of the people', although her command was only partly obeyed. The wealthy were attainted, their lands and goods reverting to the Queen, and none were pardoned unless they took the oath of supremacy.[24]

On the whole the Catholic gentry escaped lightly. Northern peers who might be regarded as Catholic or of Catholic sympathies held aloof – Shrewsbury, Wharton, Darcy, and Cumberland – and no support was given by the strongly Catholic county of Lancashire where the rebels had hoped to enlist Lord Derby. None of the prominent Catholic gentry of Yorkshire took part: 'The majority either supported the Crown or maintained a strict neutrality.'[25] A feature of the rising, however, had been the restoration of Catholic worship in the churches, and this increased the determination of the authorities everywhere to remove Catholics from positions of importance. In November 1569 the Council sent out letters to sheriffs and justices requiring a statement of their acceptance of the official services and communion, and those who would not subscribe were to give bonds for their good behaviour and appearance before the Council. Few refused to sign. There were absentees who presumably wished to evade a decision, while some who would not sign stated that they attended church. Lord Morley objected on the grounds of his rank, while James Courtney refused but acknowledged his allegiance to the Queen as his rightful sovereign in all civil matters. In several counties concern was expressed at local opposition to the State Church, but no sign of unrest was found.[26]

It was at this moment of tension that Pope Pius V issued the fatal Bull, *Regnans in excelsis*, which excommunicated the Queen and declared her deposed. On 16 February in 1570 Pius had received a letter from the Earls of Northumberland and Westmorland, written on the 7th of the previous November, in which they asked for papal support. By the time a favourable reply was dispatched on 22 February the rising was at an end. Three days later the Pope signed the Bull.

Viewed from Rome the kingdom of Elizabeth had seemed of small importance on the international scene. Of greater moment were the fortunes of the Church in the lands of the Empire, defence of Christian civilisation against the Turkish menace in the Mediterranean, and missionary work in the New World. The English Queen's abandonment of Catholicism was regretted, but her return to the fold was hoped for, without impatience. Such information as reached the Roman Curia was filtered through from foreign ambassadors and observers in London and from the English exiles in the Netherlands; the longer the Queen reigned the less likelihood would there be of a true appreciation of English affairs. For some years it was hoped that a dialogue might be opened with Elizabeth by means of a diplomatic mission.[27] Pius IV, elected in 1558, was a statesmanlike Pope of conciliatory temperament, and he made two attempts to send an envoy to England: the first mission of Parpaglia foundered on the opposition of Philip II; a second, that of Martinengo in 1561, secured the Spanish king's reluctant support but became involved with the Queen's desire to marry Sir Robert Dudley. At first the Queen gave the Spanish ambassador the impression that there would be no difficulty in admitting the papal envoy, but the opposition of Cecil won the day after a discussion in the Council. It was argued that reception of a papal envoy would give the signal for a Catholic rising, and Cecil found it opportune to discover a plot: 'When I saw this Romish influence towards one month past,' he wrote to the ambassador in Paris, 'I thought it necessary to dull the papists' expectation by discovering of certain massmongers and punishing of them.'[28] Three of the late Queen Mary's councillors were among those arrested. If Pius IV now doubted Elizabeth's sincerity he did not allow the second failure to end his attempts at negotiation before his death in December 1565. By then the Emperor Ferdinand I and Philip of Spain had experienced two rebuffs : the first to their request that the Catholic bishops should be permitted to leave England; and a second to the Emperor's request for a limited toleration for Catholics on the modest level that obtained for Protestants within the Empire.

The Bull of Excommunication therefore came after ten years of conciliatory overtures from Rome, but Pope Pius V, whose holiness impressed even the cynical Romans, was entirely different in character from his predecessor, being unskilled in diplomacy and rigid in his outlook. For that matter, his approach had little in common with the outlook of the surviving Catholic clergy and squires in England. By March 1569 he was consulting with the Duke of Alba about the likely success of a joint invasion of England by the Catholic Powers and being advised that co-operation between them was unthinkable. In the same year Nicholas Morton, a one-time prebendary of York, was sent to England to ascertain the likely attitude of English Catholics to an excommunication of the Queen. Elizabeth was now declared to be 'the servant of crime', who 'having seized the crown and monstrously usurped the place of the supreme head of the Church in all England' was guilty of heresy and with her adherents had incurred excommunication. She was now, moreover, declared to be deprived of her pretended title, and 'the nobles, subjects and people of the said realm and all others who have in any way sworn oaths to her, to be forever absolved from such an oath . . . We charge and command all and singular the nobles, subjects, people and others aforesaid that they do not dare obey her orders, mandates and laws. Those who shall act to the contrary we include in the like sentence of excommunication.'[29]

There is much that is mysterious in the circumstances of the issue of this Bull of 1570, so different in its wording from that in which Pope Paul III had excommunicated King Henry VIII. It has been argued that the sole purpose of the Pope's dramatic action was to allay the scruples of the English Catholics, who held it sinful to rebel against a lawful sovereign, in a situation where it was wrongly believed at the papal Court that a majority of the nation was ready to rebel to secure its religious freedom. The Bull did not declare that it was the duty of Catholics to rebel, and it made no reference to Elizabeth's illegitimacy, but it did include in the excommunication all who obeyed the Queen's 'orders, mandates and laws'. Some Roman Catholic historians have argued that this decisive papal action arrested the drift of Catholics to the State Church and so saved, admittedly at great cost, a faithful remnant. Yet it is doubtful if the Bull, which did not mention Church attendance, deserves this credit, although there are statistics that support this view. In Hampshire the citations for recusancy and noncommunicating numbered 303 for the years 1561–9, of which 248 were for noncommunicating and only 55 for absence from church; in 1570 245 persons were cited, 128 noncommunicants and 116 recusants, and most of these were for the last three months of the year.[30] One would, however, expect greater vigilance from the authorities after the issue of the Bull, and an overall impression is that the great increase in recusancy resulted from the missionary zeal of seminary priests and Jesuits. Their achievement was not a result of papal initiative.

To be effective the excommunication of the Queen should have come twelve years earlier, Her formal deposition was bound to be a futile gesture without the pledged support of the Catholic Powers, yet no attempt was made to enlist this or even to give them formal notification of the issue of the Bull. Philip II of Spain was gravely offended when he was advised of its publication by his ambassador in London and attributed the decision to French influence, especially that of the Cardinal of Lorraine, who was the uncle of Mary, Queen of Scots. In England the effect was twofold. The government now had cause to doubt the loyalty of the English Catholics, and English Protestants were given an excuse to propagate an image of the Popes that became a tradition for centuries to come.[31] For the Catholics themselves the unusual circumstances surrounding the publication of the Bull proved a source of division rather than unity, and in future they were to suffer under an increasing burden of penal laws.

Several attempts were made to secure the withdrawal of the Bull or at least its mitigation. The attempt of the Emperor Maximilian II, made at the request of Elizabeth, and that of the realist Duke of Alba both failed. The sole concession secured by Philip II's ambassador at Rome allowed omission of the section of the Bull that included in the sentence of excommunication all those who obeyed the Queen.[32] As for the Queen, she was more secure than ever on her throne : two years after publication of the Bull England secured an agreement from France to abandon the cause of the Scottish Queen, and in 1573 agreement was reached with Spain.

4 Government Reaction: The Sharpening of the Law

In this Parliament it was showed us a bill devised of our
safety against treasons, whereof, when we had the sight
it liked us not, being not of the mind to offer extremity
or injury to any person.

Queen Elizabeth I, 1571

Publication of the Bull of Excommunication combined with
a worsening of the international situation to produce a profound change for the English Catholics, who would soon be
regarded as potential enemies of the State. Government
reaction to the Bull was at first cautious. It took the form
of a statement by Cecil in the Star Chamber, denying rumours
that the Queen had caused any examination of men's consciences in 'matters of religion'. The statement admitted that
certain persons had been called before the Council and that
some 'have been treated withal upon some matter of religion,
yet the cause thereof hath grown merely of themselves, in
that they have first manifestly broken the laws established
for religion in not coming at all to church, to common prayer
and divine service'.[1] This may seem a dubious refutation of
the charge of religious oppression, but it was soon to be
government policy to charge Catholics under the treason
laws by a generous extension of their scope.

There was indeed some cause for alarm, with the Ridolfi
plot following on the Northern rising, followed in its turn
by the Massacre of St Bartholomew. These events were all

blamed on the Pope, who was now cast in the role of 'this bloody monster of Rome'. A sharpening of the law came with the Parliament of 1571, which was the first to contain no Catholics among the Commons for all now had to take the supremacy oath. This Parliament passed three Acts dealing with the Catholic problem.[2] First came a Treasons Act, which made it high treason to write or assert that Elizabeth was not the lawful Queen or to describe her as an heretic, schismatic, tyrant, infidel or usurper. A second Act prohibited the introduction of papal Bulls or certain Catholic articles of devotion and made it treason to reconcile anyone to the see of Rome or to receive such absolution or any Bull or writing of the Pope. A third Act dealt with the Catholic exiles. An attempt by this Parliament to make an annual communion compulsory was vetoed by the Queen, but in later years recusants would not be able to escape legal penalty by church attendance but would also be obliged to communicate.[3]

This legislation was already passed when the first seminary priests landed in England, and its penalties would have made their mission impossible from the outset had the law been enforced with determination. That did not happen, but some key appointments foreshadowed a determined drive against recusancy. Those of Grindal as Archbishop of York and of the Earl of Huntingdon as President of the Council of the North placed two men of strong puritan views over counties where, as a Member of Parliament declared in 1572, it was much more dangerous to be a Protestant than a papist.[4] Weakness in the diocese of Chester was replaced by zeal when William Chadderton succeeded Bishop Downham in 1579, while William Curteys as Bishop of Chichester after 1570 brought the full impact of the reformed religion to bear on the diocese in a manner previously unknown. Even so the success of these new appointments had its limitations. During Huntingdon's long presidency, which lasted until 1595, a large number of Marian and seminary priests were arrested, but he could not prevent an increase in the numbers of recusant Yorkshire gentry. Chadderton was very energetic but not very successful in the part of his diocese that included Lancashire – a county that contributed more recruits to Allen's college at Douai than any other part of England – and in Derby hundred in 1590 only ten out of seventy-one members of the gentry were considered reliable supporters of the new religion.[5] Bishop Curteys made the mistake of attacking a section of the Sussex gentry that had been deliberately treated with some care by the government : the crypto-Catholics who occasionally conformed for the sake of retaining public office and influence. In 1577 he summoned gentry suspected of Catholic sympathies to public consistories in his cathedral, and the few who troubled to attend were asked a series of questions : how often they attended common prayer in their parish church; since January 1576, how often they had communicated ; how many sermons they had attended; did they possess Catholic books or correspond with the exiles.[6] Complaint to the Privy Council by an indignant gentry led to an official rebuke for Curteys, and further tactlessness, though not against Catholics, led to his suspension from spiritual administration.

In the mid-1570s the government believed that recusancy was increasing, and the practice began of summoning heads of prominent families for questioning, fining and periodic imprisonment. At the same time increased efforts were made to remove Catholics from the Commission of the Peace and to secure a survey of recusancy in every diocese. The authorities were well aware that 'it is the obstinacy of the great that prevents the lower orders conforming', and in 1580 the Council advised the Ecclesiastical Commission in the Chester diocese to begin its inquiries with recusants of social standing. Special prisons were opened in various parts of the country, and Wisbech castle was set aside for the more prominent members of the Catholic clergy. To Wisbech were sent the last surviving Marian bishop, Watson of Lincoln, now blind and ailing, and the former Abbot Feckenham of Westminster. Yet it was still the official policy to attempt to win over individuals by mild treatment, persuasion, compulsory attendance at sermons, and conference with Protestant ministers. Catholics were occasionally released from prison on giving bonds for good behaviour or accepting conditions of residence in a specified place with an undertaking not to travel more than three miles from their dwelling. In return for a bond, which could amount to the large sum of £2 000, a man of wealth might obtain temporary release on account of illness, to prosecute business affairs or for family reasons. The poor were less fortunate, and the Bishop of Winchester suggested that 200 recusants from Hampshire and Surrey, 'lusty men, well able to labour', should be sent to the Earl of Leicester in the Netherlands for use with his army.[7]

Seven years passed after the publication of the Bull before the first seminary priest was put to death, sentenced under the 1571 Act, but really repressive legislation was not introduced until after the arrival of the Jesuits in 1580. By then it was evident to the government that Catholicism was not likely to die away for lack of priests and that in fact a revival was in progress. The Jesuits provided a new element that gave a remarkable stimulus to Catholicism but was ultimately divisive, and they attracted government attention out of proportion to their numbers. Historians have been given, with much exaggeration, to referring to 'a Jesuit invasion in force', when in fact the newcomers consisted of two priests, Edmund Campion and Robert Persons, accompanied by a lay brother. In a ministry lasting a single year they managed to set all England astir. It was now forty years since Pope Paul III had approved the constitutions of the new Society of Jesus, and a considerable number of Englishmen had joined its ranks, scattered abroad in its European houses and foreign missions. The first contact with English problems came when two members of the Society were lent to assist the newly founded English College in Rome, and it was mainly the enthusiasm of Dr Allen that brought them into the English mission. The Jesuit General, a Netherlander named Mercurian, had serious misgivings about the project. He was convinced that the English government would regard his men as political agents, that conditions in England would make observance of the Jesuit way of life impossible, and that the absence of episcopal authority might endanger harmony between the Jesuits and the secular clergy. In the event, Mercurian's doubts were to be well justified. Agreement was finally given on certain clear conditions : the fathers were to avoid contact with heretics, for their mission was intended for Catholics only; they were to avoid mixing in politics and mentioning the subject in writing to their superiors in Rome; and conversation about the Queen was to be avoided as far as possible, a prohibition made absolute a year later. By and large Jesuits who worked in England observed this ruling, and an absence of reference to politics can be detected in their letters to Rome. Not all observed it when outside their own country.

The arrival of the Jesuits received great publicity and raised alarm in government circles. This was due partly to the fact that Campion and Persons were both remembered in university and government circles, and partly to a natural curiosity concerning members of a new religious Order hitherto unknown in England. In later years Persons said that the true founder of the Jesuit mission was a wealthy young man named George Gilbert, a convert from Puritanism, who financed their journeys, provided horses and clothing and aided their security. Some thirty young men of gentry families shared this work and put the two priests in touch with devout Catholic families who would welcome their ministrations. They were not always discreet. The government had news of their arrival, and it was foolhardy, though characteristic of the man, that three days after Campion's landing he preached to a large congregation in the great hall of Lord Norris house at Smithfield. This meeting was arranged through Lord Paget, and it had not taken long for the two Jesuits to find influential friends. During the following year Persons journeyed through the Midlands and West Country while Campion visited Oxfordshire, Berkshire and the North, and at a time of increased government pressure these journeys brought new hope to recusant Catholics. To this exacting and dangerous travel Persons added propaganda by the establishment of a secret printing press, a task requiring great ingenuity, and six works were printed before the press was seized by the authorities at Stonor Park near Henley. Three of these works were by Persons, including *A Brief Discours Contayning Certain Reasons Why Catholiques Refuse to Goe to Church.*

In the summer of 1580 rumours were circulating of a papal league for the invasion of England. This, added to the papal support of the Irish rebellion of the previous year, intensified Protestant alarm. Before the parliamentary session a royal proclamation was issued in July 1580 that stressed the Queen's duty to keep her people free of the bondage of Rome, and a second proclamation in January of the next year dealt with students of the seminaries and the need to punish priests who were in England and their abetters. The two proclamations might have indicated the policy that the government expected Parliament to follow when it met in January 1581.[8] In a government speech made by Sir Walter Mildmay the Jesuits were mentioned for the first time by name : 'A sort of hypocrites, naming themselves Jesuits, a rabble of vagrant friars newly sprung up and coming through the world to trouble the Church of God; whose principle errand is, by creeping into the houses and familiarities of men of behaviour and reputation, not only to corrupt the realm with false doctrines, but also, under that pretence, to stir up sedition.'[9] The speaker added that many who had previously conformed 'now utterly refuse to be of our Church'. Here was a measure of the alarm that two men had created. By the end of the year only one elderly Jesuit was at large in England, multiplied by the dozen in the ordinary Englishman's imagination.

In this mood of alarm a new Act was passed to retain the Queen's Majesty's subjects in their due obedience by greatly stiffening the penalties against Catholics. In future, anyone claiming to have authority to absolve or withdraw any subjects from their natural obedience, or to withdraw them with that intent from the official religion to Catholicism, together with any persons so reconciled, were guilty of treason; anyone aiding or concealing this offence was guilty of misprision of treason. The penalty for celebrating Mass became a year's imprisonment and a fine of 200 marks; attendance at Mass incurred a year's imprisonment and a fine of 100 marks.

Neale has argued that the 1581 Act 'drew a statesmanlike distinction between being and becoming a Catholic' : the Act did not plainly define conversion as an act of treason; it was conversion with intent to withdraw a subject from his allegiance that was treasonable, thus making the approach political and secular.[10] Yet Neale has also commented on the ability of Elizabethan judges to drive a coach and six through any Act of Parliament, and in practice all conversion to Catholicism was treated as a withdrawal of allegiance. The definition of treason had now been given a sweeping extension. Finally, Parliament imposed a ruinous fine of £20 a month on every person above the age of 16 years who failed to attend church, a fine large enough in Thomas Fuller's words 'to shatter the containment of a rich man's estate'. After one year's absence the offender was to be bound over with two sureties of £200 until such time as he conformed. These were severe penalties, but two earlier Bills had proposed even stricter ones and the influence of the Queen may have been decisive in toning them down. A further Bill passed in this Parliament, which had Catholics in mind, dealt with seditious words and rumours uttered against the Queen.

The discovery of the Throckmorton plot in 1583, the assassination of the Prince of Orange in the following year, and the Parry plot of 1585 intensified anti-Catholic feeling. In December 1585 Sir Walter Mildmay was urging Parliament to pass further measures, claiming that the Pope was 'knitting together all popish princes and states to the overthrow of the Gospel in all places . . . his malicious and secret practisers creep . . . into sundry parts of the realm and are occupied to stir up sedition'.[11] The probable result of this subversion would be 'the utter rooting out of the whole nobility and people . . . and the placing in of strangers'. Parliament now passed a new Act directed against the seminary priests and Jesuits ordained overseas : its preamble declared that their purpose was 'to withdraw subjects from their due obedience' and 'to stir up and move sedition, rebellion, and open hostility within her Highness' realms'. All such were ordered to quit the realm within forty days after the ending of the parliamentary session, and those who remained would be guilty of treason by the fact of their ordination abroad. The death penalty was extended to cover anyone harbouring or helping such priests. Those also who sent money to the Catholic colleges abroad were to incur the penalty of loss of goods and imprisonment, while parents sending children to be educated abroad without licence became subject to heavy fines. Anyone now failing to give information of the whereabouts of a priest became liable to fines and imprisonment at the Queen's pleasure. The supposed treason of a priest was, however, to be pardoned if he took the oath of supremacy within three days of landing.

While this Bill was under discussion a group of Catholic laymen decided to petition the Queen to withhold her assent. They included Lord Vaux, Sir John Arundell (the 'great Arundell of Cornwall'), Sir William Catesby and Sir Thomas Tresham, members of families that had served the Crown well in past days. Arundell had been active in public affairs as late as 1574, inspecting the coastal defences with the Earl of Bedford, and was a son-in-law of Lord Derby. His determined recusancy may have been influenced by the execution of a young priest, Cuthbert Mayne. By 1584 Sir John was in the Tower; it was charged that he had permitted his nephew to go overseas and that 'besides the old matters concerning Mayne the traitor he hath received divers priests since the proclamation, had Masses in his house in the Easter week, confessed by the priest'. Tresham also suffered years of imprisonment and has been described by Rowse as 'good-natured, whimsical, loyal, fantastic, cheerful in misfortune'. He had need to be.

The petition was delivered to the Queen by a Sussex recusant, Richard Shelley, who had also suffered imprisonment for religion, 'as she walked in her garden at Greenwich at the time of the Parliament then holden'. It was a lengthy document and described the dilemma of the Catholic laity should it become treason to shelter priests:

. . . if we shut our doors and deny our temporal relief to

our Catholic pastors in respect of their function, then we are already judged most damnable traitors to Almighty God . . . Let us not your Catholic native English and obedient subjects stand in more peril for frequenting the Blessed Sacrament and exercising the Catholic religion (and that most secretly) than do the Protestants enjoying their public assemblies under divers Catholic kings and princes quietly . . . Grant O merciful Queen that we may do the work of mercy to God's priests, so long as they pray for your Majesty and use themselves dutifully to your Highness.[12]

The petitioners rehearsed the sufferings of the Catholic laity from fines, imprisonment and torture and concluded with the hope that 'now at length our approved patience will move your most tender heart to have some pity and compassion on us'. The Queen's most tender heart remained unmoved. Shelley was arrested and died in prison; his brother Edward was put to death 'for receiving and aiding and comforting one William Deane, a seminary priest'.

Stringent legislation was followed by an increase in recusancy. In 1585 the Clerk of the Peace in Hampshire complained of the extra labour involved : 'not only by himself or by his deputy and a servant or two, a great deal of time before and after every sessions, but also the most part of the sessions itself in drawing and engrossing the indictments, judgements and processes thereupon'.[13] The sessions were lasting longer, and other cases had to be postponed. Yet the application of the 1585 Act was never consistent, and it was used by the government as a useful weapon of intimidation. Of 183 priests, laymen and laywomen put to death during the remaining years of the reign sixteen were condemned under the medieval Treasons Act of 1352 and the remainder under the new laws; 123 were priests and sixty layfolk. Considering the many priests who fell into the hands of the government the number is not large, and many were left in prison or deported. Fifty or more died in prison. The government was always alert to the anti-English propaganda the executions occasioned abroad, and even the Jesuit Robert Southwell felt it necessary to ask his superior in Rome not to judge his fellow countrymen by the government persecution of Catholics.

If the death penalty was sparingly applied the financial penalties of these Acts fell more heavily. The process may have originated in 1577 with a letter from Bishop Aylmer of London to Walsingham, which called attention to the increase in recusancy. He noted that imprisonment was of little avail and 'hath also been a means of sparing their housekeeping greatly to enrich them'.[14] Fines were considered preferable, and 'this manner of fining will procure the Queen a thousand pounds a year for her coffers'. Aylmer's suggestion of 'round fines to be imposed for contemptuously refusing of receiving communion' was followed three months later by a government order that bishops should make a return of the numbers of recusants in their dioceses, and the enormous fine of £20 imposed by the 1581 Act gave the government an effective weapon. The shilling fine for absence from church on Sundays and holydays had proved a trivial sum for the wealthy, although in corporate towns it tended to be doubled and obstinate recusants were disfranchised. As the cumbersome procedure of the 1581 Act led to widespread evasion of payment, the law was tightened in 1587. Henceforth a Catholic recusant once convicted need not be further indicted, but he must pay the monthly fines twice a year to the Exchequer, and failure to do so would lead to the loss of all his goods and two-thirds of his lands. Failure of an indicted recusant to appear in court was to be treated as refusal, and conviction became automatic. This achieved some success in increasing both the numbers of church papists and the revenue from fines, a fourfold increase in the year 1589–90 over the years before 1587.[15]

In 1592 the Exchequer set up a special department to deal with recusant fines, and three years later churchwardens were ordered to make a valuation of recusant estates in order to determine names of those against whom it would be uneconomic to take proceedings. In the latter cases seizure of goods could be applied forthwith on conviction and the goods sold at auction. Robert Southwell described the sufferings of the humbler victims :

> . . . where poor farmers and husbandmen had but one cow for themselves and many children to live upon, that for their recusancy hath been taken from them. And where both kine and cattle were wanting, they have taken their coverlets, sheets, and blankets from their beds, their victuals and poor provision from their houses, not sparing so much as the very glass of their windows . . .'.[16]

In 1597 Thomas Felton was appointed at a salary of £200 a year with expenses, to review leases, raise rents of recusant estates and treat with those in arrear of fines. Felton and his agents travelled round the country searching out subjects for prosecution, and it has been claimed that by the end of the reign Catholics hated him more than any of Elizabeth's officials.[17] By 1601 the Exchequer income from recusant fines had risen to £9 126, and by 1609 to £12 965.[18] This burden was carried mainly by wealthy recusants and possibly by fewer than 200 of them. In addition to the regular fines recusants were asked occasionally to pay extra taxation : for example, in 1580, 1584, 1585 and 1598 there were levies for the supply of light horsemen for the wars in Ireland and the Netherlands.

During the 1580s enforcement of the law was being removed from the Justices of the Peace into the hands of commissions. The commissioners were selected from zealous Protestants and were given powers more extensive than those of the bishops or justices. Some of the Sussex gentry held that the methods these commissioners used were illegal, and in 1588 Lord Buckhurst, one of the Lords Lieutenant, warned a deputy lieutenant who proposed to imprison a recusant that 'it was very injurious' to assume that a recusant was a dangerous man 'before his case be first heard and tried'.[19] These moderate views had no influence with the Council. In 1592 the deputy lieutenants were given general warrant to search the houses of recusants for priests and forbidden books and to commit suspicious persons to prison. Five years later the sheriff was authorised to pay five shillings for every recusant brought to trial.

In 1593 a Bill was introduced into the House of Commons that exceeded in its ferocity all previous anti-Catholic laws.[20] The penalty for refusing church attendance was now to include seizure of all goods and the profits of two-thirds of a recusant's estate; no recusant would be permitted to lease, rent or sell land; recusant wives were henceforth to lose their dowers; the penalty for marriage to a recusant heiress was to be forfeiture of two-thirds of her inheritance; Catholics were to be excluded from all offices and the learned professions; anyone keeping a recusant guest or servant in his house was to pay a fine of £10 a month; and children were now to be removed from recusant parents at the age of 7 years and educated as Protestants. Thus, in the words of Neale, Catholics were to be treated as 'an alien pest in society, immobilised, rendered impotent by virtual expropriation . . . and eradicated in a single generation'. Queen Elizabeth has won great praise for her moderation in religious matters, yet it seems unlikely that, as Neale has suggested, she was unaware of this proposed Bill. The initiative came from the government. The Queen must also surely have known of the proclamations put out in her name. An unusually fiercely worded one had been issued in 1591.[21]

The proposed Bill of 1593 was criticised in the Commons, and some members objected that the vagueness of some clauses might even trap good Protestant subjects, they did not want to suffer financially on behalf of recusant wives and disliked the removal of children from parents at a tender age. The Bill was abandoned, and a far milder law passed.[22] Recusants must now remain within five miles of their homes or forfeit goods and income from land; They must report to the minister and the parish constable, and their names were to be kept in a parish register and certified to the justices of the peace; Those who lacked a property qualification sufficient to enable them to pay the fines now became liable to banishment; and one clause that had condemned to death arrested persons suspected of being Jesuits, or secular priests who refused to admit their priesthood, was scaled down to imprisonment without trial. The history of this Act of 1593, which completed legislation against Catholics, suggested that Parliament was able to take a stand against the government in favour of reduced severity if not of moderation.

Catholicism was not, however, to pass without comment in the final Parliament of the reign.[23] The shilling fine for absence from church was falling into disuse although it was still being levied in the North in 1599, and an attempt to enforce it was made in the Parliament in 1601.[24] This was an attempt to catch humble offenders, and a Yorkshire member claimed that in his county there were 'at least twelve or thirteen hundred recusants most of which this law . . . would constrain to come to church; I mean only those of the humbler sort.' During the debate another member alleged that he knew of parishes where 'half the people were perverted by Jesuits and seminarists, the poorer and meaner sort of the people'. The proposed Bill failed to win approval by a single vote.

Appendix: Some effects of the financial penalties
Although the financial burden fell on under 200 of the recusants and never more than seventeen paid the full fine, the results could be crippling for those affected. The great wealth of a Sir Thomas Tresham enabled him to survive, although he died in debt. The record of payment might have been held by John Sayer, a Yorkshire landowner, who paid the full fine between 1592 and 1627.[25] The richest recusant in Lancashire was John Townley who was able to pay enormous fines over a long period. However, the single Essex recusant who paid in full during the ten years from 1583 – Ferdinand Paris, a brother of Lady Lovell – had lost most of his fortune when he died in 1600. Another Essex recusant offered a composition of £40 per annum on the ground that he had a family of ten children to support; he paid a total of £397 over a period of ten years and spent much of the time in prison.[26] The Gage family of Sussex in its various branches was strongly

recusant. John Gage fell into arrears with his fines but paid in full from 1585 until 1593; in 1587 his goods were valued at £2 000 and his yearly income at £800. Lady Elizabeth Gage, his mother, owed over £1 000 at one time, and in 1593 the Exchequer sequestrated lands that were producing an income of £253 per annum; Six years earlier her total income had been estimated at £200.[27]

Fines were sometimes levied on those who were obviously too poor to pay, and in 1590 the Council complained that commissioners sent into Cheshire to discover the amount of goods and lands held by convicted recusants found nothing because most of those indicted were wives, daughters, yeomen, labourers and serving men. In one case it was reported of a man who had spent terms in seven prisons and suffered seizure of his land over twenty-two years that 'he hath nothing to live upon but that his friends do give him'; Even so he was assessed to contribute £25 for the 1585 levy for light horsemen, a sum that was eventually paid.[28]

Extra taxation was regarded as a test of loyalty, and recusants were told that co-operation would lead the government 'to qualify in some part the extremity of punishment that otherwise the law doth lay upon them'. In 1585 it was found that a number of those assessed were in prison or could not be found, while many pleaded inability to pay, as did the Sussex man who was excused by the sheriff: 'Since my last commitment into the Marshalsey I have lost upon the statute of recusancy all my leases and goods; and now have not to supply the necessity of which my poor old wife and I have and much more by means of my long imprisonment.'[29] Thirteen Suffolk gentry contributed to the levy, but in Lancashire 138 individuals provided £7 133. The levy of 1598 met with less success, and the collectors found open refusal. When the Bishop of Chester was ordered to summon defaulters he wrote to Cecil of his failure: 'We missed good success because of the recusants withdrew from their abode . . . These men have so many spies, and such great kindred and alliance, that it is most difficult to surprise their persons; of late they have grown very desperate.'[30]

Recognising the inability of most men to pay the full fine, and professing itself satisfied with the recusant response to the levy of 1585, the authorities decided that listed recusants might be permitted to make a composition of the full fine and to pay such proportion of their income as would leave enough for a decent living. The response was discouraging, for not all were willing to make an offer and those who did so suggested sums that varied from £100 to 5 shillings, well below the statutory sum. Sir John Arundell had £2 000 in goods and an annual rental of £1 000 from property held jointly with his wife, but he offered only £100, having recently paid a fine of £666 in the Star Chamber.[31] When a recusant paid a composition on his remaining income after part of his estate had been sequestered, the arrangement might be annulled if the value of his remaining lands increased. Thomas Gawen of Wiltshire suffered the loss of 1 700 acres, retaining only 300 after a revaluation demanded by the government agent, Thomas Felton; He had also spent some time in prison (see p. 154).[32]

After the passing of the 1581 Act recusants were at risk from the common informer, who could obtain a third of the fine in the event of a conviction, one–third going to the Queen and the remainder to the poor of the parish, at least in theory. In the Hilary Term of 1581–2 Hugh Cuffe sued twenty-four recusants living in twelve different counties, but his occupation had its risks, and in 1599 Catholics living in the Whitby district attacked and drove out a common informer and his companions.[33] One of these men, Richard Heaton, specialised in catching recusants living in London, and gentry visiting the capital might be at greater risk there than with their country neighbours.

5 Confrontation:
Pope and Queen 1570-1603

The slightest text in his hand gives a strange impression
of violence and presence . . . He lived in a supernatural
element, lost in his devotions, and the fact that he was
not of this world made Pius V a great historical force,
unpredictable and dangerous.

Braudel, *The Mediterranean*

Pope Pius V has not fared well at the hands of English
historians, but in a different context he is almost the hero of the
second volume of Braudel's great work, a reminder that Anti-
Christ was not exclusively concerned with the 'Elect Nation'.
For Pius V and the Popes who followed him the conflict with
Elizabeth was only one aspect of a battle fought on two
fronts: for the spiritual regeneration of the Church from
within, and for the defence of the Church against militant
Calvinism attacking from without. The Council of Trent had
concluded its work in 1563, but its decrees amounted to little
more than the paper on which they were written. Fifty years
of effort lay ahead before the moral regeneration of the
Church could be considered as secured. That task was everywhere challenged by the spread of militant Calvinism, and
Calvin's death in 1564 served as a reminder that the fortunes of
Catholicism were still finely balanced. To both sides it seemed
that they were locked in a battle with the forces of evil that
admitted no compromise. It is against this background that
papal hostility to Elizabeth's government must be weighed,
for the policies followed by the Queen almost from the begin-

ning of the reign involved the promotion of militant Calvinism – for political motives, not religious – through both open and underhand support of rebellion in Scotland, France and the Netherlands. This policy had met with considerable success by 1570. In Scotland the Calvinist cause had been strengthened by the early expulsion of the French, and the flight of the Queen of Scots in 1568 boded ill for the still influential Catholic members of the Scottish nobility. In France the expeditionary force that Elizabeth had sent to help the French Calvinists had met with disaster, but that country was now sliding into civil war and the future of Catholicism was in doubt. In Ireland an attempt, neither energetic nor successful, had been made to introduce the Elizabethan settlement of religion, but an appeal by the O'Neill for French aid had been followed by a successful English expedition that proved the prelude to a long and costly war. Yet as Pius V considered the political situation during the first year of his reign, its most significant event, unrealised at the time, was the outburst of mob violence in the Netherlands in 1566, which resulted from fanatical Calvinist preaching and led to the dispatch of Alba's army in the following year. Here too the English government had been at work, helping to promote unrest by the use of paid agitators. The arrival of a Spanish force was a check to English policies and a potential menace to both England and France, which neither country could ignore. It was to have great influence on the failure of papal policies towards England.[1]

There was a reverse side to the coin. At a time when almost every European government met with internal discontent and opposition, the rulers could expect to find aid in their neighbours' territories, and in this respect England might be vulnerable. Other governments could play Elizabeth's game. So far as religion was concerned her government at the outset was a minority one. Moreover, although it was strongly established by 1570 it still controlled a religious minority that might respond to foreign aid, while after 1568 an alternative claimant to the throne was held in confinement, a focus for discontent. So long as Mary lived some of Elizabeth's most important councillors, including Lord Burghley and Walsingham, would try to keep a line open with a view to the possibility of her accession if Elizabeth died : 'They thought it prudent to assure Mary of the reversion of their loyalty.'[2] The success of Elizabeth's policies had been greatly helped during the early years by the support or benevolent neutrality of Philip II of Spain, who was unwilling to see an increase of French influence; such influence seemed involved with the cause of Mary Stuart. Yet Spain became increasingly alienated by Elizabeth's meddling in the Netherlands and by the raids of English seamen in the Caribbean, patronised by the Queen with finance and ships. A breach occurred in 1568 when Spanish treasure ships were impounded on their journey to the Netherlands. A state of undeclared war was reached when Leicester's expedition was sent to the Netherlands in 1585. Then open war became inevitable. In the words of Neale, 'the question remained, how long could Elizabeth go on with impunity fostering trouble for everyone else and escaping it herself'. Conyers Read has supplied an answer : 'It is pretty clear that the immediate cause of the despatch of the Armada was the aggressive tactics of the English themselves.'[3]

Since England was the patron of policies that might ensure the success of Calvinism in Europe and the overthrow of Catholicism, it was not to be expected – quite apart from the question of the English Catholics – that the papacy should stand aside. Confrontation was inevitable, and in an age that accepted without question the use of force to further the cause of religion the papacy too would resort to force, though never with any degree of efficiency. Protestant princes constantly feared the formation by the Pope of a league of Catholic princes, and the first rumours of such a league seem to have resulted from a meeting of Catharine de Medici with the Duke of Alba in 1565. We know that no such league ever existed, for the papal diplomacy directed to that end constantly foundered on the rivalries of the Catholic Powers, just as the efforts of Pius V to renew the league against the Turks after Lepanto were shipwrecked on the selfish interests of

Venice and Spain. Here again we find Walsingham in later years urging the Turks to renew their attacks on Italy and Sicily.

To many if not most Englishmen Philip II appeared to be hand in glove with the Pope. The reality was different, and the Spanish king found no difficulty, as did many English Catholics, in being loyal to his religion while opposed politically to its head.[4] He was at war for two years with Paul IV; he was in conflict with the conciliatory Pius IV; Pius V refused to be bullied, but the sound advice he gave that Philip should go himself to the Netherlands was rejected; Gregory XIII had a personal liking for Philip, whom he had met in earlier years when on a mission to Spain, but there was very little co-operation between them; Sixtus V had a strong dislike of him, which Philip returned. To the Popes it often appeared that the Spanish king used his religion, sincere though it undoubtedly was, as a cloak for political objectives. The policy of Spain, as of other Catholic States, was in fact determined by *realpolitik*, not by religion. Spain's increasing power, especially after the conquest of Portugal, was of concern to the Papacy and feared by Catholic countries as well as by England.

The Protestant fear of a league of Catholic Powers was therefore without foundation. Nevertheless, it was the consistent policy of the Popes to work for such a league, and a small group of Catholic exiles tried to exert an influence, centering their political schemes on Mary, Queen of Scots. The importance of their influence may be doubted save in so far as they may have misled the Roman authorities. Dr Allen, Robert Persons and Sir Francis Englefield were welcomed at conference tables for their supposed knowledge of English Catholic opinion, but events revealed how mistaken their assessment was. Their co-religionists in England were mostly unaware of their plotting, and when they finally discovered the extent to which they had been pledged to Spain they were ill pleased. The Spanish authorities gave the exiles a sympathetic hearing but ignored them when it came to action. In 1591 Robert Persons commented that three years earlier Spain had 'showed no confidence in any living person of our nation both within and without the kingdom', yet he continued his attempts to influence events. In 1596 he forwarded a memorandum to the Spanish Council of State with suggestions for a proclamation to be issued when a landing had been made.[5]

After the failure of the Northern Rising in England the Roman authorities gave a hearing to an Italian banker, Ridolfi, who had been living in London for some ten years and who, as apparently a sound man of affairs, had become intimate with members of the Court circle. He might have had a hand in the rebellion of 1569 and was held under arrest in Walsingham's house, but if so his credit was undiminished. In 1571, after a private interview with the Queen, he left for the Netherlands, having obtained a commission to treat on matters of trade with the Duke of Alba. He also had a mission of a very different nature, for he took with him letters from the Queen of Scots and the Duke of Norfolk and a plan for the seizure of Elizabeth, the release of Mary and the restoration of Catholicism. Alba formed no great opinion of him and found him very 'liberal of speech', and his judgement on the whole affair was that 'in the case of men of such little balance as those who treat these topics, and have such little comprehension of what is practicable, nothing at all should be risked upon their words'. Moving on to Rome Ridolfi obtained papal encouragement, and his schemes were given a sympathetic hearing by Philip II and his Council, but ultimately Alba's advice prevailed. It was not difficult for the English government to unravel the plot once it had captured letters that Ridolfi had sent into England, and in January 1572 the Protestant Duke of Norfolk was tried and executed. In August the government also eliminated a Catholic rebel when it bought the Earl of Northumberland from the Scots for £2 000. The Ridolfi plot made it clear that the papacy would encourage any scheme to destroy Elizabeth's government.[6].

Pius V died in May 1572. His successor, Pope Gregory XIII, took up with even greater enthusiasm the attempt to form a Catholic league, but again the scheme was without success. It would be a mistake to judge Gregory XIII by the failure, and indeed the futility, of his political intervention in English affairs, for he was in many ways a remarkable and successful ruler of the Church. His activities ranged far and wide : the foundation of a university and national colleges in Rome; the development of Christian missions in India, China and Japan; mediation of peace between Russia and Poland, and successful intervention in North Germany when the policies of the Cologne Elector seemed to open the way for Protestantism to triumph in the Rhineland. In 1572 the new Pope at once instructed his nuncio in Madrid to press the enterprise of England upon a reluctant king, and soon a bizarre character appeared on the scene, 'sent from heaven' as one of the exiles foolishly remarked.

Ridolfi was a hopeless plotter but a solid man of business; Sir Thomas Stukely was an adventurer, a mercenary soldier and a man of dubious religious beliefs, with a background of service for Elizabeth in Ireland. Stukeley had first been received in Madrid. Later he moved on to Rome where the Welsh exiles gave him a welcome, possibly because he had fought bravely at Lepanto. He was in Rome when Dr Allen was summoned there in 1576 to advise on a project put forward by Don John of Austria for an attack on England from the Netherlands. Nothing came of this, and it was decided instead to take advantage of the Irish rising and, as the papal secretary of state remarked, 'to plant a thorn in the side of Elizabeth such as Orange is in ours'. A plea for help was also voiced by James Fitzgerald, a cousin of the Earl of Desmond and a man who was, unlike Stukely, both a devout Catholic and a sincere Irish patriot. Stukely sailed but went off to join the King of Portugal's crusade in Africa. Fitzgerald sailed for Spain, where he obtained unofficial help from Philip II and took on board the Englishman Nicholas Sander as papal representative. Their landing at Dingle Bay in July 1579 led to a rising in Munster, and in September 1580 reinforcements arrived from Spain commanded by 'a captain and general of his Holiness'. However, the papal expedition ended in disaster. Yet Gregory XIII's interest in Ireland was not unproductive, for the foundation of Irish colleges abroad trained a new missionary clergy who planted the Counter Reformation firmly in the country. Elizabeth's government had pacified the whole island by the end of her reign but had lost the battle for the spiritual allegiance of its people.

It was one thing for the Pope to work by diplomacy for a Catholic league, but the open sponsorship of a military expedition could not fail to have adverse consequences for the English Catholics. The two Jesuits, Persons and Campion, were dismayed when they first heard of it. From that angle 1580 was a most unfortunate year for their journey through England on the work of spiritual renewal. One result of their activities was the increased circulation of Catholic books. This caused official concern, for, although little had been published from the Catholic side during the 1570s, in the twenty-one months between the entry of the Jesuits and the execution of Campion eleven Catholic works were published and attracted much attention.[7] There were also renewed rumours of a papal league, and in July 1580 the English ambassador in Paris forwarded a list of ten articles that purported to be a plan for invasion. The document was a forgery, but a similar warning was received from the Prince of Orange. In fact, and in spite of papal disapproval, Philip II was planning the annexation of Portugal. However, the English government felt it necessary to issue a royal proclamation warning the people that rebels and traitors abroad had invited the Pope and the King of Spain to invade.[8]

The next five years were a time of special danger for the Queen and bore out Bacon's dictum that among 'the causes and motives of sedition are innovations in religion'. For a brief period it seemed that the Counter Reformation might win the day in Scotland when a cousin of the young King James VI – Esme Stuart, later Duke of Lennox – returned from France and, secure in the confidence of the king, overthrew the pro-English Regent Morton. The Duke of Guise now prepared an elaborate plan to restore his cousin Queen Mary and to invade England through Scotland. Two Jesuits, the Scottish Crichton and Robert Persons, were sent as envoys to enlist support from the Pope and King Philip. *A coup d'état* that drove Lennox into exile caused a change of plan, and it was then hoped that Guise could lead a detachment of Parma's army for a direct attack on England. Philip, however, was not prepared to supply the troops, and the Pope was unwilling to assist with finance until the expedition had begun. When Crichton was captured at sea by the Dutch and handed over to the English government much was learned of these schemes, while the arrest of a young Catholic, Francis Throckmorton, revealed an enemy within. He had been acting as a channel of communication with the Queen of Scots. The extent to which English Catholics supported these plans must remain a matter of conjecture. Robert Persons had promised their lavish support, claiming in 1582 that 'all Catholics without exception regard the invasion with approval', but in the next year the Spanish ambassador in London declared that it was hopeless to expect help of that kind as the Catholics were 'paralysed by fear'.

More real was the fear that the Queen might be assassinated at a time when European opinion on both sides of the religious conflict regarded the removal of a tyrant by murder as morally justifiable. In France two Dukes of Guise, Coligny and two kings were removed by the assassin's hand. Elizabeth herself agreed to a plan to hand the Queen of Scots back to the Protestant government of Scotland, provided that that government consented to put her to death without implicating England.[9] The murder of William of Orange in 1584, with the approval of Spain, alarmed Protestant Europe and led in England to the passing of an Act for ensuring the Queen's Safety. A year earlier a mentally unbalanced Catholic, Somerville, had set out from Warwickshire loudly proclaiming his intention to kill the Queen, and ten years later a Puritan fanatic, also unbalanced, was arrested for the same intent. The trial of a Member of Parliament, William Parry, revealed in 1585 that the papal secretary of state had approved of the 'removal' of the Queen as a good deed.[10] One year later came the discovery of the young Anthony Babington's plot, which included the murder of Elizabeth and the release of the Queen

of Scots. Fourteen people were put to death for this conspiracy, including a youth who had taken food to two of the
plotters who were hiding in a wood near his home. Also among
them was a seminary priest, John Ballard. Persons later
stated that Ballard had entered England without Dr Allen's
permission, and he seems to have been a freelance of somewhat dubious standing.

Given the dangers that menaced the country and the life
of the Queen, the government cannot be criticised for taking
stern action against all who were involved in plots, and much
has been made, perhaps too much, of these conspiracies. It
was the lot of all Tudor sovereigns to suffer from conspiracy
and rebellion, and towards the end of the reign an accusation
of plotting to kill the Queen was lightly made. In 1594 a
suspect under examination made a joke of it : 'It were foolish
to think of killing the Queen who is continually mewed up in
a chamber, that it were better service to kill the Lord
Treasurer's horse, for he would take it so grievously if the old
jade were dead that he would die also.'[11] Like all Tudor conspiracies those directed against Elizabeth were incredibly in-
competent in plan and execution : Walsingham's agents
usually discovered them at an early stage, while Dr Parry and
others had a background of spying in Walsingham's service.[12]
There were English Catholics at the time who believed that
the government was capable of staging plots in order to discredit them before public opinion :

> To urge a doubtful speech up to the worst
> To broach new treasons and disclose them first.

At the end of the reign Sir Thomas Tresham referred in a
letter to what he termed 'the cursed Machivelian projects
visored in former times on us in ugliest vise', believing that
Watson's plot might be another 'Atheistical Anthonie Babington's complotment'.[13] The most important person to die as
the result of conspiracy was the Protestant Duke of Norfolk.
Others, like Throckmorton, Parry and Babington, were not
themselves men of great standing; some of the plotters were
very young.

How did the government react to papal hostility and the plots? It could not touch the Pope or the Catholic Powers directly, but it waged an unofficial war on Spain and so far as possible brought pressure to bear on the Catholic exiles through the governments of their host countries. The real sufferers were the Catholics in England, and in that sense they were, as Cecil said, martyrs for the Pope. Dean Nowell's sermon at St Paul's in 1563 urging that 'maintainers of false religion should die by the sword' resembled the cry from other pulpits such as that of Archbishop Sandys of York demanding 'death, exile, confiscation, incarceration' as punishment for those who 'join themselves unto the harlot inseparably'.[14] The government controlled the means of influencing public opinion by its proclamations, its control of printing and especially its control of the pulpit. Well before the issue of the Bull of 1570 official propaganda had been building up a new picture of the Pope. Phrases of the *Homilies* and orders for prayers on special occasions might make a deep impression on simple people such as the Meditation of 1563: 'For thou knowest O Lord what a sort there are which, bewitched by the Devil and the Pope's doctrine do utterly abhor Christ's holy communion and, saving fear of the law, would never come at it'; or the later prayer of thanksgiving: 'Confound . . . these priests of Baal, the hellish chaplains of Anti-Christ, accursed runagates of their God and prince, the bellows and fuel of these flagrant conspiracies . . . but let our Queen still reign and rule in despite of Rome, and Reims, Spain and Hell.'[15]

Throughout Elizabeth's reign the Pope was commonly identified with the Anti-Christ of St John, the Beast of Revelations, and the Man of Sin of St Paul, a theme used by Bishop Jewel, Archbishop Sandys and many others.[16] Whitgift made it the subject of a doctoral thesis at Cambridge, and as late as 1596 a sermon on this topic was preached before the Queen, its effect marred by a tactless reference to her age. Hooker also identified the Pope with the Man of Sin, while prepared to concede that 'the church wherein Anti-Christ sitteth' might be considered Christian. When Sir Walter Mildmay – a faithful servant of Elizabeth and Chancellor of the Exchequer

– listed all the arguments against the French marriage in 1578, in his opinion 'th'offence beside to God is of all other the greatest, if our Queen being the patron of the Gospel shall be coupled with a papist'.[17] Hatred of the Pope and his Church was reinforced by Foxe's *Book of Martyrs*. William Haller has claimed that, by explaining the dangers from the Papacy as the last gasp of Anti-Christ and promising ultimate victory in this confrontation with the powers of evil, Foxe played a vital part in building a national identity and confidence.[18] This thesis has met with some criticism, and it has been suggested that Englishmen were more impressed by the 'apocalyptic proportions of their enemy than with their capacity to subdue him', finding in the Church of Rome 'the very epitome of the orderly nation they wanted so much to be'.[19] Hence came the excessive stress on the monolithic power of Catholicism and on the ability of the Popes to unite the Catholic Powers in a league against England.

The puritan Francis Hastings attributed most of Elizabeth's actions to the miraculous intervention of divine providence and could therefore feel confident of final victory. On the other hand, Lord Burghley with his cool and statesmanlike approach saw that divine intervention could not be relied upon to counter the missionary labours of the seminary priests and Jesuits. When he composed his *Memorandum on the Dangerous State of the Realm* in 1584 he listed three points: the diligence of the Jesuit missionaries, the lethargy of the State Church in meeting their challenge, and the influence of the Catholic nobility and gentry in promoting recusancy among the people. One remedy he suggested was the removal of those bishops 'who were of no credit with the people'.

More drastic action was taken against the Catholics themselves. The 1581 Act had already made conversion to Catholicism treason, and the 1585 Act made possible the condemnation to death of a priest without his having committed an overt act of treason. This approach had been foreshadowed in 1581 when Edmund Campion with twelve priests and laymen, including William Allen and Robert Persons in their absence, were tried under the Treasons Act of 1352 and charged with plotting to kill the Queen, to change the government and 'to incite, procure and induce divers strangers and aliens . . . to invade the realm and raise, carry on and make war against the Queen'. For this offence Campion and others were duly hanged, disembowelled while still alive, and quartered on 1 December. No historian believes that they were guilty, and many did not believe it at the time. We cannot expect a Tudor treason trial to be fair by modern standards, and many illustrious persons had preceded them to the scaffold on equally flimsy charges. Catholics, however, claimed Campion as a martyr for religion, and the government felt the need to state its case to a wide audience by the issue of a proclamation in April 1582 that emphasised the charge of treason: 'The Queen and her Council assured her subjects that from both overt acts against the realm and from the priests' own handwritings it was manifestly clear that they had been sent to prepare Englishmen to assist when invasion should be mounted and to rise up to deprive the Queen of her life and crown.'[20]

Thus began a battle of propaganda by both sides to convince public opinion at home and abroad, and the government proclamation suggests some sensitiveness concerning the effect of Campion's execution. The Frenchman Bodin had warned the government of its probable effect: 'The greater the pain inflicted on man for religion the less good is done.' The government argued not only that the Catholic clergy were, like their lay brethren, a potential danger to the State but also that they were actively engaged in treasonable activities. Catholic propaganda stressed the themes of religious persecution and, more dubiously, loyalty to the Crown. In his *Defense of English Catholics* Dr Allen evidenced the trial of Robert Cottam, who claimed in court that he had been asked under torture to reveal the sins he had acknowledged in confession. When this was denied by the Lieutenant of the Tower Cottam appealed to the consciences of other commissioners present at his racking and claimed that 'in truth all your torture and demands . . . were of no other treasons but matter of mere conscience, faith and religion'.[21]

As part of the task of educating public opinion the government devised the so-called 'Bloody Questions', which covered a prisoner's attitudes towards the deposing power of the Pope, whether he thought the Queen should be obeyed in spite of the Bull of Deposition, and which side he would take in the event of an invasion sponsored by the Pope. Answers were often extracted by means of torture. This procedure was not part of the common law under which the trials were heard : it was never part of the law of treason that a man could be punished for treasonable thoughts, and in 1588 the Solicitor General warned the Council that refusal to answer these questions did not bring a man within compass of the law. In practice, refusal to answer was often taken as implying guilt. We tend to think of these questions mostly in connection with the Catholic clergy, but in one instance they were put to a Lancashire serving maid who gave satisfactory replies but was returned to prison for refusal to attend church.[22]

The Jesuit Robert Southwell sent his Roman superiors an account of the trial and interrogation of Catholics arrested after the Armada. The questions were put to them 'not simply about what they have done, but about what they are likely to do . . . If they are reluctant to answer it is counted against them as rebellion and treason, if they say they would never do anything against their just and bounden duty to Queen and country they are reviled as hypocrites and liars.'[23] Answers given to the Bloody questions were by no means uniform, and the Catholic clergy were clearly not, as one might expect, drilled by their superiors on this vital matter. Many spurned the accusation of treason, as did Alexander Rawlins to Huntingdon : 'I never committed treason in my life . . . But if to be a priest were to commit treason then by their law they might make me a traitor.' There were also those who declared their complete acceptance of the Bull with all its consequences, unmindful of the words of the psalmist : 'I will keep my mouth as it were with a bridle.' Satisfactory replies to the questions did not necessarily save a priest from the death sentence.

The two opposing points of view can be illustrated by a government proclamation and a contemporary Catholic account of a priest's execution. In May 1586 the government published a proclamation to explain why two seminary priests had been put to death.[24] They were Robert Anderson and William Marsden, old friends of Oxford days who had been reconciled to Catholicism on the same day. In view of their profession of loyalty they had been sent up to London for examination by the Council from the Assizes at Winchester. Both acknowledged Elizabeth as lawful queen, but when asked what attitude he would take in the event of invasion Robert Anderson replied that he could not answer hypothetical questions 'until such case should happen'. Marsden stated that he felt bound to obey the Queen 'so far as his obedience impeached not his duty to God and the Church (meaning the Church of Rome)' and in the event of invasion would do the duty of a priest, 'that is he would pray that right might take place'. The proclamation concluded with the priests' statement that they felt bound in conscience to deal in matters of religion with the Queen's subjects and to persuade them to Catholicism : 'Thus they cannot hide their malice and treasonable intentions.'

The contemporary Catholic account deals with the execution of Oliver Plasden, a young man of 28 years.[25] Sir Walter Raleigh heard him pray for Queen and country on the scaffold, and as a result of favourable replies to questions about the priest's allegiance he asked the sheriff if he would stay the execution in order to consult the Queen. Topcliffe, a notorious torturer of Catholics, intervened to ask if the priest would resist the Spanish king or the Pope if such came to establish Catholicism by force, and Plasden answered that he would counsel all men to maintain the right of their prince. At this point Raleigh was satisfied, but Topcliffe had a final question : 'Dost thou think that the Queen hath any right to maintain this religion and forbid yours.' To this came the reply : 'No . . . I would never fight nor counsel others to fight against my religion, for that were to deny my faith.' 'Then lo they cried he was a traitor and the cart was drawn away.'

Royal proclamations were a means of educating people at home, but public opinion abroad could not be ignored, and the treatment of English Catholics made a profound impression in foreign countries wherever accounts of the executions circulated. Great crowds were drawn to view an enormous painting of them that was set up in the churchyard of St Sévérin at Paris, and soon the Catholic League was warning Frenchmen that the persecution of English Catholics showed what they might expect if they accepted an heretic king.[26] This propaganda reinforced an impression that the English were a barbaric nation, and it was for this reason that William Cecil composed his *Execution of Justice in England* : foreign princes must be shown that if such persecution existed it was for traitorous deeds, not for religion. His work was published in December 1583, and a second edition included a *Declaration of Favourable Dealing of Her Majesty's Commissioners.* The books were translated into five foreign languages and distributed abroad through official channels.[27]

Cecil began by recalling the Northern rising for which he blamed the Pope, and the Irish rebellion, which, he claimed, had been led by a group of English Catholics. Since, he was careful to emphasise, the rebels could not find foreign princes inclined to their wicked purposes, seminaries had been founded 'to nourish and bring up persons disposed naturally to sedition', and if the secret labours of these had not been stayed there would have been 'manifest bloody destruction of great multitudes of Christians'. All who accepted the Bull of 1570 were declared to be 'in their hearts and conscience secret traitors', merely needing opportunity to become open ones. Priests, it was claimed, were sent into England to recruit men for an invading army, and their evasive answers to the bloody questions were quoted in evidence.[28] It was also claimed that the clergy who suffered as traitors did so not by new laws but by the law of Edward III, which was of course true of Campion and others but not true of Cuthbert Mayne who had died under the law of 1571. In the *Declaration* the argument was developed to a point that, as its editor has commented, strains credulity : 'and the Queen's servants, the warders whose office and act it is to handle the rack, were ever by those that attended examinations specially charged to use it in as charitable a manner as such a thing might be'. The victims, Cecil added, were stretched upon the rack slowly, reluctantly and with relative gentleness.

On this last point a commentary was to be added later by a young Jesuit, Robert Southwell, in his *An Humble Supplication to Her Majesty.* He was himself destined to suffer torture before his execution :

> Some are hanged by the hands, eight or nine or twelve hours together . . . Some are whipped naked so long and with such excess that our enemies, unwilling to give Constancy her right name, said that no man without the help of the Devil could with such undauntedness suffer so much . . . Some have been watched and kept from sleep till they were past the use of reason, and then examined upon the advantage when they could scarcely give accompt of their own names. Some have been tortured in such parts as is almost torture to Christian ears to hear it . . . Some with instruments have been rolled up together like a ball, and so crushed that the blood sprouted out at divers parts of their bodies.[29]

Some months after the publication of Cecil's *Execution of Justice* William Allen produced his reply : *A True, Sincere and Modest Defense of English Catholics.* The government took drastic steps to prevent its circulation, but an early copy reached Mary, Queen of Scots. Allen was concerned to refute the supposed link between the seminary movement and treason, claiming that the Bull had never been posted up in his college, that the political authority of the Pope was never discussed at lectures and that public discussion of politics was discouraged :

> . . . the governors of the students always of purpose prohibiting . . . that in the course of our school questions and controversies concerning the Pope's pre-eminence, no matter of depriving or excommunicating princes should be disputed; no, not so much as in generalities, and much less the particu-

larising of any point in our Queen's case. Which matter
notwithstanding it is determinable by divinity and do come
in course to be handled in schools as other questions do,
yet because it is incident to matter of state . . . it was
thought best to pass over all in silence.[30]

Allen pointed out that only two English Catholic writers had
dealt with the Bull and that, because many Catholics had
wished 'the matter so offensive had never been touched', Dr
Bristow had omitted this section in a second edition while Dr
Sander had suppressed his own work so that no copy was
extant. Dr Kingdon has argued that some of Allen's claims
must be rejected, since his own eloquent defence of the deposing power was surely read by his own students; however,
Allen claimed not that the students were ignorant of the
subject, rather that the subject was barred in his own college.
A more serious criticism of Allen is that he himself had been
engaged in political activity and that, although he kept a clear
distinction between politics and his college, he could not
expect the English government to accept the distinction. In
private correspondence Allen and Persons proposed to warn
the principal English Catholics through their priests when an
invasion was to be launched, but there is no proof that the
clergy were aware of this intention and little evidence that the
English Catholics were prepared to take their politics from
their priests.[31] Cecil on his part evaded the main point at issue :
Catholics in England were forbidden under penalty even the
private practice of their religion and were compelled by law
to attend the Protestant services. In 1603 his son, Sir Robert,
made a more honest comment to the Venetian envoy : 'There
are laws and they must be obeyed, and there is no doubt that
the object of these laws is to extinguish the Catholic religion
within this kingdom.'[32]

The government built its case on the wording of the papal
Bull of 1570. We can only conjecture what the position of
the English Catholics would have been had no such Bull been
issued. Possibly it would have been no different, but their

attitude to the Bull was by no means one of total acceptance. For many years it was virtually ignored by both Catholics and the government, the majority of people knowing little about it and the government probably content with its ignorance. When some of the Elizabethan bishops persuaded the Swiss Bullinger to write a reply, Grindal expressed doubt to Archbishop Parker as to whether the Queen or Council would permit its publication : 'It is possible they would not have the multitude know that any such railing bull had passed from that see.'[33] Catholics too kept silent, and Persons and Campion were warned by their Roman superiors to steer clear of politics when they left for England. There are indications that in Rome, in some quarters at least, the Bull was regarded as something of an embarrassment, and the Jesuits' instructions were strengthened when they secured a papal decree that the Bull, as matters then stood, did not bind until its execution became possible. When this instruction was discovered by the English government it was naturally unimpressed, but a Roman jurist had previously expressed the view that the Bull was no longer in force, having been issued for a special occasion.[34] Moreover, some years earlier the Duke of Alba had told Pope Pius V that it was morally impossible for Catholics to obey the Bull, and the Pope had then replied that no Catholic would incur excommunication if he failed to obey its commands.[35] Short of a complete withdrawal of the Bull it does seem that canonists were doing their best to rescue the English Catholics from an impossible situation in the 1580s, but much earlier the young Earl of Southampton had been told that it did not bind in conscience when he put his scruples to the Bishop of Ross.[36]

There were indeed sound theological reasons for ignoring the Bull of Deposition, as well as the fact that papal Bulls in the past had been regarded as political statements as well as religious ones. The deposing power of the Pope was not a formal part of Catholic religious belief but rather a subject of discussion and argument among theologians. Two schools of thought hedged it about with limitations, one to the point of depriving the theory of real meaning. In France there were reputable theologians who taught that the Pope had an 'accidental' power in temporal affairs, which made him a spokesman of great moral authority but gave his verdict no juridical effect; the ultimate right to pass sentence on princes belonged to their peoples. French theories were of course influenced by the position of Henry of Navarre as an excommunicated claimant to the throne, and both Catholic and Huguenot writers bore this in mind. A former lecturer in the English College at Rheims, William Reynolds, revealed an extreme view of papal authority in a work published in 1590. It was one thing for theologians living in France to argue for a limitation of papal authority in temporal matters but quite another for theologians living in Rome, where the Pope was temporal sovereign. Robert Bellarmine had also lectured in his time at Rheims, and notes of his lectures were circulating in England in 1581. Five years later when he was a Cardinal he published his *Controversies*, in which he claimed an indirect power for the Pope in temporal affairs : a papal sentence of deposition on a wicked prince was not effective without popular action. Temporal rulers, he argued, like the Pope also held their authority from God, but they held it indirectly through the consent of their peoples. Bellarmine was a Jesuit, but a Dominican, Vitoria, had published a treatise in which he claimed that it was lawful to resist an unjust command of the Pope. These two theologians both fell foul of the autocratic Pope Sixtus V, who decided to place their works on the Index of Forbidden Books, but eight days later Sixtus died and his successor reversed the decision.[37]

Some historians have judged that the Bull of Pope Pius V created a tragic dilemma of conscience, and this might possibly have been true of the clergy for they could not all be expected to be conversant with the subtle reservations of the theologians. At a time when the spiritual allegiance of Catholics to the Pope was being called in question by the State, priests might have tended to stress papal authority more than they would have done in normal times. If a missionary priest expressed public opposition to the deposing power there was a risk that the authorities might use such statements out of their context with possible scandal caused to laymen. Campion was one example of a priest who said at his trial that he regarded the deposing power of the pope as a matter of discussion between theologians and not *de fide*. The laity certainly regarded it as a highly disputable question, and it has been remarked that, just as the conservative Catholic gentry resented interference by the Queen with their own 'estates', so they regarded interference by the Pope : 'they took no notice when he relieved them of their duty of fidelity to the Queen.'[38]

As the years passed and the full consequences of the Bull were made clear, opposition began to show itself from the Catholic side. An early work (1574–80) not intended for publication but claimed to be written by a recusant Catholic, John Bishop, was the *Courteous Conference with the English Catholikes Romane*. It stated very plainly that the Pope had no right to depose princes.[39] A number of the appellant writers expressed opposition, and a Jesuit opponent of theirs, Richard Walpole, compiled thirteen such propositions from their works, describing them as 'temerarious' though not heretical. In 1605 the Archpriest Blackwell refused to approve publication of Richard Smith's *Answer to Thomas Bels late Challenge* unless he altered a statement that the deposing power was not a doctrine to be held as of faith. Smith refused to make the alteration, and his work was delated to the Roman Inquisition after Robert Persons had drawn attention to numerous 'scandalous' passages. Significantly, it was not placed on the Index of prohibited books.

It has sometimes been argued that Elizabethan Catholics were bound in conscience to support an invasion against an heretic prince. They did not think so. A complaint was made to Philip III of Spain that the students of the Irish College at Salamanca were being taught that 'the Queen may be obeyed and arms taken against your Majesty and they confess and absolve and do admit to Mass and other offices such as do it'.[40] The exiles had always claimed that the English Catholics would rally to an invasion, but in 1588 Sir Thomas Tresham and his friends petitioned to fight for the Queen and expressly denied support for the deposing power :

We for our parts utterly deny that either Pope or Cardinal
hath power or authority to command or license any man
to consent to mortal sin . . . Much less can this disloyal,
wicked and unnatural purpose by any means be made lawful, to wit, that a native born subject may seek the effusion
of the sacred blood of his anointed sovereign . . . We do
protest before the living God that all and every priest and
priests who have at any time conversed with us have
recognised your Majesty their undoubted and lawful Queen
tam de iure quam de facto.[41]

Permission to take their place with the armed forces was
denied, and leading recusants were put under arrest at the
time of the Armada, deprived of horses and weapons and
forbidden to move outside their dwellings. It was inevitable
that it should be so. Englishmen were serving under Parma
in the Netherlands, and Cardinal Allen signed two manifestos
in support of the invasion. It would have been difficult for a
Catholic to have played a part in resisting invasion when
some feared a Catholic rising in its support. 'It were hard
for any man to face the enemy with a stout heart', wrote a
protestant, 'if he thought his house like at any time to be
burned behind his back.' The patriotism of Tresham and his
friends was therefore rejected but the government used it to
discredit the Catholic clergy. Two government pamphlets
were published after the Armada. One, possibly composed by
Lord Burghley, was entitled *Copy of a Letter Sent Out of
England to Don Bernardino de Mendoza,*[42] and it was falsely
claimed that the letter had been found among the papers of a
priest named Richard Leigh after his execution. Under cover
of regretting the defeat of the Armada the letter stated that
Catholics had been loyal to the Queen during the crisis and
ready to die for her, but it also claimed that the seminary
priests were men of dissolute life who preached treason.

The defeat of the Armada was followed by an increase of
persecution, and a number of Catholics were put to death.
When Parliament opened in 1589 the Lord Chancellor had
a word for them in his opening speech: 'I may not forget

those vile wretches, those bloody priests, and false traitors here in our bosoms.' In 1590 when a second Spanish attack was feared leading Catholics were again imprisoned, and once again the irrepressible Tresham complained to the Council : 'We Catholics have ever demeaned in all actions of civil duty both before our imprisonments and in the furnace of our many years' adversity, as becometh faithfullest true English subjects,'[43] By 1589 the lesson had sunk in for the Catholic exiles if not with the government at home. Sir Francis Englefield was one of many who had abandoned hope of the reconversion of England, because 'the Catholics are resolved to resist Spain'.[44]

6   The Exiles:
Writers and Educators

O mihi praeteritos referat si Iupiter annos
Vergil, Aeneid

It has been claimed with some exaggeration that in no other period of English history did the ruling class have less personal experience of the Continent than was the case in Elizabeth's reign.[1] Lord Burghley certainly thought that foreign travel had its dangers for the young : 'Suffer not thy sons to pass the Alps for they shall learn nothing but pride, blasphemy and atheism.' His advice was often disregarded, and the young Elizabethan aristocrat made the grand tour as a part of his education, sometimes even visiting Rome. As he travelled he often met Catholic exiles, who were to be found in most European countries and in the New World. As bishops of foreign sees, including that of Rheims in the next century, as members of cathedral chapters, as professors in universities and as mercenaries in foreign armies, exiled Englishmen were familiar figures of the age. Catholic exiles were to be found in the households of the Dukes of Parma, Savoy and Guise, at the Court of Philip II of Spain, and as secretary of Latin letters to Catherine de Medici. Several Welsh exiles were sheltered at Milan in the great household of its archbishop, Charles Borromeo, while two musicians of distinction found safe harbour : John Pickford as organist to the Cardinal Regent of Portugal, and Peter Phillips as master of music in the Archduke Albert's chapel royal in the Spanish Netherlands.

There were also those who found the struggle for survival

unendurable and were compelled to return to England. Robert Persons often appealed to the generosity of Philip II : 'Eminent persons have written . . . saying that some have died of hunger . . . others are on the verge of doing so.' More fortunate was a merchant, Robert Hicks, who presented the Duke of Alba with testimonials signed by emigrés who had known him in England and in 1569 was given a licence to trade. Also fortunate was Raphael Letherbarrow, who was reported by a spy in 1580 as being 'the banker to whom all the fugitives and papists make over their money by exchange and send cloth over under a colour as if it were his.' There was strong competition among those qualified by status to secure a place on the extensive pension list of the Spanish king, and in time the best method was to write to Sir Francis Englefield, who spent the last years of his life in this service for his fellow countrymen at Madrid. Pensions were normally paid from the Spanish military subsidy for the Netherlands and like the pay of the soldiers were often in arrears, but if pensioners suffered from the delays of Spanish bureaucracy they gained by its tolerance, for pensions were sometimes paid to Englishmen known to be anti-Spanish in politics. Philip III continued to pay pensions after Elizabeth's death, and Spain seems never to have attempted to use the pensioners as an instrument of policy.

No organised exodus occurred at Elizabeth's accession such as had taken place in the reign of Mary. Bishop Goldwell of St Asaph was in Italy at the time and did not return, and two of the Marian bishops later escaped to the continent. At the request of the Count, later Duke, of Feria – Philip II's special ambassador – the religious communities were permitted to leave, but their passports were limited to those who had taken vows during the reign of Henry VIII. Younger members were therefore officially excluded, but in the event this was not insisted on, and among those leaving were Henry V's Bridgettine foundation of Sion and the Carthusians of Sheen. During his stay in England the Count of Feria had married a former maid of honour to Queen Mary, Jane Dormer, and she left with a retinue reminiscent of that of the Duchess of

Suffolk in 1553. Her passport included six ladies in waiting, five gentlemen, two pages, chaplains, seven servants and a laundress.[2]. Her grandmother, Lady Jane Dormer, obtained a temporary licence to live abroad, and when this expired the Spanish ambassador in London asked that she might be permitted to stay on in the Netherlands or allowed to have Mass said in her house if she returned to England. Both requests were refused, but the old lady stayed on in Louvain where her house became a centre for the exiles living in that town. In later years the Duchess of Feria gave considerable financial help to her fellow countrymen in Spain.

A government licence was required to leave England, which was not easily obtained, and several priests were arrested attempting to leave without permission. In 1567 one of these was found to have been collecting funds for poor scholars at Louvain. Under torture he revealed the names of subscribers, who included Sir Henry Copley, a convert to Catholicism and a connection of the Queen. Copley was fined and imprisoned and went abroad without licence after 1570, but although his revenues were sequestrated his wife and children were permitted to join him in 1574.[3] When Sir Francis Englefield opted for exile in 1559 he was permitted to leave but cautioned not to live in Rome, and he left with eight servants, 600 ounces of plate and 100 marks. In 1563 he refused an order to return home and his estates were confiscated and granted to the Earl of Leicester. Englefield then became a pensioner of Philip II and active in politics.[4] Sir John Southworth was one of many refused permission to leave 'for conscience sake', and there was always a risk that the government might take revenge on those who left without licence. The imprisonment in the Fleet of Lord Morley's son during 1573 might have been linked with the departure of his father.

The collapse of the Northern rising introduced a new and to many an unwelcome element : the political refugee. In May 1570 nearly thirty had arrived at Antwerp, and during the next months they were joined by the Countess of Northumberland, the Earl of Westmorland and Lord Dacre. Their coming provoked some discord. They considered the earlier refugees to be 'too severe and too scrupulous' in their religious and political attitudes, while the English government was led to take a closer and unwelcome interest in the affairs of the exiles and to press the government of the Netherlands to expel them. Such pressures had a brief effect in 1575 when the English Catholics were given fifteen days' notice to leave. Some moved to France, others to Liège where Elizabeth's ambassador attempted unsuccessfully to persuade the prince bishop to refuse them entry.[5] With the arrival of Don John of Austria in the Netherlands this expulsion order was lifted, for Elizabeth's government had not honoured its undertaking to expel the Dutch refugees from England. The outbreak of civil war in the Netherlands made the lot of the exile precarious. Nevertheless the Countess of Northumberland managed to live in some style, and Lord Westmorland, although heavily in debt, retained a dozen servants. The 1571 Act was fairly effective in cutting off the supply of funds from England.

In the early days hopes ran high that sojourn in foreign lands would not be prolonged. The passage of years that saw the firm establishment of Elizabeth's government dimmed such hopes, though it did not altogether quench them, for self-deception is the natural lot of exiles at all times. As hope of return by peaceful means faded away some turned to schemes of violence and plots, but the attention that the plotters have since naturally attracted does not mean that their number was large. When war with Spain broke out the Spanish pensioners among the exiles were in a difficult position. Many shared the view of Lord Morley, who wrote to England pledging support for the Queen but maintaining the attitude he had expressed in a letter to Cecil: 'I would rather lose everything than give up my faith by returning to England.'

The importance of the exiles lies not with the plotters but with the university scholars and the college that William Allen founded at Douai in 1568. The first Elizabethan visitation of Oxford and Cambridge led to the first exodus of scholars by voluntary resignation or deprivation, although the oath of supremacy was not at first rigidly enforced. In his edition of Sander's *Rise and Growth of the Anglican Schism*, published in 1585, Edward Rishton wrote of 'the very flower of the two universities' being carried away 'as it were by a storm, and scattered in foreign lands'. Among the scholarly emigrés were fifteen or so heads of colleges.[6] Most were attracted at first to Louvain where a colony of English exiles had formed as early as 1549, and this university town became the main centre of English Catholic scholarship. Among those who settled at Louvain were : Nicholas Sander, a former Fellow of New College, Oxford, who became a writer of European reputation; William Soane, the Oxford Regius Professor of Divinity; Francis Babington, Vice-Chancellor; and John Bavant, the Reader of Greek. Cambridge provided its Regius Professor of Divinity, Thomas Sedgwick, and several Masters of colleges including Thomas Bailey of Clare.

A group that included some of the most distinguished English humanists naturally turned to writing. Among them was Thomas Stapleton, who managed to hold on to his prebend at Chichester until 1562–3.[7] Summoned home he was called before Bishop Barlow and was willing to swear only that part of the supremacy oath that recognised the Queen as supreme in temporal matters. Deprived of his prebend he left England with his parents and taught first in the new university of Douai and later as regius professor at Louvain. Stapleton edited the Latin works of Thomas More and published a number of apologetical works in English. He then became interested in the refutation of Calvinism and wrote in Latin for a European public. Of his English works the *Fortresse of the Faith* and *Counterblast to M. Horne's Vayne Blaste against M. Fekenham* were perhaps the most important. After 1568 Douai became the chief exile centre, but during the four years before this some forty works were published at Louvain. Many of these were works of controversy arising from the publication of Bishop Jewel's *Apology* in 1562. Thomas Harding, a Hebrew scholar and former Fellow of New College, was the chief protagonist in this 'great controversy', which was still rumbling in 1580 and drew in some twenty writers on both sides.[8] Not all the Louvain writers were occupied with controversy, however, and the *A*

Catechisme of Christian Doctrine necessarie for Children and ignorant people, published in 1567 by Laurence Vaux, had a large circulation. At least eight editions had appeared by 1605.[9]

A second wave of writers arrived during the years 1568–75, members of a younger generation who were mostly Oxford converts to Catholicism and had known Elizabeth's Church from within. Their outlook was less tolerant, and the Counter Reformation training they received in Allen's college reinforced their unwillingness to wait passively for a change of heart among their countrymen at home. They included: Richard Bristow, a prominent Fellow of Exeter College, Oxford; Gregory Martin of St John's; William Rainolds of New College; and Thomas Alfield, a Fellow of King's College, Cambridge. To this group belong the two Jesuits, Campion and Persons. Alfield was to lose his life in 1585 for distributing copies of Allen's *Defence* of the English Catholics. From 1570 to the end of the reign nearly 150 works were published. Among them were a number of influential devotional works, including the popular translation by Richard Hopkins of a work of Luis de Granada, *Of Prayer and Meditation*. This might have supplied some inspiration for the religious poems of Vaughan and Crashaw in the next century.

In 1582 appeared the Rheims New Testament, a Catholic translation that was to be used by the translaters of the 1611 Authorised Version of the Bible.[10] William Allen was deeply interested in scriptural study and regarded it as an essential part of the curriculum of his college. In 1579 he was appointed by Cardinal Caraffa to assist in the preparation of an amended edition of the Hebrew Septuagint as an aid to the revision of the Vulgate Bible. Allen needed an English translation for his students, who knew the Bible only in Latin and who therefore, as he wrote, in their sermons when ordained priest 'are obliged on the spur of the moment to translate some passages which they have quoted into the vulgar tongue; they often do it inaccurately and with unpleasant hesitation'. The work of translation was the task of Gregory Martin with Allen, Bristow and Rainolds acting as revisers. Martin translated from the text of the Latin Vulgate, aided by the Greek texts of Erasmus and Beza and sometimes adding the original Greek or Hebrew word in the margin. The 5,000 copies of the first edition that were printed were welcomed with enthusiasm when they began to circulate in England. A Cumberland man, Andrew Hilton, wrote to the priest John Boste for a copy: 'for I can neither, eat, drink nor sleep until I see it'.[11] Martin also published a handbook entitled *A Discoverie of the manifold corruptions of the holy Scriptures by the Heretics of our Daies, Specially of the English Sectaries,* and his accusation that Protestants were corrupters of the Biblical text led to a literary war. Leicester and Walsingham financed a reply by Cartwright, but as his puritan views were unacceptable to Archbishop Whitgift the work was not published until 1618. By then a second edition of the Rheims New Testament had appeared.

The execution of Campion and others in 1581 and the government proclamations with their charge of treason led to the appearance of a new type of writing : the martyrologies. An early accusation that Catholics were traitors was made by the puritan divine William Charke, who was commissioned by the government to reply to Campion's *Challenge.* After the trial several Protestant works appeared, including Anthony Munday's *Breefe Discourse of the Taking of Edmund Campion,* and *Discoverie of Edmund Campion* the latter work being rewarded by the Council. Mundy had witnessed for the prosecution at the trial, but the man actually responsible for Campion's arrest, 'Judas' Eliot, also printed a *Very True Report . . . of the Taking of that Arch-Papist Edmund Campion* in which he attacked Munday's version as a book 'as contrary to truth as an egg . . . to an oyster'.[12] A Catholic reply to these works was to be expected, and the government was soon to complain that 'some traitorously affected have of late by letters, lives, pamphlets and books . . . given out that the said most horrible traitors were without just cause condemned and executed'.[13] On the Catholic side the most impressive book to appear was that by Thomas Alfield, which was circulating in London in March 1582 : *A True Reporte of the Death and Martyr-dome of M. Campion*; to this was added a *Caveat to the Reader touching A. M. his Discoverie*. William Allen used much of this work in his own *Briefe Historie* of the martyrs, but perhaps more influential among continental readers and therefore more annoying to the Council was the *De Persecutione Anglicanae* of Robert Persons, which in its English version had a prefatory letter addressed to the council charging it with religious persecution unsurpassed in Europe.[14]

The literary output of the exiled writers, both in its earlier phase at Louvain and in the second phase at Douai and Rheims, had a marked effect on the morale of educated Catholics in England. Allen testified somewhat complacently to the result of this apostolate : 'Books opened the way for a change of heart among Catholics for in these books, written in a way adapted to popular understanding, almost all the frauds of the heretics . . . were made remarkably clear; so that not only by the learned but by the popular voice we were judged to be superior to those whom we opposed.'[15] Bishop Pilkington of Durham believed that the circulation of these books did much to keep Catholicism alive in the North, and knowledge of them was spread by the practice of Protestant controversialists of printing the text of an offending work with their reply. It is not clear how the heavy cost of printing the books was met, but the smuggling of them into England was occasionally aided by the connivance of sympathetic officials at the ports, as was the case at Newcastle.

The government never managed to suppress the illicit importation of Catholic books in spite of heavy penalties on those caught in the act. When Grindal's official searched the house of the London antiquary Stow in 1569 the report was sent to Cecil : 'His bokes declare him to be a great favourer of papistry.' Thirty-eight unlawful books were found in Stow's house, and a list of 'trayterous and popish bookes' was intercepted by agents of the Master of the Stationers' Company in the 1580s, included 430 copies of six printed books and 700 loose sheets.[16] Eight printers and publishers, members of the Stationers' Company, stocked Catholic books, which suggests a steady demand for them. Gabriel Cawood, who became Master of the Stationers' Company in 1597, published two works of the Jesuit Robert Southwell: *Mary Magdalen's Tears* and *Saint Peter's Complaint*; he also stocked other Catholic texts.[17] Some of the Catholic devotional works were widely read, and when Edmund Bunny decided to pirate an edition of Persons' *Christian Directory* he gave as a reason, in the preface dedicated to the Archbishop of Canterbury, that so many people were reading the book that it seemed wise to produce an expurgated edition, removing all specifically Catholic references.

Of greater importance than this literary activity was the educational work associated with William Allen and Robert Persons, for its result was to produce the priests without whom English Catholicism would have died. Allen was destined to become the unofficial but unchallenged leader of the English Catholics, endowed with the rare ability to drive a great work forward through every difficulty while lesser men doubted and bickered. When he died in 1594 his place remained unfilled.[18] Born in 1532, the year before the one that saw the marriage of Henry VIII and Anne Boleyn, he belonged to a family of Lancashire gentry who had widespread connections in the county. He took his degree at Oxford in 1550, was elected a Fellow of Oriel College and seems to have avoided taking the oath of supremacy during the reign of Edward VI. When Queen Mary came to the throne he was appointed Principal of St Mary's Hall and Proctor in the university. He was marked out for promotion, but, as the Jesuit poet Robert Southwell was to write, 'The sea of Fortune doth not ever flow.' Allen could not in conscience accept the Elizabethan settlement of religion. Consequently, he resigned his Oxford appointments and soon went overseas to Louvain.

Illness drove him back first to his native Lancashire, then to Oxford, and finally to the household of the Duke of Norfolk who gave shelter to Catholics while himself accepting the new régime. During this period Allen wrote his *Certain Brief Reasons concerning the Catholic Faith,* and although not

himself a priest he spent much of the time urging Catholics not
to attend the new church services. He was shocked at the
spinelessness of many who accepted while not believing in the
change of religion, at the laymen who might attend both a
secret Mass and the official service on the same day, and at
priests who conformed but celebrated a secret Mass and then
went off to administer the new Communion service in church.
This state of things has been described by Sander in his *Rise
and Growth of the Anglican Schism*, where he mentions
clergy who carried to church altar breads consecrated at Mass
and gave them to Catholics at the communion while giving the
official communion to others.[19] This period of Allen's life ended
in 1565 when the authorities got on his track, and he was
forced to return abroad.

On a journey to Rome with his old Oriel tutor, Allen made
the momentous decision to found a college in exile. As his
ideas developed he planned to include a home for scholars that
would provide an environment suitable for literary work, a
school for the education of young Catholics, and finally a
seminary that would train and supply priests for missionary
work in England. Allen lacked the funds and the influential
sponsors that an ambitious adventure of this kind would surely
need, but this did not deter him. His assets were personal ones :
family relationships among the English gentry; the Oxford
background, which gave him authority as a scholar and
teacher; and above all the trust and affection that his own
character drew from others. He was to prove not only a great
and inspiring teacher but also a remarkable peacemaker in
the uneasy world of the exiles, and the success of his college
was to bring him increasing influence and distinction. It was
one of the first of the seminaries that the Council of Trent had
urged for the training of the clergy. He was fortunate in the
early days to have the advice and encouragement of a distinguished Netherlander, Jean Vendeville, who was destined
to become President of the Council of Justice and an influential figure in the government of his country.

It seemed sensible to establish the new college in Douai,
for the town's new university owed much to Oxford men. Its

first Chancellor was Dr Richard Smith, a former Oxford Regius Professor of Divinity, and its professor of canon law was Dr Owen Lewis, who had held that chair at Oxford with a Fellowship of New College.[20] Allen acquired a large house and in September 1568 established a régime resembling the collegiate life that he and his associates had known in England. It was the forerunner of a series of future foundations of seminaries, schools and religious communities that through centuries to come were to train generations of young Englishmen. There was never a lack of applicants for entry, itself a remarkable fact when we consider the future to which its scholars were dedicated, but before it was firmly established it had to endure more than the average share of vicissitudes.[21]

Allen's training of the future clergy as it developed in the college was far removed from both the haphazard system of medieval England and the system of Elizabeth's Church. The student's life was austere in its physical hardship and contained in a spiritual framework that included daily attendance at Mass, private prayer and recitation of the breviary Offices. A rigorous course of studies was organised on a three-year basis, although many students did not follow the full course. Great importance was attached to biblical study in the light of current controversies, and to this end Greek and Hebrew were taught; emphasis was laid on preaching, scholastic theology and the history of the English Church. Moral theology also had an important place in the curriculum. The religious divisions of the age had produced a series of moral problems unknown to the medieval churchman, and a Catholic priest in Elizabethan England was likely to be called upon for advice and decision beginning with the obvious question about the lawfulness of attendance at the official church services. After 1581 the Douai college used a textbook by the Spanish Jesuit Martin de Azpilcueta, a manual for confessors in an edition published at Antwerp.[22] This also dealt with the subject of casuistry, with the application of the principles of moral theology to particular cases, and especially with the circumstances that might excuse a normally forbidden course of action.

These studies were supervised by Robert Bristow, a former Fellow of Exeter College, Oxford, aided by a highly qualified staff of teachers. The financial administration was in the hands of Thomas Bailey, one-time Master of Clare Hall, Cambridge. In time Bailey was assisted by Robert Hargrove, who as a cloth merchant was able to make journeys to England, raising funds and convoying students back to Douai. Hargrove was included in 1582 in a list of papists known to be frequenting the North and was described by an informer: 'low, slender, black and thin haired, small legs and a childish voice'. But the atmosphere of the college was at first determined by the personality of William Allen and maintained with the minimum of regulation: 'A little government there is and order, but no bondage nor straightness in the world. There is neither oath nor statute nor other bridle nor chastisement; but reason and every man's conscience in honest superiority and subalternation each one towards others.'[23]

Financial stringency made life difficult at times and frustrating for Allen with his ambitious plans, for in addition to the college the expense of publications had to be met and in time also that of sending his young priests to England. At first all depended on casual gifts, and the first permanent income came from the university salary drawn by Allen when he obtained a chair in the university; a papal grant was not made until 1575, and the pension promised by Philip II was often in arrears. Funds were always needed, and somehow they always arrived, but the flow from England was made more difficult by the Act that Parliament passed in 1571. This complained of fugitives who practised rebellion and made fraudulent conveyances of their estates in England by which they retained the income. Such conveyances were declared void and trustees who did not report them became liable to penalty. The government at home did not find it easy to disentangle such arrangements, and in the case of Sir Francis Englefield a special Act was needed in 1593.

By 1576 it was reckoned that there were 236 Englishmen studying in Douai, and although it could be claimed that in seven years no Englishman had been brought before the magistrates on any charge the townspeople found this foreign invasion disquieting. With growing disorder in the Netherlands and a combination of anti-Spanish and anti-English feeling, it became necessary in March 1578 to remove the college to Rheims where it could enjoy the protection of the Duke of Guise. Two years before this upheaval the first four priests had left for England. The first to land was Lewis Barlow, a former student of the Middle Temple; he was arrested in 1587 and banished but returned to his ministry in England and died in 1610. Thomas Metham was a nephew of George Lord Darcy and was destined to die in prison. Martin Nelson was arrested in 1594; he recanted and was pardoned but returned to his Catholic faith and was still active as a priest in 1625. The fourth, Henry Shaw, also had a lengthy ministry before he died in 1607.

As the English penal laws made it increasingly difficult for Catholic parents to secure a religious education for their children, Allen widened the scope of the college and began to accept young boys for a course in humanities. By 1580 a division of the college into two sections, a theological college and a school for boys, was marked by separate staffs and meals[24] The boys followed the curriculum of the Jesuit schools of the day, based on the classics, and at first much of the teaching was obtained in schools of the town. Increasing numbers increased the financial problems : in 1583 fifty young men arrived from England, many from the universities, and in the next year the Roman authorities pressed for a reduction of numbers.

Allen was unwilling to turn applicants away, and in 1585 Thomas Bailey was sent to Rome to ask for an increased grant from the Pope. Gregory XIII was discouraging, and the mission returned unsuccessful. However, when the Pope died in the same year Allen went himself to plead with his successor a journey from which he did not return, for in 1587 Pope Sixtus V created him a Cardinal resident in the Curia. Meanwhile Thomas Bailey ruled the college until the appointment of Richard Barrett, who also succeded to the canonry Allen had held in the cathedral of Rheims. This appointment was only moderately successful. The new president found it difficult to work with Thomas Bailey, who retired to the old buildings at Douai, but he was no more successful with his new vice-president, Thomas Worthington, who succeeded as president in 1599 and embarked on a stormy and disastrous term of office that ended with his resignation in 1613.[25] As vice-president Worthington was something of an absentee, and it was Richard Barrett who led the college back to Douai in 1593.

The assassination of the Duke of Guise in the Armada year and the outbreak of civil war in France made Rheims unsafe for Englishmen. At Douai the college would have no rent to pay on its buildings, and a return to Spanish territory might secure a renewal of Philip II's grant. The return was successful, but the loss of Cardinal Allen's talented guidance was apparent, and the college, inevitably affected by dissension among the Catholics in England, entered on a period of decline. An official visitation in 1599 revealed insufficient revenues and pressing debts, poor discipline and a lack of proper food and clothing for the students. Allen had been proud of the fact that for twenty years there had been no need for written rules or constitutions, but the visitors found it necessary to establish a stringent set of rules and ordered a reduction in the numbers of students. Yet there were signs of a more promising future. In 1602 the foundation stone of permanent buildings was laid with a chapel dedicated to St Thomas of Canterbury, and new exiled foundations were established in the town, among them an Irish and a Scots College and the first monastery and school of the English Benedictines.[26]

Within ten years the steady flow of young men from England had proved too great for the capacity of one college. Rome was a natural place in which to found a second, for it already contained a suitable building : the English hospice that had served English pilgrims for centuries under royal patronage.[27] For several years after Elizabeth's accession the hospice had afforded an easy going refuge for a number of Marian priests, and these did not wholeheartedly welcome its transformation into a college for young candidates to the priesthood. The first students arrived in 1577, and the college was form- ally founded two years later at the instance of William Allen and Owen Lewis, who gave his books, furniture and some money for endowment. Lewis, who held a legal post in Rome and had at one time hoped to play a part in providing for a native Welsh clergy, had some influence on the appoint- ment of the warden of the hospice as the first rector. This was Dr Maurice Clynnog, an elderly Welshman who had in Marian days been himself a young man of promise. He had been nominated by Queen Mary to the diocese of Bangor but never confirmed by Rome or consecrated as bishop. All the same he seems to have been at sea in dealing with young men. He had settled in the hospice to a comfortable régime, anticipating the ultimate recovery of England for Catholicism but not feeling a sense of urgency or need for action. He also favoured his fellow countrymen among the students. Quarrels were fomented, and finally the Englishmen left in a body, causing a scandal in Rome. Dr Clynnog was removed from office, and the direction of the college was delivered to an Italian Jesuit. Robert Persons was in Rome at this time and mentioned these early troubles in a letter to Allen : 'The best borne Englishmen went all this winter with naked thighs and full of lice and all the Welshmen double apparrelled . . . Who can stay young men or old once incensed on both sides by national contentions. You know what passeth in Oxford on like occasions.' Contention, however, had now subsided after a spiritual retreat during which the preacher had 'left hot coles in the bosom of many'.[28]

Under Jesuit control the English College at Rome had its ups and downs, but by 1585 it had already sent thirty-three priests into England and its future was assured. The flow of applicants continued. Writing to his colleague at Rome in July 1590, the president of the Douai college urged him to take more men :

New students are constantly arriving. Your reverence must take at least sixteen or seventeen at once. Reverend father this is not the time to ponder how we are to make both ends meet. Between Easter and now twenty have arrived, others are announced and already on their way. We dare not refuse them; God sends them to us. I have reduced the quantity of food in the refectory to the smallest possible amount; their clothing is worn out, but never were the brigade happier or more content. Better youths more full of promise in virtue and talents than these we have never seen.[29]

This picture of austerity contrasts with the account of the English College at Rome given by the spy Anthony Munday gave in his work of 1582, *The English Romayne Life.*

Pressure of numbers and the energy of Robert Persons led on to the foundation of more colleges in Spain and, in the next century, of one at Lisbon.[30] In 1589 some English and Irish students already studying at the university of Valladolid received help in their financial difficulties from Philip II generous as always to the exiles. In that same year the president of the Rheims college sent some students for further study to Spain, but it was a dangerous year for Englishmen to be travelling in that country. Five were arrested by the Inquisition on arrival in Valladolid and three more at Burgos as 'followers of Drake'. Their release was secured by Persons, and from his interest in their problems he conceived the project of founding a permanent college. By 1592 his new college of St Alban at Valladolid held seventy-five students, undeterred by the English proclamation of 1591 that had attacked the seminary priests as 'dissolute young men'. Philip II paid a royal visit to the new foundation and endured addresses from ten students in ten different languages: Hebrew, Greek, Latin, English, Scots, Welsh, Spanish, French, Italian and Flemish – a trial that Philip III was spared in 1600. On that visit he and his queen were greeted by the customary *Te Deum* in the college chapel and also by 'the musicians in the other room adjoining who . . . began to play upon their viols and virginals with a very grand and pleasant song of eight parts'. By 1592 another college had been established at Seville, and the English merchants of the fraternity of St George had presented their house and chapel at San Lucar de Barrameda as a hospice for priests and students travelling to and fro from England.

In all these projects Persons had Joseph Creswell as his assistant, a Jesuit who took charge of the finances and was greatly trusted by the Spanish Court.[31] He had a talent for begging, and it was part of his duties to secure payment from the Spanish Treasury of the annual grant that had been promised for the English College at Douai and for Persons' school at St Omer. By 1603 he had a list of thirty-two members of the Court who helped to support students in the colleges, among them the Duke of Medina Sidonia of Armada fame. Seville became familiar with the sight of the English students and was generous to them. Spanish ships sailing to the Indies often carried an alms box for the English colleges.

After his work in Spain Persons turned next to the establishment of a school for English boys.[32] He had already in 1582 persuaded the Duke of Guise to support a small school for thirty boys at Eu with a Mr Chambers as its master, and this also served as a preparatory school for Allen's college. In 1592 the president of the college bought a house at St Omer to which the boys from Eu were transferred, but the magistrates made it a condition that the rector should not be an Englishman and limited the number of boys. A year later Persons obtained the support of Philip II for the foundation of an English Jesuit school on a far more ambitious scale : by the end of its first term thirty-three boys had arrived, mostly from England, and in 1599 the numbers reached 100. Persons described the object of his foundation : 'To receive the first fry that cometh out of England, which before must either have stayed there and been in danger of infection, or else lose their time and lack maintenance on this side of the seas, for that there was no fit place for to receive them here.'[33] He was pleased with the situation of St Omer 'for no part thereof liked him better than the Low Countries in regard to their nearness to England and air most like unto the air of our English climate'. It was hoped that the school would encourage vocations to the priesthood, but it was also intended that the school would provide the laity with the Catholic education that was not to be obtained in England.

Although the foundation of other schools was to follow, notably by the English Benedictines, the Jesuit school at St Omer was a pioneer and has been termed the supreme symbol of Catholic persistence throughout the seventeenth century, well known to and greatly disliked by the English government. By contemporary standards it was a large school, and by 1635 it held a record 200 boys. No boy was admitted under the age of 14 years, and a full statement of family background and a knowledge of Latin were required. The boys rose at 5 a.m. and retired to bed at 9 p.m., save at recreation conversation was supposed to be in Latin, and a religious observance that seems excessive by modern standards required a fifteen-minute examination of conscience every evening. Some rudimentary games were played, including football, but it has been noted that English was not taught as a class subject.

By 1600 when this educational system was firmly established there were also signs of the remarkable revival of the religious life that was to be a feature of the seventeenth century. The communities that had left England under the wing of the Count of Feria had survived great hardships, and by 1600 the Carthusian monks were settled in Flanders and the Bridgettine nuns at Lisbon. From 1569 to 1609 some twenty-five English nuns were professed in the Flemish community of Augustinian Canonesses at Louvain, and in the latter year they were able to establish their own independent community (the present-day community of Dames Anglaises at Bruges). However, the first Elizabethan foundation was of Benedictine nuns led by Lady Margaret Percy, daughter of the seventh Earl of Northumberland, followed by seven more foundations after 1600. The blessing of the first abbess was duly reported to England by a spy :

There are sixteen English gentlewomen in this town who wish to set up a nunnery. The Archduke gave them £2,000 and they bought a house. A daughter of Sir John Berkeley

and sister of Sir Nicholas Pointz was solemnly created
Abbess by the Archbishop of Malines . . . The Infanta
made a banquet for 100 persons, the great ladies, Abbess
and nuns dining at one table.[34]

This foundation was followed by two of Benedictine monks.

The first recruits came mainly from members of the English
College at Rome, who left to join abbeys of the Congregation
of Monte Cassino. Their departure from the college was peaceful, although Robert Persons viewed it without enthusiasm,
but a similar movement from the colleges in Spain was accompanied by much controversy and opposition. By 1600 several
abbeys in Italy and Spain had English members who hoped
that they might be permitted to work as monks in their native
land. There were also Catholics in England who believed, with
undue optimism, that the entry of Benedictines would provide
an impartial third force between the Jesuits and their
opponents. Permission to work on the English mission was not
readily obtained. The Cassinese Congregation was in the full
flower of a strict reform, so much so that Augustine Baker,
who was a novice at Santa Giustina of Padua in 1605–6,
could write of it later as the 'most exactly regular' monastery
in the world. Fourteen years were to pass, 1588–1602, before
the English monks were permitted to leave their monasteries
for the mission. The tradition of the Spanish Congregation of
Valladolid was also one of reform, but it was more activist
than the Italian with an emphasis on higher studies and
preaching.[35] The Spanish superiors were therefore more
sympathetic, and it was from Spain that the first three English
monks came back to England shortly before the death of
Queen Elizabeth. Others from Italy soon followed, and within
a few years two communities of English monks were founded
in exile: St Gregory's at Douai, and St Laurence's at
Dieulouard in Lorraine.

Meanwhile, waiting as it were in the wings were two contrasting figures who had their part to play in this revival. One
was the last surviving monk of Westminster, Dom Sigebert
Buckley, a former member of the Evesham community. Born

in 1517, he had lived on in prison throughout Elizabeth's reign, refusing conformity to the religious changes. It was through this 'venerable piece of antiquity' that a thread of continuity was established with the restored Westminster community and pre-Reformation monasticism. This was achieved when in November 1607 he formally aggregated two of the English monks from Italy to the Westminster community. Legal advice on this procedure, which was attested before a notary, was given by a young lawyer named David (in religion Augustine) Baker. David Baker, born in 1574, was the son of a Sheriff of Monmouth and nephew of David Lewis, who became Master of Requests and the first principal of Jesus College, Oxford. He became a Catholic in 1603 and later a member of the restored English Benedictines. As a mystical writer of note he was to have a lasting influence on the formation of generations of English monks.[36]

There were also Englishmen who entered foreign communities and were lost to the mainstream of English Catholicism but achieved distinction in their own spheres. One remarkable character was the son of a puritan shoemaker of London. He appears in the seventeenth-century history of the Friars Minim as a Frenchman, Jean François de Binans, but he has been identified as Samuel Debenham, a protégé of Robert Crowley, the puritan vicar of St Giles, Cripplegate.[37] Debenham was probably educated at Merchant Taylors' School and Pembroke College, Cambridge, and when he became a Catholic in 1583, despite his puritan upbringing, he does not seem to have found it difficult to contact a priest or to obtain help for the journey overseas. By 1605 he had become Provincial superior of the Friars Minim of Provence and had achieved distinction as a theologian, preacher and Hebrew scholar. A second Englishman who achieved considerable renown in France was the Capuchin Benet Canfield, born in 1563 at Canfield in Essex. He returned to England as a priest in 1599 and was later released from imprisonment at the request of Henry IV of France. His *Rule of Perfection* was widely read, and he has been judged to have had a decisive influence on the religious revival in France that was in progress during the early seventeenth century.[38]

The controversial writings of the exiles passed in time into oblivion, while some of the devotional works were constantly re-edited and widely read by Englishmen of all creeds. The exiles' work also endured in the field of education, and until the French Revolution compelled their transfer back to England the colleges and schools continued the work of training priests and educating the children of the Catholic gentry, in circumstances so different from those of contemporary life in England. For the greater part of Elizabeth's reign this education was greatly influenced by the tradition of the English universities, but in time the stricter imposition of religious tests at Oxford and Cambridge diminished the flow of university recruits. It was unfortunate that the education of English Catholics tended to develop apart from the national tradition.

7 Robert Persons and the Political Exiles

It is a world to see the emulation here . . . They are strange people and have strange humours.

Charles Paget to the Queen of Scots, 1585

In 1565 an exiled Englishman, Nicholas Sander, was riding through the woods on an estate of Cardinal Hosius, Bishop of Ermland. He was in distinguished company, that of Cardinal Commendone, papal nuncio to Poland, and with their host they had just completed a tour of Poland, Lithuania and East Prussia to set in train the decrees of the recent Council of Trent. The nuncio and Sander were engaged in a theological discussion, and Commendone suggested that the Englishman should write a book on the papal primacy, a suggestion that led to the publication of the *De Visibili Monarchia Ecclesiae* in 1571. Disturbed by its circulation in England the authorities commissioned a reply from a Cambridge scholar, and Archbishop Parker ordered the printer to suspend all other work and produce it by 1573.

Sander had travelled far by 1565 and not only in distance : he was by then a cosmopolitan, but one whose roots were firmly grounded in the English tradition. With many of his fellow exiles he shared memories of school at Winchester and of a Fellowship at New College, Oxford. It was shortly after the accession of Elizabeth that he had abandoned his Chair of Canon Law and had taken the road to an exile that led him first to Louvain, then to Rome, to attendance as a theologian at the Council of Trent and the Diet of Augsburg, and

now in 1565 to Eastern Europe. How adaptable these Elizabethan Englishmen were in carving out fresh careers in foreign
countries. Ahead lay a period of residence at the Court of
Philip II, membership of the expedition to Ireland in 1579,
and a miserable death as a fugitive from an English army.[1]
A distinguished and unfortunate man, and to some extent a
controversial figure even among the Catholic exiles, he was
well known in English government circles where he was
denounced in 1576 as 'a most wicked Englishman named
Nicholas Sanders who has set forth the most detestable works
. . . wherein he speaks most irreverently of Henry VIII'.
Irreverence to that departed monarch was not his worst
offence, for his writings were influential and the government
ban failed to prevent them from circulating in England. They
were sometimes read in strange surroundings, as by the young
man who in 1591 passed his time during Raleigh's voyage
to Guiana in the *Black Dog* with Sander's *Rock of the
Church*.[2] Literary work for Sander, however, was not enough.
He was all for action, for 'the stout assayling of England', if
that was the only way to expel the wicked men who had
deprived Englishmen of their traditional religion, and he
became a notable rebel when he joined the expedition to
Ireland. Even so a modern scholar has paid him tribute : 'For
courage and devotion to the cause for which he fought it
would be hard to find Sander's equal, Protestant or Catholic,
in Elizabethan England.'[3]

   There were other Englishmen who took part in open war
against their country. Some were members of Parma's army,
ready to cross the Channel in 1588, and when Drake captured
the great ship *Our Lady of the Rosary* an Englishman named
Tristram Winslade was on board. One of several exiles who
had sailed with the Spanish fleet, Winslade had been involved
in the troubles in Cornwall that had led to the execution of
the first seminary priest. Topcliffe was allowed to rack him
after his capture, but he was fortunate to escape a death
sentence. Such men were guilty of treason although in many
cases their country had treated them harshly. They had a
point of view to justify their actions, for they too believed

in the struggle with Anti-Christ and saw it seated in the government of their native land. At first in writings they sought to distinguish between the Queen and her ministers; later they set their hopes on a future when Mary Stuart would inherit the Crown. With Mary's death came division : some looked wholly to Spain, others to James VI of Scotland.

These exiles were mostly men of high character with all the patriotism of typical Elizabethans, and for most their love of country was heightened by a sense of loss, of being spectators at a time when great and stirring events were afoot. This can be seen in the lives of that contrasting pair of men, William Allen and Robert Persons. Allen lamented 'that for our sins we should be constrained to spend all, or most, of our service-able years out of our natural country, to which they are most due, and to which in all ages past they should have been most grateful; and that our offices should be acceptable, and our lives and services agreeable, to strangers, and not to our dearest at home'. All we know of Allen suggests that he would gladly have exchanged his position as cardinal, with all its splendour, for that of a humble parish priest in his native Lancashire, had that been possible, Persons wanted to end his days preaching in the towns and villages of England, and he too, for all his travelling through Europe and his hobnob-bing with the great, remained a West Countryman to the end. For him everything English, save Elizabeth's religion, was the best in the world, and he was accused of national prejudice against the Celtic fringe : many of his Catholic opponents were Welsh exiles. Both Allen and Persons looked back on Oxford as the best of all universities and were happy if they could reproduce something of its atmosphere and learning in the exiled colleges of their creation.

Dr Allen and his friends were firm believers in the enterprise of England and looked to Spain to provide the means for invasion, but they claimed that, having reconquered England for Catholicism, Spain would withdraw and leave Englishmen to manage their own affairs. Allen's position as the unofficial but accepted leader of the exiles made it inevitable that he should be drawn into politics, so that when summoned to

Rome in 1576 he could not refuse, for his entire missionary enterprise depended on the goodwill and support of the Pope and Philip II. On that journey he was joined by Sir Francis Englefield, who had in former days been made a privy councillor to Queen Mary at the age of 31 and Master of the Court of Wards, losing these offices when that Queen died.[4] The loss of his English revenues left Englefield little choice but to enter Spanish service, and in 1568 Philip II gave him a pension and sent him as adviser to the Duke of Alba. The discussions at Rome in 1576 made it clear that the exiles were far from united in their political views, but Englefield left with the impression that 'the enterprise would probably begin within twelve months', as he wrote to a friend. He was soon disillusioned, and moving permanently to Spain in 1580 he devoted the rest of his life to furthering the claims of his fellow countrymen for financial assistance. The English government was aware of the large correspondence that he conducted, including contacts with the Queen of Scots, and during the Throckmorton trial he was charged with having announced in a letter that Spanish troops stood poised for invasion. This was unlikely, but *in absentia* Englefield was attainted of high treason.

It is also unlikely that he had real political influence at the Spanish Court, but he was useful in discovering possible English spies. When Anthony Poyntz came to Madrid he was interviewed by Englefield, and Stafford, the English ambassador in Paris, later wrote to warn Walsingham that Poyntz 'sent by you into Spain' had been declared by Englefield to be 'either a spy or at least unfit to do what he offered'. The offer was to secure the death of Elizabeth for 4,000 crowns. When Englefield died he left a letter for Philip II pleading for action against England but urging him, if successful, not to claim the crown for himself.

Throughout his life Englefield remained on friendly terms with Dr Allen and Robert Persons, who became increasingly influential after his return from England in 1582.[5] Allen, in the early days, may have been a reluctant politician, but for Persons the travelling, the planning and the intimacy with the great that political activity involved were congenial from both conviction and temperament. He was a natural diplomat and in some spheres a successful one, but it is remarkable that two such dissimilar men as Allen and Persons were able to work in harmony for so long : the calm North Country gentleman, and the explosive and energetic Somerset man of the people. Person's enemies – and they were never lacking – claimed that he was the son of a blacksmith of Nether Stowey, and it was a Catholic opponent who spread the story that he was the illegitimate son of a priest. His brother, a clergyman of Elizabeth's Church, rejected the charge of illegitimacy as an impudent and palpable slander, and Persons himself claimed to be of yeoman stock, a status that he once tried to explain to a papal nuncio. At Oxford he achieved some distinction, becoming dean and bursar of his college, but his Oxford career turned sour for he quarrelled with the Balliol Fellows and either resigned or was dismissed in 1574. Persons gave an account of this episode in his *Autobiography*, concluding that 'when Robert had called to account some of his friends for eating meat in time of Lent within the College bounds contrary to the statutes . . . they even with public ringing of bells shut him out from the College'.[6] Christopher Bagshaw was another Fellow of Balliol of this period who left the State Church for the Church of Rome, and he carried his enmity towards Persons into Catholic circles. It may be that Person's departure from Oxford was connected with his attraction to Catholicism, and if he never lacked enemies he never lacked friends : the father of a former pupil gave him at this time the financial support for a European tour.

Persons was reconciled at Louvain when he was 27 years of age, and after a year of study at Padua he decided to enter the Society of Jesus, thus embarking on a career that eventually made him a confidant of Philip II, of the Dukes of Guise and Parma, and of the Pope. He was the only Fellow of Balliol of the age to achieve international fame. A permanent relationship with Philip II resulted from his mission of 1582 to enlist support for schemes against England sponsored by the Duke of Guise. This proved important during the period 1588–97, which Persons spent in Spain furthering his educational projects and the work of the Society.

Not all the Catholic exiles approved of the reliance on Spain of Dr Allen and Persons. Opposition developed around Dr Owen Lewis, later Bishop of Cassano, which was linked by another Welshman, Thomas Morgan, with a group of laymen headed by Lord Paget and his brother Charles.[7] Charles Paget was sent to England in 1582 to sound out the leading Catholics, and he returned with the impression that they had no enthusiasm for rebellion or foreign intervention. In later years Persons accused Paget of having deliberately sabotaged this mission, but by 1584 opposition was having effect and he wrote to the Queen of Scots :

> Dr Allen and I, having had a meeting together, had con-
> cluded upon consideration of our thwarts and oppositions
> that we received daily in all our doings, and men of our
> side, and of the small success our former labours had
> brought forth – we resolved, I say, to leave cogitations of
> such matters and to follow only our spiritual course, where-
> on all dependeth though in longer time.[8]

It was, however, against his nature for Persons to remain in-active, and he and Allen continued to press the Spanish authorities. In March 1587 in a memorandum for the Spanish Secretary it was urged that the special interest of Philip II in the English succession should be concealed from the Pope and the English Catholics : 'It is not unlikely that the Pope himself and some of the Cardinals, for reasons of state, would begin to indulge in divers reflections and suspicions . . . and that possibly His Holiness would not collaborate in it.'[9] Only after a successful invasion, it was suggested, should the Spanish king's right to the throne be publicised in a book that could be secretly prepared beforehand. Here was Persons proposing to hoodwink the Pope and coolly casting the claims of Mary Stuart aside : either she would be dead, 'and it is possible that the heretics . . . being under the impression that the expedi-tion is being made in support of her cause will put her to death', or she 'if alive can be bestowed in marriage by His Majesty'. In 1588 when the Armada was preparing to sail Allen signed an *Admonition to the Nobility and People of England*, which attacked the Queen and called on Englishmen to rise against her. The *Admonition* was to have been issued after the Spaniards had landed and was never published, but the government secured a copy and thus fresh ammunition against the Catholics at home.

The role of Thomas Morgan during these years was an equivocal one, and he was much distrusted although he controlled the correspondence of the Queen of Scots as cypher clerk to her ambassador in France, Archbishop Beaton. As a result Morgan suffered from both sides. Elizabeth's government tried to secure his extradition for alleged complicity in the Parry Plot and did obtain his imprisonment in the Bastille for two years from 1585 : In 1590 the Duke of Parma ordered his arrest in the Spanish Netherlands as a suspected English spy, and at this point some of the exiles claimed that Morgan, a former secretary to the Archbishop of York, had never become a Catholic. He failed to inspire confidence although Bishop Owen Lewis and Lord Paget protected him. In 1585 the Paris nuncio had written to the papal secretary of state : 'This Morgan is considered by many here and particularly by the Jesuits to be a knave; yet the Queen of Scots relies upon him more than her own ambassador.'[10] Seven years later when Cardinal Allen wrote to Charles Paget the picture had not changed : 'I see no Jesuit nor other priest, clerk or religious of our nation that detesteth not Morgan's foul dealings towards me and consequently against the common cause.'[11] The Duke of Parma agreed. When he forwarded a dossier on Morgan to Spain he commented on the latter's 'attempts to sew cockle and intrigues and to undo everything that Cardinal Allen and Father Persons and other good Catholics are doing'.

This dissension among the exiles increased after Allen's death, some intriguing to obtain the elevation of Bishop Lewis to the cardinalate, others working for Persons although he flatly declined any pretension to such honour. In 1595 John

Slade, the confidential secretary of Sir Francis Englefield, fled with all his cyphers and papers intending to hand them over to bishop Lewis, but he died on the journey to Rome and the papers were recovered. The loyalties of some of these opponents of Allen and Persons may have been suspect, but a growing number of Catholics in England were opposed to reliance on Spain. This opposition found expression after the defeat of the Armada in a book published by a priest named Wright, who argued that in spite of papal policy Catholics in England were fully justified in taking arms to defend their Queen and country against Spain.[12]

Many Englishmen were interested in the question of Elizabeth's successor, but this was a delicate topic and the Queen forbade public discussion. Peter Wentworth had been confined in the Tower in 1593 when he attempted to secure its debate in Parliament, but the government veto on discussion did not deter the authors of a book that appeared in 1595. This was *A Conference about the next Succession to the Crowne of England,* and although published under the name of Doleman it was a composite work by several authors in which Persons had a major share.[13] Its first section argued the concept of monarchy as a contract between an elected ruler and his people, who could depose him if he violated the contract, and for this reason the book was reprinted during the constitutional struggles of the next century, in 1648 and 1681. A second section discussed the claims of possible aspirants to the Crown, including James VI and Arabella Stuart, Beauchamp and the Earls of Derby and Huntingdon; the Infanta Isabella, daughter of Philip II, was also included on account of her descent from the House of Lancaster. Persons was to claim that the book was impartial and did not attempt to decide between the claimants, but the main purpose of the *Conference* was to argue for a Catholic successor and only the Infanta could fulfill this condition.

The work soon came under fire. Wentworth criticised Doleman for attributing too great powers to Parliament, while Dr Gifford, a Catholic opponent of Persons among the exiles, claimed that 'in every way Persons will make England an

absolute monarchy'. By raising this delicate and controversial
subject Persons and his colleagues gave offence not only to the
English authorities but also to James VI, the future King of
England. The editor of his political works has written : 'James
was right in regarding it as the most dangerous book of the
time . . . It is hardly too much to say that this book was the
chief storehouse of facts and arguments drawn upon by
nearly all opponents of the royal claims for a century, Protestant as well as Catholic.[14] A group of Catholic opponents
persuaded the papal nuncio in the Netherlands to forward a
summary of the book to Rome where it made an unfavourable
impression. In due course the English government received a
report that Persons had been criticised for his political activities at a General Congregation of the Jesuits, which had
decreed that members of the Society of Jesus should not
meddle in State affairs, directly or indirectly. Among those
who protested against the *Conference* was the Scottish Jesuit,
Creighton, and students of the English College in Rome were
reported to have objected to a reading of the work in their
refectory. In 1600 a group of Catholic laymen published a
reply at Paris, *A Counterfeit Conference,* in which they gave
wholehearted support to the claims of James VI. By this time
laymen were getting restive at the meddling of clergy in
politics, and Charles Paget was not alone in his belief that
priests should stick to their breviaries and spiritual matters,
leaving politics to the laity.[15]

In 1690 a work of Persons called a *Memorial for the
Reformation of England* was found among the papers of
James II and printed for the first time for use as anti-Jesuit
propaganda, but although the author did not intend it for
publication in his lifetime its ideas were fairly well known.[16]
On the assumption that a Catholic sovereign would succeed
Elizabeth, Persons was concerned to map out a programme
for action, for the lesson of the unplanned Marian restoration,
with its lack of genuine spiritual revival, must be learnt. At
first, he argued, there must be no persecution, for he was
convinced that full and equal disputation in public must
carry conviction and destroy the credit of all heresies. He

stressed, however, that he was not urging toleration : 'I think no one thing so dangerous, dishonourable, or more offensive to Almighty God.' Ultimately 'a good and sound manner of inquisition' should be established to replace the Court of High Commission, but not one on the severe model of Spain.

A central Council of Reformation was to direct the restoration and ascertain the needs of every diocese, controlling the economic affairs of the Church, founding seminaries and appointing clergy who, like the bishops, would be removable. A learned and reformed clergy was essential, and Persons thought it preferable to leave benefices vacant rather than to fill them with ignorant or unsuitable priests : it was better that a good layman should summon the people for the reading of homilies and spiritual books rather than that the minister should be unworthy. Funds were to be obtained by the restoration of alienated Church property, a key issue, but Catholic holders might be permitted to pay an annual rent and retain former church lands. Income from this source was also to be used for the support of schools, hospitals and universities. There was much in the *Memorial* that was enlightened, especially its stress on the need for social reform and a sound educational system, which might include the foundation of a third university in the North. Persons considered that there was 'overmuch beating of boys' in England and that the brutality of its legal system needed reform, while the 'bare and needy husbandman' deserved protection from bad landlords. By these wide-ranging reforms a new England was to be created as 'a light and lantern' to other nations. The *Memorial* throws much light on its brilliant author, but Persons' Catholic opponents, aware of its contents even if they had not read it, found little to praise in an 'ecclesiastical Utopia' or 'Jesuitical Common wealth'; it was regarded as one more example of arrogance. To one modern historian it has appeared to be one of the most influential unread books ever written, providing a link between the Tudor Commonwealth and the radicals of the seventeenth century.[17]

Much of Persons' writings consisted of controversy, and he was a master of invective, writing under many pseudonyms.

In his *Temperate Ward-Word to the Turbulent and Seditious Watch-Word of Sir Francis Hastings*, published anonymously, he wrote as a detached friend of the Jesuits and in a tone of respect for the Queen and her Council, but respect was abandoned when news of her death reached him. A hasty *Addition* was made to the first volume of his *Treatise of Three Conversions*, in which he thanked God for his mercy in delivering Catholics from their old persecutor and praised the learning and judgement of the new king. Five years later when James published his apology for the oath of allegiance, *Triplici Nodo, Triplex Cuneus*, Persons entered the lists against him with his *Judgement of a Catholike Englishman, Living in Banishment for his Religion* and greatly shocked the king by placing Elizabeth in hell. James was convinced that every anointed sovereign must be predestined for the other place.

Persons had always been profoundly influenced by memories of the year spent in England in 1580–1, and he never appreciated the decline in the numbers and influence of the English Catholics that resulted from the steady grinding of the penal laws. After he had seen the death of his political hopes from Spain with the failure of the last Armada of 1597, Persons wrote to a Jesuit college in 1603 in terms that indicated a change of view, and in the course of an apologia for his past political activities he counselled patience for the present in the hope that toleration might result from a peace between England and Spain. This hope was also to be dashed, but he stressed the policy of Pope Clement VIII towards James I: 'His Holiness here is so far embarked to try what may be done by fair means with him', and warned that the English Catholics must take heed 'lest upon passion some break out and be oppressed in the mean space or cause more severity to other'.[18] Would that the Gunpowder plotters had followed such advice.

During the reign of Clement VIII the Jesuits were out of favour, and the death of Philip II in 1598 had ended any influence that Persons still retained in Madrid. The days when the carriage of the Pope's nephew had waited daily outside the English College to convey Persons to the Vatican were over, and for a brief period he was exiled from Rome. For some years he had been at the centre of the Appellant controversy, opposed in England by his former Balliol colleague, Bagshaw, and by some very vocal members of the secular clergy. In the course of this quarrel a respected secular priest wrote to him : 'The trouble and scandal you have wrought in our church these late years by your politick courses do quite cancel all your former deserts.' Yet the services of Persons to the Catholic cause had been immense : his flair for organisation had served the English mission well, his educational work was of enduring importance, and his literary work amounted to some thirty publications. The high quality of his prose, which helped to make the *Christian Directory* a spiritual classic, has won increasing recognition, and its influence was spread by translations into Latin, German, Italian and Welsh.[19] A man whose spiritual teaching was reprinted more than forty times by English Protestants before 1640 must have had remarkable qualities of mind and heart. To many of his contemporaries, however, he seemed a dangerous and cunning man, and when he died in 1610 there were those among his fellow Catholics who shared the relief of government circles in England.

During the 1590s the ranks of prominent exiles were thinned by death, and Cardinal Allen was soon followed to the grave by Bishop Owen Lewis and Sir Francis Englefield. Sir William Stanley lived on into the reign of James I when Charles Paget returned to England. Stanley's betrayal of Deventer while serving in Elizabeth's army was never forgiven, although he could plead a patent from the Earl of Leicester permitting him to leave the English service at any time.[20] He had led a frustrating existence after the events of 1587 when some 600 men had followed him into the forces of Spain. At first he took command of an Anglo–Irish Regiment, but no special employment was found for it, and his suggestions were not adopted. In 1596 national quarrels made necessary the separation of English and Irish. Stanley lost his command but, possibly as compensation, was made a member of the Archduke's Council of War in 1602 and later appointed governor of Malines. In 1605 he was denounced in England by a former ensign, Guy Fawkes, and put under arrest at the request of James I. On release he held a public thanksgiving in the cathedral of Malines, and a protest by Sir Robert Cecil elicited an official reply that Sir William was very devout and fond of music. Stanley lived on in honour in the Spanish Netherlands until his death in 1630; it was then fifty years since he had seen his native Lancashire.

The English Regiment, however, had a future, and when peace was signed in 1604 between England and Spain James I permitted recruitment in England and approved of the appointment of the newly created Lord Arundell of Wardour as colonel.[21] Arundell (1560–1639) had been a fairly typical Elizabethan courtier of the younger generation. At the age of 20 he was banished from Court after imprisonment for religion, and later he was under suspicion of political activity during travel abroad. When the imperial army was besieging the Turks at Gran in Hungary during 1595, Arundell appeared in front of the army and attracted attention : 'By reason of my plumes of feathers, of my armour bases and furniture full of gold and silver . . . I was presently marked of all men's eyes.' First into the breach he scaled the citadel and fixed the imperial standard in place of the crescent, being made a Count of the Holy Roman Empire by the Emperor Rudolph II as his reward. Returning to England he met with a chilly reception from the Queen, who gave her opinion of his new title before committing him to the Fleet prison : 'I would not have my sheepe branded with another man's mark; I would not they should follow the whistle of a strange Shepherd.' He was soon released but was back again in prison in 1597 and found guilty of harbouring a priest. However, the legal penalty was not invoked, and Arundell's father was told to keep an eye on him. The old gentleman mistook this to mean that his son and daughter-in-law would be permanently quartered on him, and disliking the lady he asked that they might be kept at least 'two flight shots away'. Soon afterwards the father died, and on inheriting Arundell was created a baron and allowed a passport in order to take up his new command.

An aspect of the exiles' life that was a constant source of suspicion and distrust was the ease with which the home government could obtain information about their activities. It was a simple matter to plant informers in the colleges as bogus servants or students, to purchase information and to keep a watch on political activity.[22] It was the duty of English ambassadors abroad to keep an eye on their fellow countrymen, and some exiles maintained a correspondence with Cecil and Walsingham. In 1585 Sir Charles Arundel, who had left England with Lord Paget, warned that Elizabeth's councillors were bribing one of the Roman cardinals. Such was the atmosphere of suspicion that in the same year Arundel was himself accused of being an English government spy but was declared innocent after an investigation by the Paris nuncio.[23] Yet when Arundel died Elizabeth's ambassador in Paris, Sir Edward Stafford, wrote to Walsingham : 'No man of this side served my turn as he did for her Majesty's service . . . he had continually letters from Sir Francis Inglefield and Pridieux, whose letters I ever saw afore he deciphered them.'[24] This may imply that the letters were intercepted without Arundel's knowledge or that he was of assistance to Stafford. Conyers Read has argued that Stafford himself sold information to his Spanish colleague, a charge that Neale has found it difficult to accept, but it has been found that in this curious world of the exiles agents of Cecil and Walsingham were spying on each other.

Allen and Persons were both spied on by servants, and a copy of Allen's 1588 *Declaration* was obtained by a government bribe to the printer. An accurate and detailed account of 285 Englishmen living abroad was supplied to the government by John Sledd, who lived in Rome for some months and denounced priests travelling back to England. A memorandum of 1586 suggests that an agent intending to spy on the exiles should first pretend to be a Catholic and make friends with priests by visiting the London prisons :

He is to yield himself, as it were, under shift to have advice and ghostly counsel . . . being desirous, if it might please Jesu for his dear mother's sake, to gain some friends for his better access into foreign parts and Catholic countries, there to pass the time with the quiet and comfort of his conscience and in the causes of his poor distressed countrymen.[25]

If the government found it important to keep a watchful eye on the exiles the same was true in reverse, and the exiles were well informed of affairs at home. A centre through which much information passed was the Antwerp house of Richard Verstegen, the well-known printer, publisher and writer.[26] On one occasion he received copies of letters sent to the Privy Council and reported to Persons : 'fifty sheets of paper, being the confession of Mr Anthony Tirrell written by himself, and others in authority unto him, besides divers articles, interrogations, practices of Walsingham'. In 1598 Persons obtained copies of letters that Charles Paget was writing to members of the Council.

A talent for languages gave one of the Welsh exiles a key position in the gathering of intelligence. Hugh Owen was one of three brothers : the eldest was a Welsh squire, Robert became a canon of Mantes, while Hugh mixed in the inner circles of the exiles. Hugh Owen supported Spain and was highly esteemed by Philip II, the Duke of Parma and the Archduke Albert.[27] Among his successes was the interception of dispatches sent to Leicester during the Sluys campaign, and he also obtained summaries of secret discussions that some Walloon nobles were conducting with the English government unknown to the Spanish authorities. In 1605 he was one of those arrested at the request of James I on the charge of complicity in the Gunpowder plot, but no evidence was forthcoming from England. Owen applied for aid to the Duke of Lerma, enclosing a memorandum in his defence for the Spanish Council of State. He claimed that in his confidential papers, which had been impounded, 'not a word will be found which touches the said conspiracy, for I take my oath that no human being ever wrote to me about it, nor did I write to anyone about it, nor did any other person do so by my order'.[28] In the absence of any firm evidence from London Owen was released but he was tried in his absence in England when Lord Salisbury reminded Sir Edward Coke : 'You must remember to lay Owen as foul as you can.' Two years later Owen discovered a plot by one Thomas Wylfourd to kidnap him and take him to England. After his brief imprisonment the Spanish authorities had increased his pension, and they now offered him a refuge in their embassy at Rome, where he died in 1618. There he had an opportunity to renew his friendship with Robert Persons, and the two old conspirators were able in tranquility to recall their life of exile. It had not lacked excitement, danger, hope and frustration, but it was Persons alone who could look back on work that would endure.

8 The Scorching Wind: Catholic Life under Repression

> A scorching wind shall be the portion of their cup.
>
> Psalm 11

In spite of fierce legislation a Catholic minority survived throughout the reign of Elizabeth, whereas in Italy and Spain the fate of Protestants was one of virtual extermination. The reasons for this distinction are clear enough. In the Latin countries a very small Protestant minority held to a religion that offended and was alien to their neighbours, who consequently offered no protection against the Inquisition. In England a minority, large in number for part of the reign, retained a faith that had been the religion of the country for over 1000 years : as late as 1593 a writer complained that 'the common people for the greater part' persisted in calling Protestantism 'the new religion'.[1] The government itself had no wish to enforce its legislation to the letter, and throughout England Catholics might hope to rely on the connivance of relations and friends. In times of national stress they could expect to suffer the full rigour of the law, but there were intermittent periods when persecution was more than usually relaxed. This was notably the case during the negotiations for the Queen's French marriage, which ended in 1579, for a brief period after 1582 and for a few months at the end of the reign.

Catholicism was never entirely banished from Elizabeth's

Court, and it has been estimated that a third of the peerage held to the old religion : of sixty peers in 1580 ten were strongly puritan, twelve might be termed Anglican, twenty-four were indifferent to religion, and twenty might be described as Catholic.[2] Lord Burghley himself had Catholic relations, and Walsingham's daughter married a Catholic, the fourth Earl of Clanricarde. Although the Catholic peers held a very privileged position they were not entirely immune from vexation, especially if in any way politically suspect. The troubles of Lord Vaux have been fully investigated, the young Earl of Southampton was for a time under house arrest, and Lord Lumley was heavily fined. The two Catholic sons of the Duke of Norfolk were both briefly imprisoned in the Tower, where their half-brother the Earl of Arundel was destined to die. There were other young men who began hopefully at Court and ended like Thomas Pound, nephew of the first Earl of Southampton, who spent thirty years in prison for his religion. Contact with the Catholic clergy was never impossible for members of the Court, and conversions were not unknown; besides that of Arundel there was the conversion of the eighth Earl of Northumberland, which led him to the same fate. Burghley's former ward, the young Earl of Oxford, was attracted to the old faith but did not persevere. The Earl of Essex, while not himself a Catholic, drew a number of young Catholics around him all hoping for political change, a point that was stressed at his trial : 'such a Catiline, popish, dissolute and desperate company of traitors'; Coke went on to depict the Essex rising as a popish plot engineered by Spain.[3] There were also defections and conversions among Elizabeth's Maids of Honour and Gentlemen Pensioners, and it was claimed that Mass was sometimes secretly celebrated at Court.

It is therefore not surprising that a fortunate few were at times able to invoke Court influence in order to escape the penalties of recusancy. The 1571 Act against the exiles had specially exempted Jane Dormer, Duchess of Feria, from its penalties, and the Queen herself occasionally aided recusant friends. Prominent members of the Court, including the Earls of Leicester and Warwick and notably Sir Christopher Hatton, also protected recusants. There were limits to such favours. The Earl of Shrewsbury was temporarily banished from Court on the charge that members of his Derbyshire houshold had intimidated local officials so that they 'did find means to keep notable recusants from appearing at sessions and from being indicated at assizes'.[4] The greatest English musician, William Byrd, was an uncompromising recusant. Protected by special licence of the Queen and Council and undeterred by the knowledge that publication was impossible, he continued to compose for the Latin Liturgy, dedicating such work to peers of Catholic sympathies: the Earl of Worcester, the Earl of Northampton, Lord Lumley and Lord Petre. His contemporary John Dowland

> whose heavenly touch
> Upon the lute doth ravish human sense

was less fortunate, having committed the offence of conversion to Catholicism while in the service of the English ambassador at Paris.

Court favour secured the release from prison in 1585 of Lady Lovell and her son, who were given immunity from further prosecution. In 1595 a particularly steadfast Lancashire, recusant, Lady Egerton, was declared by the Archbishop's Visitors to be 'specially dispensed withall from Her Majesty's laws and not to be dealt withall by justices or ecclesiastical judge'.[5] Lady Constable of Burton was indicted in the same year of harbouring a priest and was saved by influence in high places: she was a sister of Lord Scrope and her husband, Sir Henry, was a nephew of the Earl of Westmorland and the wealthiest church papist in Yorkshire. Two years later her brother-in-law of Upsal Castle was arrested, guilty of the same offence, but although the Council of the North was anxious to secure conviction he too escaped punishment.[6] The daughter of Sir Thomas Cornwallis even enlisted Sir Philip Sidney, a good Protestant, to put in a word for her father with Walsingham. With so many connections and friends it is understandable that some Suffolk recusants claimed to receive previous warning from Court in times of persecution. In Court circles also originated a plan that had the Queen's approval : to found a colony for Catholics in America. For this plan Sir Humphrey Gilbert made assignments to three Catholics : Sir George Peckham, Sir Thomas Gerrard and Sir William Catesby. The scheme foundered on Spanish hostility.[7]

In time the Catholic gentry tended to restrict their social contacts. However, they were not necessarily cut off from the society of their neighbours, and sometimes good relations were maintained with clergy of the State Church. It was charged against Bishop Freke of Norwich by local puritans that he held convivial gatherings with recusants and employed a Catholic lawyer and butler. Bishop Babington of Worcester was invited to join the hunting parties of John Lyttelton at Frankley.[8] The autobiography of the Jesuit John Gerard mentions social calls made by Abbott, a future Archbishop of Canterbury, on local Catholic gentry at a time when he was Master of an Oxford College. No doubt it was sound policy for recusants to keep on good terms with powerful neighbours, but Sir Thomas Tresham's friendly connection with the Bishop of Lincoln seems to have been genuine, and he exchanged cordial greetings with Archbishop Mathew of York, who had been of service in the recovery of stolen horses.

Recusants were not restricted in their marriages, but a protestant husband or wife inevitably brought religious difficulties. Consequently there was a tendency for closely knit groups of related Catholic families to form in most counties, and it was among these that the clergy were most likely to find some security. In Sussex the Shelleys of Michelgrove, who ranked just below the peerage, were related to the Earls of Southampton and linked with a number of lesser families : Gages, Copleys and Brownes. In East Anglia the Rookwoods, Timperleys, Bedingfields and others were all related, and some were connections and followers of the Norfolk Howards. In

the Midlands, where there were some forty-five houses of recusant gentry in the county of Northampton alone, the Lords Vaux
and Monteagle, the Treshams and the Brudenells were linked
by marriage. The Northern counties had similar networks.

Apart from imprisonment and fine, exclusion from office
involved a considerable loss of prestige and financial gain in an
age when the gentry laboured to maintain and increase their
family position. In time most recusants were excluded from
the Commission of the Peace. Some might have slipped
through the net, however, and William Lambarde claimed to
have known some justices in the 1590s who had successfully
evaded taking the oath of supremacy.[9] In 1578 the Hampshire
justices bound over Sir Benjamin Tichborne as 'an obstinate
papist', but the senior circuit judge, Manwood, made him
a justice on his next visit with the words : 'Now you are fellow
with those that bound you to the peace.'[10] In 1582 the
Bishop of Chichester complained that the Earl of Arundel's
steward, Edward Caryll, a member of a strongly recusant
family, had been restored to the commission 'being a knowen
papist'. Caryll was dropped after his imprisonment in the
Tower but was restored again in 1591. He might have been
an occasional conformist but his daughter was a nun in a
convent abroad and in 1614 his son was keeping a Jesuit
chaplain.[11]

Catholics also maintained a hold on the legal profession.
They were strongly represented in the Inns of Court, and if
they entered into litigation they did not find it impossible to
retain a Catholic attorney. Edmund Plowden was one of the
most distinguished of the Elizabethan lawyers and treasurer
of the Middle Temple, his recusancy dating from 1569. In
1563 he defended Bishop Bonner and in 1578 was counsel
for the Archbishop of Canterbury, even appearing for the
Crown a year later and obtaining judgement for the Queen.
He also acted for Francis Tregian when the latter was a
prisoner in the Marshalsea and was reported that year by an
informer as being one of the papists 'wont to hear Mass at
Baron Browne's in Fish Street Hill'. Plowden's *Commentaries*
became a standard authority on the common law.

Of all the well-known recusants Sir Thomas Tresham was the most indefatigible in his resort to litigation, and at one and the same time he was involved in no less than nineteen law-suits. He put on record his recognition that justice could be obtained in spite of recusancy, although 'the then Marquis of Northampton (my near kinsman and one of my mightiest adversaries) and the judges of the circuit, also the preachers and the puritans, combined therein against me'.[12] One circuit judge, appointed in 1589, had a recusant wife and brother. This was the Lancashire man Thomas Walmesley, who soon gained a reputation for sympathetic dealing with recusants, and when magistrates with recusant wives were barred in 1592 he was not removed from the bench but was changed to another circuit.[13] Litigation by a Catholic risked the raising against him of a charge of treason. At the end of Elizabeth's reign three fanatical puritan landowners in Yorkshire, includ-ing Sir Thomas Posthumous Hoby, were engaged in enclosing common land, and this brought them into collision with Catholic neighbours who were following the same policy. A quarrel was pursued before the Council of the North and in the Star Chamber, and in the course of a series of lawsuits the puritan gentry charged the West Riding Justices, together with the Council of the North, both with protecting recusant families and with neglecting a Catholic conspiracy. On the whole their proceedings were not favourably viewed by the Yorkshire gentry, and a conviction secured against a Catholic neighbour of ridiculing the State Church was a poor result of their efforts.[14]

There were obvious dangers if the patients of a Catholic doctor failed to recover. When Edmund Brudenell's puritan wife was dying a family struggle ensued for her estate. Her brother-in-law – Richard Topcliffe, the notorious hunter of Catholics – was disappointed, and he accused the doctor of being 'a notorious recusant and maintainer of popery, and a doer of much hurt with his persuasions therein under cover of ministering physic'. Topcliffe was not a popular member of the family, and Sir Edmund had once threatened 'to entertain him with a case of pistols' if he dared to visit Dene.[15] When

Abbot Feckenham was permitted to visit Bath for reasons of health the authorities did not object to his residence with a Catholic doctor, Reuben Sherwood, and Catholicism proved no bar when Sir Robert Cecil recommended George Turner for membership of the College of Physicians in 1602.

After 1571 Catholics were barred from the House of Commons unless they took the oath of supremacy, and by the end of the reign it was not expected that they should take part in parliamentary elections. Recusant peers were still summoned to the House of Lords, and Lord Vaux was present at the Parliament of 1589 shortly after imprisonment for recusancy. In 1595 he wrote to Burghley to excuse his absence from the Parliament of that year : 'My debts and miseries beyond measure multiplied, I am come up raggedly suited and clothed unfittedest to give dutiful attendance on royal Presence . . . Moreover my parliament robes are at pawn to a citizen.'[16] Although Catholics might not sit in the House of Commons it seems that the exercise of patronage was not impossible, and the case of Lady Copley suggests that such patronage was not lost by voluntary exile. Her husband, Sir Thomas – a distant connection of the Queen, who was godmother to his son – was returned as a member for Gatton in three Parliaments, but the election was a formality as there were no inhabitants. In 1570 he was reconciled to Catholicism and went abroad to become, in the words of Neale, 'one of the most eminent of the non-political exiles, a victim of conscience'. By the 1571 Act the rents of his estates were sequestered, but Lady Copley was permitted to join him in 1574. She returned to England after his death in 1587, where she was soon imprisoned for harbouring a priest, and her son was under restraint in a London alderman's house. As a result of her imprisonment she lost the nomination of two burgesses for Gatton, but she had apparently retained it up to that time.[17]

One of the rare disputed elections of the reign, at Rutland in 1601, showed that although it might be unusual for Catholics to take part it was not impossible. A number of

Catholic recusants were persuaded to support one of the candidates. James Digby, a member of a former leading family of the county, was told that as a recusant he had no voice, but he replied: 'Though I be a recusant yet I have a voice here and will have a voice, for I pay subsidy and fifteenth and have more freehold to lose than you.'[18] A recusant brother-in-law of the Earl of Shrewsbury was ordered to give up his office as a justice of the peace in 1593, but he acted as agent for the earl's candidate in the Nottingham election of that year. Conversion to Catholicism involved resignation of a parliamentary seat, and a member might be forced out if his wife and children were convicted as recusants. Ralph Sheldon, a former Member of Parliament, had a long history of recusancy when the Council wrote to him in 1601 to warn him against opposing a local candidate for Parliament who was an ardent Protestant: 'It is not our meaning in any sort to restrain or hinder the liberty of a free election which ought to be amongst you, but because it is suspected that some undue proceeding may be used against him, especially out of animosity of religion which would greatly displease her Majesty . . . we thought good to admonish you.'[19] The government candidate was duly returned.

A man of ambition, anxious to play a part in local or national affairs in accordance with family tradition, might be driven into conformity by the disabilities and humiliations attached to recusancy, but more serious were the legal penalties. Yet it is clear that the death penalty was only sporadically enforced in the case of the laity, and many escaped the penalty for harbouring priests or for helping to reconcile or being reconciled to Catholicism. Figures for one county give some indication of the extent. Of seventeen laymen and women put to death in Yorkshire, two died for denying the royal supremacy, one for being reconciled and eleven for harbouring priests. A further twenty-one were charged with harbouring priests and not put to death, and thirty of the county's gentry were informed on without result in the 1590s for the same offence.[20] The government was obviously reluctant to face the odium of executions on such a scale among the gentry. Nevertheless, the statutes acted as a great deterrent, and we cannot estimate the mental strain endured by those who gave hospitality to their priests.

The danger of detection for harbouring priests produced the system of building hiding places in country houses, and recusants evolved remarkable legal skill in evading the penalties of imprisonment and fines. As proof of absence from church on four successive Sundays was required, the well-to-do recusant could evade the £20 fine by moving house before the month expired, an easy matter for those owning houses in more than one county or with an abundance of relatives. Distraint for the debt was also evaded by collusion with neighbours for the lease of land to friends, who might later return it to the original owner or a member of his family. It was difficult to suppress this type of evasion even after the 1581 Act had been tightened up in 1587, although the 1587 Act increased both the income from fines and the number of church papists. The process of evasion can be followed without difficulty in the case of particular recusants.

Thomas Meynell of Kilvington in Yorkshire escaped conviction by shifting from the house of one relative to another over a period of years. Then the death of his father and his succession to the estate compelled him to sue his livery from the Crown, and he thus became liable to the oath of supremacy. He received livery in London but escaped having to take the oath, probably by bribing a clerk. By 1596, five years after his father's death, he had paid no recusancy fines but his arrears amounted to £3 400. The Exchequer appointed three commissioners to supervise seizure, and the Bishop of Durham's steward had to appoint a jury of inquest to value the estates. No list of jurymen was produced in court, and another recusant, whose estate was also due for valuation, gave the commissioners a list of his own jurymen, who were conveniently in attendance. The list was accepted, and Meynell's estate was valued at £5 a year although it was worth £300. A Member of Parliament was involved in the affair and became farmer of the small part of the estate that was sequestered, and one of the commissioners was also a friend of the two recusants. The bishop complained to London, and a new valuation was ordered. Meynell then began litigation, dragging the case out until 1603 when a valuation of £15 a year was secured. He proved that all but £15 was the property of his unconvicted brothers or was held in trust, and Aveling has pointed out that his success depended on the brothers' ability to escape conviction.[21]

The connivance of neighbours was also shown in the case of Nicholas Timperley, who succeeded to the Hintlesham estate in 1594. He should have taken the oath then, but fourteen years passed before he was convicted of recusancy. His opinions were well known, and one of his relations was the Rookwood who was gaoled in 1578 after the Queen had enjoyed his hospitality. Timperley's wife and three sisters were certified as papists before a judge of assize in 1595, but at that time they were not residing at Hintlesham where they had enjoyed the connivance of the rector and tenantry. The law caught up with Nicholas in 1606, when he seems to have been a victim of a common informer.[22]

When Ralph Sheldon was indicted before a grand jury at Worcester in 1587, after an earlier imprisonment for recusancy, the charge was rejected as the jury stated that one of their number would testify that Sheldon had attended church. The evidence was not accepted for it amounted to little more than a claim that he had been seen in the nave of the cathedral and going to prayer in his house chapel. The judge asked if any of Sheldon's servants would testify on oath to having seen him at common prayer in any church or chapel, and finally he appealed to the sheriff, 'as a dear friend and great familiar of Mr Sheldon'. The sheriff, himself reputed as 'a great and vehement papist', was unwilling to commit perjury. Sheldon's daughter made an unhappy marriage with John Russell, the elder brother of Shakespeare's friend, and in 1585 Russell complained in the Star Chamber that Sheldon had tried to remove his daughter, alleging 'for the difference between them in cause of religion'. Sheldon counterclaimed that Russell had attacked his house with forty evil-disposed

persons, but he had to admit that his own son Edward had
attacked Russell's house in Ludgate.[23] These affrays of the
gentry, with their religious background, remind us of the
troubles brought on families by religious divisions.

Many families remained on good terms despite differences
of religion, but in some they ran deep with tragic results.
Edmund Sykes was a seminary priest who worked for four
years in Yorkshire; he was imprisoned, then banished in 1585,
but when he returned to England he was informed on by his
brother and put to death. There were also cases of fathers
betraying sons; on the other hand, when Mrs Lee, a daughter
of the recusant Thomas Tankard, was denounced as a
recusant by her brother, it was considered unfitting to accept
the evidence of a blood relation and she escaped conviction.
Much evidently depended on local feeling. John Tippett was
a Catholic youth of 18 years who was arrested on his return
from Douai and condemned for his religion; his Protestant
father wrote to him in prison:

> I tell you briefly that, if you do not quickly amend and
> abandon these evil opinions, you must not in future look
> upon me as a father, but as a stranger and unknown . . .
> Do you think it was not the greatest of sorrows to me to
> hear that my son had been whipped through the city tied
> to a cart, his ears pierced with hot irons like a criminal?
> Truly it made me wish I had never begotten you.[24]

The Catholic father of Laurence Chadderton, an under-
graduate of Christ's College, Cambridge, took a similar view
when he found that his son had been converted to Puritanism:
'If you renounce the new sect which you have joined you may
expect all the happiness which the care of an indulgent father
can secure you; otherwise I enclose in this letter a shilling to
buy a wallet with. Go and beg for your living.'[25]

Some families tended to extremes of Catholic and puritan
recusancy. Sir Robert Brandling, a former Member of Parliament and mayor of Newcastle, seems to have been a church
papist. In his will he left vestments to local churches 'provided

always that those vestments shall not be given except the old accustomed service be used according to the Catholic usage of the church'. This was in 1562–3. One nephew, Richard, became a merchant adventurer, a pirate, and was mentioned in 1587 as a secret conveyer of priests; in 1596 he was indicted of recusancy. Another nephew, William, may have been one of the pursuivants who captured two priests in 1592; over thirty years later he achieved the feat of locking the Court of High Commission in the chancel of the church at Alnwick, from which the members were obliged to escape by making an undignified exit through a window.[26]

For the devout Catholic the education of his children presented a considerable problem. Their baptism was less of a difficulty : failure to have a baptism entered in the parish register might raise later problems of legitimacy and inheritance, but it was easy to plead that the child had been baptised at birth as in danger of death. Richard Danby of Masham admitted to the commissioners that he had himself baptised all of his six or seven children in the absence of a priest.[27] The law ignored the existence of recusants' children under the age of 16 years until 1593, and from that date those under the age of 9, so there was no difficulty in keeping children from attendance at church. The wealthy could afford a private tutor, and some Catholics were able to send their sons to one of the illicit schools that operated in various places : at one time thirty-two were reported to be working in Lancashire.[28] There were also men of Catholic sympathies teaching in some grammar schools, and in 1590 Sir Robert Cecil complained that there was no worse house in Lancashire than that of Mr Yates, master of the grammar school at Blackburn, whose recusant wife, daughter and maid were reported as having an evil influence on the scholars. In 1599 the headmaster of Westminster School became a Catholic and went off to France, while the headmaster of the school at Worcester sent his own son to the English College in Rome. Earlier, the former suffragan Bishop of Hull, Robert Pursglove, had opened a school that survived from 1560 to 1575.

The authorities were aware of an unsatisfactory situation, and a draft of *Regulations for Schools and Schoolmasters* stated that three out of every four papists 'were not twelve years old when the Queen came to her crown, but have learnt it in the time of her reign. So it appeareth that the Queen's trust hath been deceived in the education of her subjects.'[29] In the early 1580s Lord Burghley addressed a memorandum to the Queen: *Advice in Matters of Religion and State.* He suggested that Catholic children should be forcibly taken from their parents to be educated in the Protestant faith and held as 'hostages for the parents' fidelities', and he stressed that 'the greatest number of papists is of very young men'.[30] Whether this was so is doubtful, but Walsingham made the same point in 1586 and urged that 'the said recusants be ordered by my Lords to send their children by a day named to the bishops, to such place as by them shall be appointed'. The government Bill of 1593 would have removed the children of convicted recusants and financed their Protestant education from a third of the parents' estates. The Bill was rejected, but there were instances where this was done by royal prerogative when the death of the father gave the right of wardship to the Crown. The details of wardship of Catholic children were closely watched by Lord Burghley, who took charge of the third Lord Wharton and the third Earl of Southampton; the latter was removed from his mother at the age of 8 years, and both boys were educated as Protestants. The third Earl of Cumberland was removed as a boy from the care of his uncle, the Catholic Viscount Montague, and handed over to the devout puritan Earl of Bedford.[31] Some children escaped, but when Lord Vaux died his widow had to satisfy the Council that she would employ Protestant tutors for the education of the heir. By contrast, Sir Thomas Guildford left a request that Lord Leicester would preserve his son Henry from a Catholic education, for the boy's mother was a Catholic Shelley. His wish was frustrated, for Sir Henry Guildford appeared as a recusant in the next reign, as did the fourth Lord Eure, whose father had been President of the Council of Wales.[32]

The determination of Catholic parents to secure the education of their children was reflected in the rapid growth of numbers in the Jesuit school at St Omer after 1592. Parents who attempted to send their children out of the country accepted great risks, and if caught the children might be given into Protestant care. The authorities were alert, and a number of boys and girls were intercepted on the well-tried route from Chester to Ireland and hence to France and Spain. One boy so caught was sent to the Bishop of Ely 'that such order may be taken for his education as shall be thought meet by his Lordship', and a second was sent to the Lord Mayor of London.[33] Another group containing 'certain young striplings of England . . . who had in purpose to transport themselves beyond seas to places of popish religion' was captured after it reached Ireland. The young striplings included the sons of a merchant, a lawyer, a draper and a husbandman. One boy who planned to escape in a French ship was released from prison after capture on condition that he avoided any company of his father 'so long as his said father shall continue as a recusant and an enemy of God and her Majesty', but two years later he successfully found his way overseas; he returned to England as a priest in 1607.[34]

The classic case was that of the four Worthington boys, arrested in 1584 with their uncle, a priest. The boys, aged from 12 to 16, were taken for examination before the Earl of Derby and the Bishop of Chester, and when they refused to attend church they were flogged and marched to the service under guard. After several attempts all four eventually got abroad, and in time two became priests on the English mission. From an examination of the family background of some 400 entrants to the English Colleges abroad Professor Beales has concluded that in late Elizabethan times there was an even chance for Catholic children to retain their faith, a one in three chance of Catholic schooling or tutoring, a one in four chance of a higher education in the universities, and a remarkably slight risk of lapsing from the faith after a fully Catholic education.[35]

Education was a serious matter to the Elizabethans, encouraged by the interest and benefactions of members of the ruling class. As the two universities revived after the Catholic migration in the early years of the reign, the gentry increasingly appreciated the value of a university course for their sons, and Catholics followed the prevailing fashion.[36] Attendance was made possible by the lack of any requirement of the oath of supremacy during the early years, so Catholic sympathies survived in some colleges, especially at Oxford, which Dr Allen noted as more sympathetic to the Catholic cause than its sister university. The government reached the same conclusion and the activities of two former Oxford Fellows, Campion and Persons, emphasised the danger of contamination of the young. In 1581 the Oxford Vice-Chancellor received a reminder from the Council that 'most of the seminary priests which at this time disturb the church have been heretofore scholars of your university', and in that year the Earl of Leicester, as Chancellor, ordered that subscription must be made to the Thirty-Nine Articles of Religion by students who had reached the age of 16 at the time of admission. A further effort to exclude Catholics was made by ordinances that forbade residence except in a college where chapel attendance could be enforced. At Cambridge, which provided most of the men who guided Elizabeth's Church, puritan feeling was strong, but no tests existed until James I insisted on them, and even then they were not required until the first degree was taken. Some Catholics were still taking Cambridge degrees as late as 1591. The authorities were active enough. Dr John Caius was forced to resign his mastership of the college he had practically refounded after the discovery of enough Catholic vestments 'to have furnished divers massers at one instant', and Archbishop Sandys of York soon accused his successor of welcoming sons of Northern papists and training them 'able to dispute in defence of popery'.[37] By the end of the reign the number of seminary priests who were graduates of Oxford and Cambridge, at one time a high proportion, showed a definite decline. In the long run this strengthened their foreign background and cut them off, to some extent, from important spheres of influence in England.

The devout Catholic incurred the dangers and disabilities of his recusancy in order to follow the dictates of his conscience in the practice of his religion. It is necessary to ask what exactly was left to him of the external side of an institutional religion, what form of spiritual life was open to the devout layman. No great problems faced the Catholic gentry during the first twenty years of Elizabeth's reign when their religion has been termed survivalism – Catholicism regarded as 'a complex of social practices rather than a religion of internal conviction', which could be maintained without difficulty given a house chaplain and at the price of occasional conformity. If this was so a transformation was brought about by the impact of the seminary priests, who came armed with the dogmatic certainties of Trent and with a rejection of compromise. They preached an interior religion and the need for an interior life, which demanded far more than external observances. The atmosphere of two Oxford colleges, Exeter and St John's, which housed many members of Catholic families in the late 1560s and produced many seminary priests, seems to have exerted a strong influence on one generation. The change can be noted dramatically when a seminary priest replaced the old chaplain of Lord Montague, who had occasionally, with his chaplain's approval, attended the official church services. The new chaplain registered a strong rebuke, which was accepted : 'Instantly putting off his hat and falling to his knees . . . he most humbly submitted himself to the censure and promised never thenceforward to be present at heretical service which all the rest of his life he exactly observed.'[38]

Within a gentry household, depending on its size and the importance of its owner, a fairly elaborate religious observance might be possible, and at Battle Abbey the Montagues had a chapel with a stone altar and a pulpit, with a weekly sermon and a sung Mass with musical instruments on solemn feasts. At Harrowden the Vaux family had a chapel with splendid fittings : six massive silver candlesticks, a silver crucifix, ornaments of silver and gold, rich vestments embroidered with gold and pearls – all of which were finally seized in a raid on the house in 1611. These were houses of peers, but in the Buckinghamshire house of Richard Bold, with the musician William Byrd present, it was possible to have a sung Mass. In these houses with one or more priests in residence there was the ordered round of Mass, the sacraments and the Sunday sermon. As a child Mary Ward (1585–1645) grew up in several great houses with a number of young people where the daily routine included family prayers and the recitation of the Rosary and of the day hours of the breviary. These Elizabethan households influenced the great expansion of religious houses for men and women on the continent that was a feature of the next century. Attention has been called to a Jesuit manuscript written in 1604 : 'An instruction and direction for the spiritual help of such English gentlewomen as desire to lead a more retired and recollected life than the ordinary in England doth yield'.[39]

Where scattered congregations held together it could only be by dependence on such houses, the tenants and neighbours joining with the family of the great house. After the death of Sir John Arundell in 1588 his widow retired to the Dorset manor of Chideock, where four years later her chaplain, John Cornelius, was captured when Sir Walter Raleigh raided the house. A remarkable priest, he had ministered to the Arundell family and their dependents for eleven years, visiting the poor, giving the last rites to the dying and preaching with great success in 'a sweet and plausible tongue'. At Chideock he had been saying Mass for a congregation of some thirty people. Many manor houses lacked a resident chaplain and might receive the hurried visit and secret Mass in an improvised chapel such as Robert Persons described.[40]

When we move away from this atmosphere it is evident that the ordinary Catholic had very small chance of attending Mass, with the possible exception of London where Mass was often celebrated, at great risk. In 1574 a congregation of twenty-three was arrested at Lady Morley's house in Aldgate. Twenty-two were present at Mass in the loft of a Cheshire yeoman's house and seven such were present in a blacksmith's house at York in 1581, while Campion preached to forty people at Lyford. Exceptionally, John Gerard mentioned that he had seen more than 200 present at Mass in Lancashire, probably in the open air, but he added that in such parts 'people fell away easily in time of persecution'.

There was a demand for instruction in the practice of meditation and mental prayer, which the Jesuits in particular were well qualified to meet. They were also very successful in giving the *Spiritual Exercises* of Ignatius Loyola as a retreat to a succession of young men. On another level, the secular priest John Mush acted as spiritual director to Margaret Clitherow of York. Sir Thomas Tresham was accustomed in prison to having a spiritual book read to him for an hour after supper, and in some houses it was the custom to have this spiritual reading at meals if strangers were not present. We have an account of the young Sir Oliver Manners, son of the Earl of Rutland and a convert of John Gerard : 'He read devotional books eagerly and always carried one in his pocket. You might see him in the Court or in the Presence Chamber as it is called, turning aside to a window and reading a chapter of Thomas à Kempis *Imitation of Christ*.' It does not seem to have been too difficult to obtain Catholic devotional books, and Persons' *Christian Directory* and Richard Hopkins' translation of Luis de Granada's *Prayer and Meditation* were popular with men of all religions, the Protestant editions having the specifically Catholic references deleted. When a group of pilgrims was arrested in 1601, travelling to St Winefride's Well in northern Wales, Bartholomew Brooksby was found to have in his possession *A Method to Meditate on the Psalter of Our Blessed Lady* and the *Palestra Hominis Catholice*, while his son, aged 16 years, had the *Modus Orandi Deo*.[41] The Jesuits were active in spreading devotion to the rosary, and in 1593 Henry Garnet published his *Societie of the Rosary* from a secret press. In his *Rule of Good Life* Robert Southwell gave advice for the Catholic who was unable to practise his religion : every day he should kneel and offer himself to God, assisting in spirit at Masses being offered at that moment in other places; every week he should make a confession of his sins to God just as he would in the presence of a priest.

The household accounts of Lord William Howard afford some idea of the religious books that a wealthy Catholic might possess. At the end of Elizabeth's reign he retired to his wife's Dacre inheritance at Naworth in Cumberland, taking there the library that he had been assembling before the Armada year. This collection continued to grow with the help of his Benedictine chaplain. It included a wide variety of religious reading, ranging from medieval mystical treatises to the contemporary theological works of Suarez and Bellarmine, and many of the books, including a work of the Louvainist Thomas Stapleton, were liable to seizure by government officials. Some had been acquired during visits to recusant houses in Lancashire. It may be that the spiritual teaching of these writers was lived by Howard's half-brother, the Earl of Arundel, during the imprisonment in the Tower that only ended with his death.[42]

The teaching of the seminary priests seems to have influenced Catholics to regard marriage in the State Church as equivalent to apostasy : a recusant could either wait for the opportunity of marriage before a priest or marry in secret before witnesses, hoping to obtain a priest's blessing later.[43] Clandestine marriages were not uncommon in Elizabethan times, and after the Council of Trent there was the added difficulty that Roman canon law and the marriage law of the Church and State in England did not in all respects agree. The recusant as a result might face problems concerning the validity of property settlements and doubts about the legitimacy in law of his children. When Thomas Meynell was summoned before the High Commision concerning his second marriage the case was referred to the Chancery Court. Here witnesses state that they had seen him married by a Marian priest in January 1605, using a rite allegedly resembling that of the *Book of Common Prayer*. Meynell was able to prove that the priest had been ordained by Bishop Tunstall of Durham in March 1558–9, and the court issued a licence stating that the marriage was valid and licit. This established a precedent, although the priest in the case and his patron were later goaled by the High Commission, for marriages performed by Marian priests. When cases came before the High Commission, parties accused of a clandestine marriage were ordered to agree to questioning on oath with a penalty of imprisonment for refusal. If convicted they were put on bond to conform in religion and prove their marriage, and in the event of failure to offer proof they were declared to be fornicators and ordered to do public penance and to marry before a minister of the State Church. Jane Whitmore, a Catholic gentlewoman of Cheshire, was presented before the York High Commission as both a recusant and an adulterer, having contracted a Catholic marriage that was declared invalid.[44]

However, women like Jane Whitmore played an important part in the history of recusancy. Although Catholic women were unable to demonstrate in public – like the sixty puritan ladies who descended on the bachelor Archbishop Grindal in defence of a suspended preacher – they proved too much for Lord Huntingdon. He mounted a special campaign against them in 1592, opening new prisons to receive them, and in that year a York priest reported : 'The gents were much fallen off, but the gentlewomen stood steadfastly to it.' Huntingdon also tried placing Catholic wives in Protestant households but eventually had to give way and release them. Several women suffered the death penalty, including Margaret Clitherow of York who was pressed to death by the *peine forte et dure*, and age did not excuse them imprisonment for we read of a woman of 80 years held in confinement : she was 'so aged and weak that she is not able to come before us'. This was Margaret Aldersey of Chester, whose troubles over religion began in 1562 and were not ended thirty years later.[45] There were women who rented houses to shelter priests and others who conducted illicit schools for the children of recusants, no doubt resembling the Lady Bodenham of whom the Bishop of Hereford complained to the Council : 'an imperious dame of high stomach and stirring humour, who countenances all priests and recusants'. As the government came to appreciate the importance of the women it stiffened the law so as to draw them within its penalties, a process not welcome to

Protestant husbands. The 1581 Act was interpreted to make husbands pay for the recusancy of their wives, but forfeiture could not be exacted while the husband was alive. On his death two-thirds of the widow's dower was liable to seizure, and sixty widows were so treated in the recusancy rolls.[46]

Some historians have seen a link between recusancy and economic decay, and it has been estimated that during the whole Elizabethan period only two recusant families in Sussex were prospering. There were, however, some notable exceptions elsewhere : in Northamptonshire the Treshams and Brudenells, and in Yorkshire the Gascoignes and Tankards.[47] Thomas Tankard, son of a Councillor of the North who was removed for his Catholic sympathies, managed to build up the family fortunes in spite of determined recusancy and the education of two sons at Douai. The Brudenells came late to recusancy and moved steadily up the social scale to the earldom of Cardigan in the next century. An efficient manager prepared to follow the best farming methods of the day with some ruthlessness, like Sir Thomas Tresham, could improve his estate in spite of paying very heavy fines. Even a man of fairly modest means, like Thomas Meynell, could do so. On the other hand, there were families that went down in ruin and obscurity, but it is not possible to be always certain that recusancy fines were the determining factor. Imprisonment of the landlord would be no aid to the efficient management of an estate.

The effects of the system of repression were varied and uncertain. Its efficiency was impaired by the disorganisation of the prisons and the reluctance of the authorities to pay their officials a living wage, which made the officials amenable to bribery and corruption. In 1591 it was found that a recusant prisoner at Worcester was riding out with his gaoler 'into other shires, to what houses he will go unto . . . and sometimes sleeps a fortnight abroad before he comes to gaol again', while a junior clerk of the Western circuit was bribed over a period of ten years to suppress the records of local recusants.[48] More pleasing was the reluctance of the ordinary Englishman to

betray friends and neighbours, like the Yorkshire villagers –
curate, schoolmaster, churchwardens and yeomen – who were
fined and gaoled in 1590 for giving a false certificate of conformity to a Catholic gentlewoman.[49] On the whole the
recusancy laws caused great hardship. Heroism might rightly
be expected of the priest, but the endurance of the laymen
was more remarkable. He might escape death and possibly
imprisonment, but strong faith indeed was needed for a man
to face financial hardship and the loss of social and political
advancement when neighbours were improving their status.
The normal philosophy of the Elizabethan gentry was well
expressed by Raleigh to his son : 'Strive if thou canst to make
good thy station on the upper deck; those that live under
hatches are ordained to be drudges and slaves.' The recusant
tried to swim against the tide, and it may be that recklessness
and bitterness were bred among the younger generation, who
saw parents, like Sir Thomas Tresham, in and out of prison
or their inheritance dwindling year by year. This was the
generation of the Gunpowder plot.

Towards the end of the reign, when it was hoped that the
death of the aging Queen might bring better days, there were
signs that the passive endurance of Catholics was changing in
areas where they were still strong. The refusal to bury a
Catholic yeoman's wife was soon to lead to a Whitsun riot
in the Welsh Marches, which caused the government some
anxiety. The funeral of Thomas Gawen in Wiltshire was even
more extraordinary and its aftermath macabre.[50] The local
curate refused to admit the corpse to the church as Gawen
had not attended church for twelve years and was excom-
municate, but his friends broke into the church at night and
buried him in the chancel. For the whole of the following day
they tolled the church bell until ejected by the constable and
his assistants. The body was then disinterred and left out in
the churchyard for several days. Subsequently the widow
brought a case in the Star Chamber against the curate, constable and others for their ill-treatment of the corpse. She
won her case against all the defendants except the curate, who
was commended for his action.

Lancashire, however, remained the most stubborn county, and in 1598 the Bishop of Chester complained that the trials of 600 recusants had seldom proceeded beyond the initial indictment. In that year an attempt to counter recusancy was made by the appointment of four special preachers, but it ended in a mixture of failure and farce.[51] Bishop Vaughan made a point of placing them where recusants were numerous and reported good progress to the Council in 1600. His good tidings were premature. After the arrest of some local Catholics at Garstang one of the preachers was besieged in the vicarage by an armed mob, which also attacked a pursuivant and the vicar. Early in 1603 the bishop was reporting that two of the preachers were absentees and 'dare not almost look into their charge for fear of violence offered to their persons'. An arrested priest had been rescued, the Queen's Messengers had been attacked, and it was thought that no jury would convict those responsible if they could be apprehended. The bishop, poor man, gave a strong hint that he would like to be translated to a less troublesome diocese, and all this was more than forty years after the settlement of religion.

9 Three Members of the Laity: Cornwallis, Tresham and Tregian

An honest man may be a Catholic and be no fool
Henry Constable to Francis Bacon

The misfortunes of the Catholic laity and their clergy lend themselves easily to the picture of an aristocratic minority hounded by persecution and at risk of their lives, with priests living in disguise and hiding holes in remote manor houses, severed from social contact with their non-Catholic neighbours. It is a misleading picture though true of some individuals, and if we consider the lives of Sir Thomas Cornwallis, Sir Thomas Tresham and Francis Tregian it will be clear that the penal legislation had a varying impact on wealthy recusants and that it was certainly possible to survive. All three were members of families that had been good servants of the Crown in the past and had also profited by the acquisition of church lands, while the story of Cornwallis illustrates the advantage that might derive from a friendly connection with members of the Council. As members of the gentry they were protected, though not wholly, by their social class and so saved much of the humiliation and suffering of poor men about whose lives we know but little in detail. Yet this preoccupation with the gentry should not lead us to neglect the existence of working-class recusants, for there is some evidence that key positions in the organisation of Lancashire recusancy were held by humble people and that conversions of labouring and fishing folk of the Yorkshire coast were gained by the seminary priests.[1] Of forty-one recusants brought to trial at the May Quarter Sessions of 1582 in Cheshire, only seven were members of the gentry; the rest included a weaver, a draper, a tailor a blacksmith and a labourer.[2] The wealthy tended to escape the death penalty suffered by James Byrd, a youth of 19 years who was charged under the 1581 Act with having become a Catholic, or the flogging and imprisonment on the treadmill in Bridewell endured by the young Robert Colton.[3] Imprisonment for the working-class recusant was a far less comfortable state than it normally was for the well-to-do.

The career of Sir Thomas Cornwallis covered the whole reign of Elizabeth, for he was born in 1519 and died at a great age in 1604.[4] His father had been Steward of the Household to Edward VI. The son, as sheriff of Norfolk and Suffolk in 1553, was early in the field as a supporter of Queen Mary, and later as a member of the Council he achieved some prominence in state affairs as a negotiator with the Scots and the rebel Sir Thomas Wyatt. As a trusted servant of the Crown he improved his position, adding the offices of Treasurer of Calais and Comptroller of the Queen's Household, and was one of those charged with the task of bringing the Princess Elizabeth to the Tower in 1554. He seems to have discharged this duty with tact and to have opposed further action against her, and it was at this time that he formed a useful friendship with Sir William Cecil.

With the death of Queen Mary this promising career came to an end when Sir Thomas was barely 40 years of age; he was dropped from the Council and retired to his estate at Brome in Suffolk, maintaining, however, some contacts with friends at Court. Now like many of his contemporaries he devoted his time to the rebuilding of his house and the care of his estates, but these peaceful occupations were ended with the arrest of the Duke of Norfolk in 1569, for the Cornwallis family, like many others in East Anglia, had been attached to the Norfolk Howards. An inquiry began into all who had been associated with the Duke, which included Sir Thomas and his son-in-law, Sir Thomas Kitson. They were asked many questions about their attitude to religion, covering their attendance at church, reception of communion and possession of unlawful books. Kitson had not received communion for four or five years, and the answers of Cornwallis must have proved unsatisfactory for he was committed 'by the Lords of the Council . . . as a prisoner for matter of religion', part of the time to the care of Bishop Jewel of Salisbury. His stewards' accounts record the gifts that he gave in return for this unwelcome hospitality : twelve yards of satin at £7/4/0 and a ring of gold 'sett with a very fair turqueis', price £13/6/8 for the bishop; and, as befitted his station in life, three yards of taffeta for Mr Bold the bishop's chaplain, which cost only 40/-.

Back in London by June 1570 Cornwallis had to endure a discussion with a number of Protestant divines, and it is an interesting commentary on Marian Catholicism that Goodman, Dean of Westminster, formed a high opinion of him : 'I have seldom known any of that side so wise and so conveniently learned, more reasonable in Conference, or more nearer to conformity.' As a country gentleman and amateur theologian Cornwallis must have been at some disadvantage in these circles, but Cecil also brought pressure on him to conform and after a struggle with his conscience Cornwallis asked Cecil to see that 'at the first I be drawn no further than to coming to church where I will use myself (by God's grace) to want offence to any man and not by device to be pressed further, which might make me either an hypocrite or desperate'. The context makes it clear that Cornwallis was motivated largely by loyalty to the Queen. His state of mind is also shown by the letter to his son-in-law : 'The time is such in which we now live as it would comber a wiser head than I have now to give you advice which way to proceed, and therefore can do but humbly beg God to direct you to take such course as may tend to the preservation of your credit and reputation and the best safety of your person.' This was hardly an heroic attitude but was typical of the church papist, and Sir Thomas would now be regarded by recusant Catholics as a 'schismatic' though an unwilling one. Soon he was again under suspicion in official quarters. Bishop Freke of Norwich had a troubled episcopate, and in the course of bitter disputes with the local puritans he was accused of favouring Catholics and of allowing Cornwallis to influence the appointment of the diocesan chancellor. This was Dr William Masters, whose mother and wife were recusants. It was alleged against Cornwallis that at service time 'when others are on their knees at prayers, he will sit contemptuously reading on a book (most likely some Lady psalter or portasse which I have found in his pew'. It was claimed that he had helped a former secretary to become a Carthusian monk overseas, and the puritan complainants pictured the bishop and Mrs Freke with Sir Thomas and his friends, feasting together in Norwich to such effect that some of those present 'reeled home in the streets well tipled to the offence of all good people'. It was also unfortunate for the bishop that both his butler and his lawyer were indicted for attending Mass.

During these difficult days Sir Thomas made good use of his connection with Court circles, thanking Cecil for his continued friendship and getting his daughter, Lady Kitson, to pull strings with Sir Philip Sidney. Sidney wrote to her in March 1582 that his father-in-law, Walsingham, had promised a 'speedy easing of the greatness of your burden', for it was intended to permit a general mitigation for recusants. Two years later Sir Thomas reached the difficult decision to cease attending church services, but as a guarantee of his loyalty he signed the Bond of Association to defend the Queen against her enemies. He wrote to inform Cecil of the refusal to attend church, but no action was taken against him. In 1585, when recusants were asked to contribute to the levy for light horsemen, he was one of thirteen Suffolk recusants prepared to contribute, in his case £50. Next we find him journeying to London in 1587 in an attempt to secure relief from the payment of fines, and he told Cecil, now Lord Burghley, that he could only pay by closing his house and living with one of his children, a prospect that he did not

relish. Then in November came a brief period of imprisonment, but possibly on account of illness and his age, 68 years,
he was soon permitted to return home under bond to appear
if summoned again. From this time on he enjoyed the protection of the Cecils, and in December 1598 he was exempted by
the Council from an order confiscating the horses of recusants :
'Forasmuch as he has been and so continueth an ancient and
true servant unto her Majesty, and notwithstanding his differences of religion hath never been touched with any suspicion
of disloyalty or ill affection to her Majesty and the State.'

Sir Thomas was not further harassed, but it was necessary
to observe great care for he had a brother who was a priest
ordained overseas. This brother was arrested and remained
in the Clink prison until 1600, when he was released on the
ground of age and infirmity on condition that he remained at
Brome. Another brother, Henry, had been reconciled to
Catholicism before his death, and in 1598 his son entered the
English College at Rome and was later ordained priest.

In his old age Sir Thomas kept in touch with Catholic
books published abroad, especially books on prayer and church
history, and he wrote to his bookseller asking for 'that French
apology for the Jesuits, though I do not readily understand
that language I shall make shift to pick out the meaning'.
He was also willing to give shelter to those pursued by the
law. When a young Norfolk man, Edward Yelverton, entered
the English College he told how, after leaving Cambridge as
a Catholic, he had been obliged to move about from one
Norfolk house to another 'by reason of the persecution'.
Cornwallis invited him to Brome, where for three months the
young man and the old together recited every day the Office
of the breviary. In the life of Cornwallis we can trace the
career of the church papist who ultimately took the plunge
and faced the dangers of nonconformity. In his case, no doubt
because of his friendship with the Cecils, the perils of recusancy
were not great. He did not invite martyrdom, but he endured.
This is all the more remarkable since, like so many of his
generation, he had apparently accepted without demur the
religious changes of his youth.

The life of Sir Thomas Tresham provides a sharp contrast.[5] He may be considered as a leader among the recusants, and with his correspondence, his law suits, his building activity and his estate management he has left a far more vivid impression of his personality than most of his coreligionists. The Tresham family rated one degree below the peerage, and had the next generation been as able as Sir Thomas they might like the Brudenells have been able to buy entry to the peerage under the Stuarts. Strongly rooted in Northamptonshire, the family was of some antiquity and sharply aware of the rise of upstarts at a time when recusancy excluded its members from profitable employment under the Crown. A William Tresham had been Attorney General to Henry V, and the first Sir Thomas had been Comptroller General to Henry VI, dying for him on the field of Tewkesbury. Pride in his family's history and service to the Crown made it all the more difficult for Elizabeth's Sir Thomas to accept that a change of religion by Act of Parliament should make suspect his loyalty to the Queen. He represented a Catholic piety, traditional but not uninfluenced by the Counter Reformation, which made his loyalty to the distant Pope something he took for granted, inevitable and unchanged, but his loyalty to the Queen was part of his family tradition and social class.

Family pride is shown in Tresham's letters, whether he is reminding the Montagues of Boughton of their past disloyalty to the Crown or Lord Spencer of Althorp that the Treshams 'have been in this country [Northamptonshire] of longest continuance' and 'in country and court, peace and war, within this realm and forth of this realm, more used or more commanding'. He was contemptuous of James I's plan to summon for knighthood all those with a £40 income as likely to produce 400 claimants in his county alone, 'whereof some landless, many base and dosser headed clowns'. Tresham married a Catholic Throckmorton, his sister married William, Lord Vaux of Harrowden, and his daughters married into recusant families: Monteagle, Stourton, Brudenell and Parham. By the marriage of Frances Tresham with Lord Stourton the family became distantly linked with the

Arundells and Tregians. Here we have the traditional network of recusant families.

Sir Thomas Tresham's troubles over religion resulted from the Jesuit mission of 1580. In January 1581 he conveyed most of his property into the hands of twelve trustees, probably as a precaution against forfeiture, and in the following August he was arrested on a charge of harbouring Edmund Campion and confined to the 'close, noisome and moist' prison of the Fleet. Three months later he was tried in the Star Chamber; he refused the oath of supremacy, was fined £500 and returned to prison. At the trial Tresham admitted that Campion might have been in his house but would not swear one way or the other on the ground that he sometimes entertained friends and their followers to the number of 100 and did not know the names of many of them. In large households it was certainly possible for a priest to stay without the owner's knowledge, but Campion's visits were major events, and in Lancashire even members of the gentry would wait for hours at night in a barn in order to hear him preach. It was at this point of Tresham's fortunes that his younger brother William suddenly left the Court and went abroad in circumstances that would not have helped him. William was a Gentleman Pensioner of the Queen, and he not only quitted his post without her permission but also roused her anger by a letter that blamed his decision on the enmity of the Earl of Leicester.

Tresham's imprisonment for religion covers most of the years from August 1581 to 1596. Part of the time he spent in the Fleet and part released under bond but forbidden to live on his estates or in one of the three houses that he owned near London, living mostly in an 'erst tipling cottage' at Hoxton instead of in the house with 'its little orchard and less garden' that he owned close by. For seven months in 1587 he was in the Bishop of Lincoln's charge. Then he was removed to the dilapidated old palace of the Bishops of Ely, where in that 'filthy and fennish country' he experienced the mortification of watching from his window the musters drilling in preparation for the Armada: 'what greatly grieved us', he wrote, 'to be by unheard of accident exempted forth of so requisite and honourable a service'. Twice again he was imprisoned at Ely. Then in 1593, possibly through the intervention of the Earl of Essex who had taken his elder son into his household, Sir Thomas was at length permitted to return to his family home at Rushton. Here after a brief spell of freedom he was arrested once again and confined in the Fleet; final release, this time from the familiar Ely prison, came in 1596. Thus over a long period Tresham could never have felt secure, and for an enterprising landowner his situation must have been intensely frustrating while it also played havoc with his family life, depriving his sons of their father's supervision at an impressionable age. Francis, the elder, a cheerful young man, was thought 'unstayed and wild', and the rackety circle around Essex suited his temperament but was not the best of influences. During his father's absence in prison he once tried to persuade the family steward to falsify the accounts in order to cover his own debts. Worse still, his cheerful irresponsibility led him into plots and eventual disaster. The second son, Lewis, was imprisoned for a year as a student for beating an enemy with a cudgel as he sat at dinner in the Inner Temple, 'which was well liked of all the House but the Bench'.

Sir Thomas Tresham was a man of great wealth, and his financial affairs have been a subject of expert investigation and some controversy.[6] His first fine was the £500 in the Star Chamber, and later he was fined 100 marks for attending Mass in the Fleet. From October 1581 to March 1582 he paid £100 of the monthly £20 fine. From that date until 1587 payment was not enforced, but then with greater efficiency of collection he was called upon to pay the arrears of £953, and Sir Thomas had to find sureties for payment : Lord Mordaunt and a justice named Edward Watson. At this time Tresham had no excess of revenue over expenditure and was able to pay only half of the arrears, so in 1591 the sheriff seized a portion of his estates and some lands belonging to the two sureties. As a recusant he found it difficult to obtain credit, complaining that while he was in prison he could not borrow £100 whereas there had been a time when he was 'wont to have been trusted for a thousand upon a bare bill of my hand'. In 1593 failure to secure the Bishop of Peterborough's licence to travel to London led him to forfeit £2 400 for Lord Vaux and £1 500 for himself to a 'merciless gripping usurer'; Tresham could have raised the money, but his presence in London was necessary. From 1581 to 1605 he paid a total of nearly £8 000 in recusancy fines. As it has been estimated that his annual income from all sources rose to £3 500 in 1590, the fines amounted to two and a half years' income during twenty-four years, and had credit been available there would have been no difficulty.[7]

Not all Tresham's financial problems were due to his recusancy for there was the traditional hospitality and the maintenance of his houses, which in 1605 included fifty-two servants. There was a large family to support also, and his six daughters all received generous marriage settlements. The involvement of Francis in the Essex rising led to payment of a fine of £2 000, and a further £1 000 was paid to Lady Katharine Howard to prevent a charge of treason. The affairs of his brother-in-law, the impoverished Lord Vaux, were a further expense.[8] Sir Thomas lost money by standing surety for the debts of Lord Vaux and, as their trustee, was drawn into endless quarrels with the women of the family. They were a quarrelsome lot and blamed Sir Thomas because the Vaux heir, Henry, wished to become a priest. When one Vaux daughter became a nun Tresham was accused of having 'married her to a monastery' in order to avoid paying over her marriage portion. In 1594 when he was a prisoner in the Fleet Anne Vaux brought an action against him, and another daughter broke her engagement and secretly married a servant of Sir Thomas. When he refused to hand over the balance of her dowry she managed to get him again committed to the Fleet. Sir Thomas had endured imprisonment for his faith with resignation, but now he wrote that 'no malice is comparable to the malice of a woman' and complained that Muriel Vaux had cast herself away 'on a land lopper, a very beggar and bankrupt base fellow'. He wished to retain part of the dowry lest this base fellow should later abandon her and found it hard to endure the criticism of Catholics who were unaware of the circumstances: 'God forgive them and give me Christian patience to endure so intolerable a cross.'

There were other lawsuits, at one time no less than nineteen, and legal expenses must have been heavy. Financial necessity drove him to exploit his estates to the full and apply the most up-to-date business methods in their management. This involved enclosures and the eviction of tenants who could not pay higher rents, accompanied by the opposition of tenantry during years of famine and high prices. Over a period of fifteen years Tresham raised his revenue from rents by half and doubled his flocks of sheep, but even so his debts in 1605 amounted to £11 495, nearly four times his annual income.

The building activities of Tresham have attracted attention and were typical of his social class, except in so far as they illustrated his 'vein of perfervid and elaborate piety'. They included additions and alterations to his house at Rushden and the famous triangular Lodge, work at another house at Lyvedon during the 1590s, and minor works elsewhere. The cost of this was not excessive for local labour and materials were used, and the total expenditure fell short of £2 000. The plans and drawings for this activity provided an interest during the years of imprisonment. He was fascinated by religious symbolism, which, linked to his devotion to the Trinity, was expressed in the decorative work on his buildings. In prison at Ely he and other prisoners found occupation in wall painting, and Sir Thomas amused himself by outwitting the warders who tended to wash out specifically Catholic symbolism. In 1590 he was negotiating with a Mr Fletcher of Caius College, Cambridge, as a man skilful in mathematics, to come and assist him, but he found it more difficult to get a Cambridge man as law tutor for his son. From Ely again instructions were sent for the laying out of gardens at Lyvedon and for the planting of new roses, damask and red.

The devout phraseology of his letters is reminiscent of the Pastons. He began a letter to Lady Tresham in the usual recusant fashion with the words *Jesus Maria* at the heading and, referring to the lawsuit that Anne Vaux had brought against him, wrote that he would have avoided such action against any fellow Christian but 'if against one of my religion, a Catholic, I sooner would have begged my bread'. 'Farewell Tress,' he ended another, 'Almighty God bless all ours and grant us of his grace to pray for our maligners.' Sir Thomas was thought dilatory over the arrangements for his daughter Catherine to marry Sir John Webbe, and he gave his own view to another daughter, Lady Stourton : 'Lent, a season more fitting prayer than passionate wifeing' might have excused him. In 1601 he wrote to the same daughter after the complicity of Francis Tresham in the Essex rising :

> . . . I drenched up, as it were in a world of adversities. What my estate hath been, you well know, but what it is now I most feel. With the Apostle I may say that I have heretofore known how to live and abound in plenty. I wish that with the said Apostle I may say that I now know to endure and suffer penury. Truly my estate is greatly impaired . . . He who hath given all may take away all, His holy will be done.

Lines from the Latin Bible dropped easily from his pen, and very aptly he commented on his quarrels with the Vaux ladies : '*inimici hominis domestici eius.*' In a letter to Lord Henry Howard written in July 1603 Tresham referred to his imprisonment for religion as a long apprenticeship 'to prevent the forgoing of my beloved, beautiful and graceful Rachel (*videhantur illi pauci dies prae amoris magnitudine)*'. He would keep Lord Henry in his zealous remembrance 'when I forgot not to beseech our God for myself, a wretched sinner, who deliver us from the godless crew of the Puritan rakehells, multipliers of damnable drifts'.

Tresham took a leading part in the attempt to win an easing of the recusant position by petition to the Queen and James I. He disclaimed all belief in the papal deposing power and claimed that all the priests with whom he had had any dealings had been wholly loyal. His own unqualified loyalty brought him into disfavour with the Spanish party among the exiles, and in 1598 the Jesuit Henry Tichborne wrote of him : 'Sir Thomas Tresham as a friend of the State is holden among us for an atheist, and all others of his humour either so or worse.' Had he known of this Tresham might have regarded it as a compliment, but his own loyalty did not blind him to the government's attempt to discredit Catholics by all possible means. As leader of a deputation to James I he secured a promise that the recusancy fines would not be levied. The promise was not kept.

Sir Thomas Tresham was a typical Elizabethan : tough, talented, quick-tempered, but open-hearted and generous. His uncompromising stand for his religious faith did not prevent friendship with the Bishop of Lincoln, at one time his gaoler, and in his old age there was a pleasant exchange of letters with the Archbishop of York, who had helped in the recovery of stolen horses : Tresham recalled their youth at Christchurch, Oxford, with the hope that both might live in the church of Christ and die his servants. It is sad to think that the exiles could not appreciate his long endurance for the Catholic cause, but he found his own reward. In the Ely prison he was wont to listen to his servant reading a book of devotion after supper; and on one occasion their book was the *Christian Resolution*. At the page where it dealt with proof of the existence of God three loud knocks were heard upon the table 'to the great amazing of me and my two servants'. His devotion to the Trinity was correspondingly fortified.

Sir Thomas died in July 1605. The elder son, Francis, was in the Tower by December, charged with complicity in the Gunpowder Plot. The second son, Lewis, who as a youth had brawled in the Inner Temple, became a baronet and accompanied Prince Charles and Buckingham to Madrid, but he sold most of the estates and the direct line of the Treshams ended in 1643 when Lyvedon was sequestered for recusancy. Thus the long battle to preserve the family inheritance was lost by the heirs.

For nearly twenty years after Elizabeth's accession the Cornish

Catholics were left in comparative peace, until the worsening
of relations with Spain led to greater interest in the county
by the central government. Disaster struck with the appointment in 1577 of a strong Protestant sheriff, Sir Richard
Grenville, who had long been at odds with the leading
Catholic family, the Arundells. This family had frustrated his
wish to secure the wealthy Francis Tregian in marriage for
his daughter and had secured him for the daughter of Lady
Arundell by her first marriage with Charles, Lord Stourton.
The Tregian family had estates in Devon and Somerset as
well as Cornwall and had grown in wealth and social standing
by service to the Tudor dynasty and careful intermarriages.
John Tregian, the grandfather of Francis, had been steward
of the Chamber and Esquire of the body to Henry VIII and
had married into a Court family. His daughter Elizabeth
married an Edgecumbe, and his son, the father of Francis,
married an Arundell. Through his wife's connection with the
Stourton family the young Francis was related to Edward
Earl of Derby and many recusant families. It is significant
that Francis spent some years abroad, returning to England
in 1571 after Parliament had passed the Act against the
exiles.[9]

According to the account written by his grandson, another
Francis, he spent some time at Court. He was offered preferment by the Queen, which he declined, and left the Court
without her permission, an action that Elizabeth was not
likely to forget. By 1575 he had succeeded to the family
estates and embarked on the normal round of a country
landowner. It was not to endure for long. In June 1577,
shortly after his appointment as sheriff, Grenville descended
on the Tregian home at Golden Manor with a number of
justices and 100 armed men. Tregian's steward at the time was
sitting peacefully in the garden. Hearing the sound of an
affray he entered the house, was seized, found to be wearing
an *agnus Dei* of silver and crystal, and further identified as a
seminary priest named Cuthbert Mayne. Mayne was a quiet
unassuming young man, son of a Devon yeoman, who had
been provided with a benefice at the age of 17 and had pro-

ceeded to Oxford. There he was ordained in the Protestant
ministry and was appointed chaplain of St John's College. He
came under Catholic influence, met Gregory Martin and
Edmund Campion in St John's, and joined the emigration of
converts to Douai where he was eventually ordained priest.
He had been living at Golden for a year and, as its supposed
steward, had been able to ride through the Tregian and
Arundell estates saying Mass, preaching and administering
the sacraments. These Cornish Catholics evidently felt very
secure, and in the manor house the searchers had no difficulty
in finding all that was needed for the celebration of Mass and
moreover a copy of an expired papal Bull. Thirty-one
Catholics, including Sir John Arundell, were arrested. Some
were destined to suffer the worst horrors of a sixteenth-century
gaol, although only one is known to have conformed.

Francis Tregian was sent up to London and lodged in the
Marshalsea, where he spent some months in solitary confinement. The choice of prison was significant for it came under
the control of the Queen's cousin – Sir George Carey
– and it was to him that the Queen offered control
of the Tregian estates. It was therefore in his interest
to secure a conviction. Tregian secured two distinguished
counsels, including the recusant Edmund Plowden, but by a
complicated legal manoeuvre Carey obtained postponement
of a verdict until the law term ended. In July 1578 the
Council sent the prisoner back to Launceston and directed a
letter to the Justices of Assize, ordering them to proceed 'in
uprightness and indifference so that hereafter it may appear
that no partiality hath been used therein . . . and that the
trial be done uprightly and indifferently according to law
and justice'. The judges had already tried and condemned
Mayne to death, the jury had been selected with some care,
and a principal witness for the prosecution was a strolling
player named Twigges who thus briefly preserved his name
for posterity. Twigges had entertained the household at Golden
during the Christmas of 1575, and he claimed to have shared
a room with Mayne and to have been told that he was a
priest. Tregian declared that the evidence was false as Mayne

at that date had not arrived in England. When questioned the player did not know where the steward was lodged, but the judges ruled that this was irrelevant and refused leave for witnesses to be summoned who could prove that Mayne was at Douai at the time.

An important charge at this trial, as at that of Mayne, was that Tregian had abetted Mayne 'in the execution of the instrument of absolution obtained from the bishop of Rome'. This was a reference to the papal Bull that had been found at Golden. This document was a copy bought in a Douai bookshop, had nothing to do with English affairs, and as it referred to events long past had no validity of any kind. On this point the judges disagreed, but in Lent 1579 Tregian was condemned to the penalties of premunire, imprisonment and loss of goods. Carey could now take possession of the estates and arrived at Golden to expel Mary Tregian, her children and her mother, who were given shelter by neighbours. He also seized the lands that provided the jointure of old Mrs Tregian. Meanwhile Francis was lodged at Launceston in a cell twenty feet underground, in the company of condemned criminals and in conditions of filth and semi-starvation. It might have been thought that such unusual rigours inflicted on a man of his standing would lead him to conform and attend church.

From Launceston he was sent back to London as a close prisoner in the Queen's Bench prison. The Council was apparently annoyed by a petition that he should be permitted to receive alms from his friends, and in 1580 he was removed to the Fleet and found himself once again 'among a sort of bankrupts, cozeners, and forgerers'. However, his wife was allowed to share his imprisonment, and when his health gave way he was removed to better quarters in the prison. He now had a servant, and visitors were free to come and go. At this time Tregian was about 30 years old and a further nineteen years of imprisonment lay ahead.

Two sons of Tregian had been educated abroad. The elder Francis, later studied at Rheims and Rome where he became a member of Cardinal Allen's household and was described as gifted in philosophy, music and the Latin tongue. In 1594, after an absence of eight years, he was able to return to England and visit his parents during their imprisonment.

As the long years of imprisonment passed the health of the elder Tregian suffered, and in 1601 he asked Sir Robert Cecil to intervene with the Queen on his behalf : 'that I might enjoy the benefit and fruition of the open air in and about the city of London, not exceeding the circuit of five miles, yielding my body every night into the prison of the Fleet'. He also asked permission to visit Buxton or Bath for the relief of his sciatica, and at this point Lord Hunsdon intervened, urging that Tregian should not be freed but should be imprisoned at Wisbech : 'For Mr Tregian's person he is well known to be a most discontented, malicious and practising papist against the Queen and State being employed as an Agent of the Pope, and all traitorous enemies beyond the Seas . . . having a Son to negotiate all causes at Rome and to return correspondent actions from all thence'. Fortunately for Tregian Hunsdon's advice was not accepted. In July 1601 he was released on parole, and a year later he presented Cecil with two of 'a litter of greyhound whelps such as for their beauty deserved then in the opinion of many both allowance and liking'.

By 1603 both the Queen and Hunsdon were dead, and Tregian was released from his parole on condition that he left the country. He went first to the Netherlands and then to Spain, visiting the English College at Douai on the way. His long endurance in prison had attracted much attention abroad, and Philip III received him with honour in Madrid and gave him a pension of sixty gold pieces a month. Tregian ended his days with the Jesuit fathers in Lisbon, a long way from the manor of Golden and the Cornwall of his youth but probably more content than many of his Elizabethan contemporaries who were angling for places at the Court of James I. He had well fulfilled the horation line : *aequam memento rebus in arduis servare mentem.* In his excellent account of the Cornish Catholics Dr Rowse has judged him differently : 'obviously a self complacent fanatic fool of the first water'.

The story of Francis Tregian can be completed by a reference to his family. His widow was still alive in 1622 and still a recusant, but by then her elder son Francis had followed his father to imprisonment for recusancy. He had returned to England when his father died in 1608 and bought back the Cornish property from the widowed Lady Hunsdon. Six months later he was convicted of recusancy, losing two-thirds of the property but paying fines on the remaining third. By 1614 he was in the Fleet prison and described as 'a popish recusant as his father was'. In prison he collected a library and settled down to study, indeed to find enduring distinction for he copied down nearly 2 000 pieces of Elizabethan and Jacobean music before he died in 1619. This work was to become known as the *Fitz William Virginal Book*, a major source of our knowledge of Elizabethan music. When his younger brother Charles succeeded, the financial burden of recusancy led to the final loss of the last of the Tregian estates, including the manor of Golden.

10 A Hunted Life: The Clergy

A multitude of dissolute young men who have, partly for
lack of living, partly for crimes committed, become fugitives, rebels and traitors.
> The Queen's Proclamation, 1591

How many of them are Knights' and Esquires' sons,
and otherwise allied both to worshipful and noble houses,
and heirs to fair revenues, let their own friends and
parents dispersed through the whole realm bear witness.
> Robert Southwell, *Humble Supplication*

The Elizabethan government made a clear distinction between
the nonconforming Marian clergy or 'old' priests and the
seminary priests and Jesuits who were liable, after the 1585
Act, to suffer the death penalty for treason by the fact of
their ordination abroad. Its attitude was that of Francis
Bacon : 'The one is a priest of Superstition and the other is a
priest of Sedition.' The Marian clergy were also distinguished
from the new by training and outlook, and by age, for the
coming of the seminary priests, mostly young, not only ensured
the survival of Catholicism but also marked a significant break
with the past. Their professional training and missionary zeal
produced a readiness, even eagerness, to face danger and
death. This self-confidence was shown by one young priest
who wrote on the eve of his journey back to England, with a
touch of typical Elizabethan rhetoric : 'and now at length with
full sail and courageous minds most like unto Aeneas we will

cut the surging seas, and make assault towards our foes'. When death came most of them faced it with the serenity of one of the Yorkshire missionaries : 'So many of my blessed brethren have already got the victory in the same quarrel.' The frescoes on the chapel walls of the English College at Rome, which depicted the torture and execution of former students, gave its members a daily and grim reminder of their calling. This was a background that the 'old' priests could not share. Some historians have considered the continuity between the two types of clergy to have been slight, regarding the 'old' priests as representatives of the Henrican conservatives of the years 1534–58 with an outlook remote from that of the militant Catholics of the 1580s.[1] This probably does them an injustice, for some Marian priests did their best to absorb the new Counter Reformation spirit and are known to have crossed to Douai for refresher courses in theology. One deacon waited for twenty years until 1576 in order to obtain ordination at Bruges.[2]

The number of 'old' priests who carried on an underground ministry after 1558 has certainly been underestimated. In Yorkshire alone it has been estimated that 150 or more were at work in a county that as late as 1582 had been reached by few seminary priests. Seventy-five are known to have worked in Lancashire, where, it has been argued, recusancy was not the creation of the seminary clergy, who were able to build on a foundation laid by the 'old' priests.[3] A large number of the early students of the Douai College came from Lancashire, and the transition from pre-Tridentine to post-Tridentine Catholicism seems to have been made without difficulty. In time, some of the 'old' priests were numbered among those who suffered the death penalty, and in the 1570s the prisons at York and Hull usually held six or eight of them. Some ministered for a time in the State Church before taking the hard road to recusancy. Michael Bolton was one such priest. He accepted the Thirty-Nine Articles in 1569 and was installed as vicar of Burton Pidsea; in 1579 he either resigned or was deprived, and later he was gaoled at Hull as an obstinate recusant.[4] James Bell ministered in Elizabeth's Church for

twenty years until his reconciliation with Catholicism in 1581 :
'And as soon as he had learned again to say his office in the
Breviary and Mass and was admitted again, after certain
months, to the Holy Altar he was very diligent, and painful
among poor Catholic people.'[5]

We catch occasional glimpses of these 'old' priests, such as
Simon Southern, who was examined for recusancy in 1582
before Whitgift, then Bishop of Worcester.[6] Southern gave
his age as 83 and stated that he had been a priest for fifty-one
years. Whitgift described him to Walsingham as an 'old and
very ignorant massing priest', but in 1530 Southern had been
regarded as a man of some consequence, a competent critic of
Latin verse who became chaplain to the Bishop of Worcester
in 1545. In 1585 another Marian priest, James Stonnes, was
arrested in 'a very poor man's house' and committed to the
new Fleet prison in Manchester.[7] He was then 72 years old
and had been ordained by Bishop Tunstall in 1539. Examined
before the Earl of Derby he refused to incriminate anyone
else and stated that

> He thinketh her Majesty's laws spiritual are not established
> according to God's law and therefore that is the cause that
> neither since the beginning of her Majesty's reign he hath
> frequented or been at church, nor will do, because he says
> it is against my conscience. But for her Majesty's temporal
> laws established he alloweth well of them and prayeth to
> God that her Majesty may long reign over us.

This old priest was provided with everything needed for saying
Mass, together with a case for the holy oils of baptism and
the sick. There is no doubt that these Marian clergy played
a significant part in the survival of Catholicism.

Yet it is not surprising if they tended to be out of sympathy
in some respects with the younger generation from the colleges
abroad. Since 1559 their lives had been far from easy, but
the Bull of 1570 and subsequent legislation brought new
dangers for which they were ill prepared, although in the
event they faced them bravely. On the whole, Marian priests

did not condemn attendance, under compulsion, at services of the State Church; they did not approve of the new milder laws concerning fasting that had obtained abroad since the Council of Trent; and they used the Sarum rite for the celebration of Mass, whereas the seminary priests soon brought in the Roman rite as revised by order of Pope Pius V. These differences emerged at a meeting of 'old' priests, seminary priests, laymen, and the two Jesuits Campion and Persons, which was held at Southwark in 1580. On that occasion, Persons later recorded, 'a grave and ancient priest named Mr Wilson' suggested that it would be better for all if the Jesuits simply went away, a sentiment that was to be echoed later by a number of Catholics. The habit of compromise that distinguished many Marian priests was also illustrated by a reference to the Catholic Viscount Montague : 'If . . . he went to heretical churches, it was not so much to be imputed to him as to his priest, a learned and pious man indeed, but too fearful, who supposing it to be expedient something to give to the time, durst not determine such a fact to be a sin.'[8] As soon as he received a seminary priest as chaplain Lord Montague found himself called on to cease attending church. To some extent these differences resulted from the inevitable conflict of the generations. In his *Autobiography* John Gerard mentioned the 'old' priest who was chaplain to William Wiseman : 'one of those old priests who were always at odds with the young, especially the Jesuits whom they looked on as meddlesome innovators'.

The training of the seminary priests and their way of life in England necessitated the abandonment of many old traditions, and if they had their critics among the Marian priests Dr Allen had also to defend them against criticism from some of the exiles. The prior of the English Carthusians was one who complained of both their secular dress and their youth and also of their inexperience for a life that was outside normal ecclesiastical discipline. Lord Burghley also complained of their coming in disguise 'all in their apparell as roisterers and ruffians', but he could have found targets for criticism nearer home : the Elizabethan vicar of Preston in Kent was presented by his churchwardens in 1572 for driving cows through Faversham 'in a jerkin with a bill on his neck, not like a prelate but rather like a common rogue'.[9] When Robert Persons landed in England he was attired in captain's clothes of buff inlaid with gold, with a hat and feather to match, lent him by Sir George Chamberlain, and the former Ballioldon was just the man to carry it off with panache. Other priests came more modestly attired, some as sailors or serving men. In 1585 Bishop Chadderton gave a detailed description of the attire of a priest who had been arrested in his diocese : his black cloak with murry lace, straw-coloured doublet with red ornamentation, completed by 'a little black hat lined with velvet in the brims, a falling band, and yellow knit stocks'.

In whatever disguise they came the first problem was to secure an undetected landing. Some, like John Gerard and his companions, might be landed on a deserted part of the coast, where the very presence of strangers could excite comment; others might hope to enter more dangerously through the ports. Since government informers had no difficulty in collecting information about members of the colleges abroad and the names of those ordained and ready to be dispatched to England, a number of priests were at once arrested on landing. When Campion and Persons arrived they found that notice of their coming had been posted at the ports and that officials had been alerted to watch for them. Thomas Cottam returned to England at the same time for reasons of health, unknowingly made part of the journey in company with a spy, and was arrested on landing and executed. Another elderly Jesuit, unused to English ways after a long sojourn in Vilna, was arrested on landing but released from prison three years later at the intercession of the King of Poland. Some priests appear to have shown remarkable simplicity in their dealing with the authorities, as would appear from the account given by Robert Persons of the arrest of William Bishop. When he landed at Rye in 1581 Bishop was then 28 years old. On being questioned he claimed to be a merchant, but he was unable to say what merchandise he dealt in and soon admitted that he was a priest. Persons commented that Bishop had been warned before he went on board ship, but 'he seemed so absorbed in meditating on heavenly things as to be quite oblivious of human affairs'. Bishop was condemned to death on the charge of plotting the death of the Queen, but eventually he was banished and repaired for study for a doctorate at the Sorbonne. He survived to become Bishop of Chalcedon in 1623. James Lomax was another young priest who was arrested on landing and secretly scolded by the magistrate for admitting too readily to his identity. He died in prison.

Once he had landed the seminary priest became a hunted man. His situation was that of Lear's Edgar :

> No port is free, no place
> That guard, and most unusual vigilance
> Does not attend my taking.

One striking fact about these priests was that all depended on their own initiative; they did not form part of a highly organised expedition. The individual priest often had to make his own contact with Catholics; his channels of communication with Douai or Rheims were uncertain; and he was without a superior's guidance until the appointment of an archpriest in 1598. If this was a fifth column it was a singularly ill-organised one for most of the reign. The first Jesuits were in much the same position, and Persons made his first contacts in 1580 by visiting the Marshalsea prison. A further disadvantage was that many of the priests had been absent from England for many years and were out of touch with existing conditions. When Henry Garnet became superior of the Jesuits one month after his arrival in England, he had been away from his native land for eleven years. The lack of understanding of English affairs in Rome did not help them. Rome was a city where no secrets could be kept, and in 1585 the single Jesuit then at large in England wrote with some justice to Allen : 'I know for certain that whatever shall be muttered in Rome . . . will be preached here on the housetops quicker than can be believed.'[10] Over the years, and largely due to Jesuit efficiency, an elaborate organisation developed for the conveying of priests, the smuggling of books and letters, and the passing of information. A network of communications was thus set up with resting houses for priests in foreign ports and contacts with seamen and ships' captains. How all this was financed is not clear. The war between England and Spain made this traffic more difficult but never impossible.[11]

To carry out his ministry efficiently the priest needed vestments and altar furniture for the celebration of Mass and a breviary for his daily recitation of the Office, yet it was an added risk to carry such equipment with him on his journeys. Lancelot Blackburne, arrested with his 'massing stuff' by the Derbyshire justices in 1587, was one of a number so caught. William Freeman, arrested in 1595 after six years of ministry and many narrow escapes, was found to carry a breviary under his hat. Toby Mathew, then Dean of Durham, wrote to Burghley of the priest Bernard Patterson who was caught with a serving man : 'a base begotten desperate and dangerous fellow who carried in a cloke bag on his horse behind him the priest's massing vestments, books, etc.'. The priest later escaped from York castle, but the servant was still in prison in 1593. It was one of Robert Persons' many services to maintain a supply of these requirements and arrange for them to be smuggled across the channel. Writing to the Rector of the English College in Rome, in 1584, he mentioned the heavy financial burden entailed : 'In the first place I have sent to England at various times since I have been in these parts chalices, vestments, missals, breviaries, catechisms, books of devotion and controversy to the volume of more than four thousand crowns.'[12] In time many Catholic houses came to possess all that was needed to furnish a simple chapel, and the householder thus relieved the priest of one risk by accepting it himself. After a heavy fine of £1 000 Lord Lumley stored all such furnishings with a London Catholic, whose wife, after her husband's arrest, unwittingly confided to an informer that 'all books, copes, vestments, cross, chalices and all the rest' in her house 'was my Lord's'.[13]

The 1585 Act, with its drastic penalties for harbouring priests, had an immediate deterrent effect and made some Catholics reluctant to shelter them. It was said of the widowed Lady Arundell, a staunch recusant, that after the arrest of her chaplain 'she was ever fearful and . . . never bore young priests any good will'. However, the Act also influenced the gradual build-up of an organisation. Its likely effects were discussed at a meeting of a number of laymen, who included Lord Vaux and Sir Thomas Tresham, when it was decided that for the time being the clergy 'should shift for themselves . . . in inns or suchlike places', visiting Catholic houses only by invitation. A fund was raised for their support, administered by Lord Vaux, to which each layman contributed 100 marks. Government reports indicate that in fact there was no lack of houses where a priest was welcome. In July 1586 a remarkable meeting was held in the house of Richard Bold, a former Lancashire sheriff, at Hurleyford in Buckinghamshire, where a number of the laity assembled for eight days with three Jesuits : William Weston and two new arrivals, Robert Southwell and Henry Garnet, both destined to die on the scaffold.[14] With them was the Court musician William Byrd, and the occasion was marked by a sung Mass with a choir and instrumental accompaniment. Listening today to a Byrd mass sung in the splendour of King's College chapel at Cambridge one's thoughts are drawn to the celebration in that remote house of the Chiltern woods, when the composer had the rare opportunity of hearing his work in its liturgical setting.

William Weston now drew up a list of houses that would shelter priests despite the law, and Henry Garnet made extensive travels as far as Yorkshire in the North and Wales, finding out at first hand the possibilities. By 1596, where formerly Persons had noted the tendency of priests to gravitate to London and the neighbouring counties, Garnet could write of the incoming priests : 'The greater part of them we place in fixed residences. The result now is that many persons, who saw a seminary priest hardly once a year, now have one all the time and most eagerly welcome any others no matter where they come from.'[15] The Countess of Arundel, whose husband was a prisoner in the Tower, had earlier provided both finance and a house at Acton where incoming priests might be received, and here was installed a secret printing press. The increase of persecution that followed the defeat of the Armada led many Catholics to fall away but increased the determination of the remainder. When Robert Southwell was sent off for a country tour in December 1588 he gained a ready welcome and found that

> . . . people up to now who would not even speak to a priest, much less admit one to the house, do not only receive us but press us to come and stay with them . . . In the majority I have found a wonderful keenness and contempt for worldly values : men of noble family and great possessions, surrounded as they are by every advantage are yet more and more ready to risk their lands and liberty.[16]

Steps were also taken during these years to improve security against the sudden raids and searches to which known Catholic houses were exposed, and from 1580 onwards the practice began of building hiding places in country houses for priests and chapel furnishings. When this work was taken over by a Jesuit laybrother, Nicholas Owen, it became expert in design and execution. Owen, who came to England in 1586 with John Gerard, was a skilled joiner and son of an Oxfordshire carpenter. His work was mostly done at night while he was visiting Catholic houses in the disguise of a servant to Henry Garnet. Between 400 and 500 of these hiding places have been recorded, and in time justices and pursuivants found it useful to be accompanied by a professional mason and carpenter in their efforts to uncover them. Owen was arrested for the first time in 1594, but his identity was not known and he was later released. Taken again after the Gunpowder Plot, by which time his importance was realised, he was so severely tortured that he died, but without revealing any information. The debt owed him by the

Catholic body was therefore twofold, for his fortitude under torture prevented a major disaster for the Catholic gentry. He had been a familiar figure in many Catholic houses throughout the land, riding about in an old cloak 'of sad green cloth with sleeves caped with tawny velvet and little gold stripes turning on the cape'.[17]

By 1585 the number of seminary priests working in England had increased from the initial four who had landed in 1574 to about 300, including thirty-three from the new college in Rome. Their enthusiasm was reflected in the reports that they sent back to Dr Allen, with claims of success that seem excessively optimistic, although in the 1580s Lord Burghley himself complained to the Queen that 'the greatest number of papists is of very young men'. During the summer of 1586 less than half of the 300 were at liberty and exercising their ministry: 33 had been put to death; 8 more had died in prison; 60 had been banished; 50 were prisoners; and a few had died from natural causes. More executions took place during the year after the Armada, and by the end of the reign 123 had been put to death. Government measures therefore achieved a good measure of success and moreover on the whole had the effect of restricting the ministry of the Catholic clergy to recusants. Writing in 1616 the Jesuit historian More distinguished three possible ways of life for a priest on the English mission, and these would not have changed from those of Elizabeth's reign. There were the priests who could work from a rest house or centre that was in charge of laymen, riding out to minister to local Catholics, spending an occasional night in a Catholic house and saying Mass for the household before moving on. These were the most active priests, who also faced constant danger of detection. The Cornishman, John Hambley, was arrested on his way to meet a son of Sir John Fulford and his future wife before performing their marriage. Other priests might have the good fortune to serve as chaplain where 'the head of the house . . . was made either by his own virtue or by the good esteem of his neighbours, superior as it were to the action of the laws'. The servants of the house would be Catholics, and warning might be expected in times of danger. Here, possibly acting as steward, the chaplain might have some opportunity to come and go. The third and worst experience for the priest was what More termed 'a private life'. This was the lot of those who were chaplain in a household whose head was extremely timid, who 'lived in such servile fear as though the liberty either of the priest or of themselves was likely to suffer' and did not trust even Catholic servants. The priest lived in a remote part of the house, careful of opening windows or showing lights at night, and if he left the house at all he might only do so after dark. In a household of sixty to eighty persons he might spend weeks or even months alone, except at the hour of Mass or with an occasional visit from a member of the family. 'How oppressive this constant solitude was . . . no one can imagine who has not tried it.'[18]

It is not surprising if the strain of this life of danger and loneliness proved too much for some, and under torture and the threat of death some priests apostatised and informed on their fellow Catholics who had sheltered them. One such was Thomas Bell, a former Protestant minister. He abandoned his priesthood in 1592 and entered the service of Huntingdon, revealing details of the Lancashire mission, its centres, priests and the names of individual Catholics. The Yorkshire mission also suffered from the apostasy of Thomas Clark, who gave the authorities the names of thirteen priests and was responsible for the arrest of Edward Osbaldeston, who suffered death at York. Clark is known to have repented of his apostasy before he died, an unhappy man. The career of another priest, Anthony Tyrell, was a strange mixture of farce and tragedy. Brought to St Paul's Cross in 1588 to make a public abjuration of his faith in the presence of the Lord Mayor of London and a large crowd, he caused consternation by proclaiming instead his belief in the 'Roman and Catholic Church from which by the instigation of the devil I fell away'. Persons wrote an amusing account of this extraordinary episode :

. . . all was in marvellous hurly and burly at Paul's Cross where the people heard three sermons in one hour, all contrary the one to the other; the first of the preacher in praise of Tyrell; the second of Tyrell himself in derogation of the preacher; the third of Justice Young threatening death to those who should believe in Tyrell.[19]

A further sojourn in prison, however, aided Tyrell once more to see the light, and he was rewarded with a pardon and a Crown living. He must have pursued an uneasy ministry in the Elizabethan Church, for conscience moved him in his old age to abandon his parish for exile and reconciliation with the old faith.

This danger from false brethren was one that both priests and laymen had to face. It is impossible to know exactly how many Catholic clergy went over to their enemy and conformed or how many were like Tyrell and in the end returned to Catholicism. As Anstruther has pointed out, systematic record of a priest ceased when he left his seminary, and the special pardon sometimes granted on condition of taking the oath of supremacy was given to some who were later found working as trustworthy priests. Of the 800 or so names listed by Anstruther, perhaps twenty-eight might be regarded as having apostatised, some of whom returned to Catholicism. An approximate 4 per cent of failures seems a remarkably small number for men engaged in such a dangerous enterprise. There were also Jesuits who conformed. One of these was Sir Christopher Perkins, and it is significant that when first invited to join the English mission he had expressed his willingness provided he received papal permission to take the oath and attend the official church services.

Restricted in his ministry by the constant danger of detection and arrest the priest often found more opportunities once he was in prison, provided he was not held in solitary confinement. Prison conditions were sometimes lax with gaolers open to bribes and visitors often permitted. It was against this state of affairs that the Bishop of London made protest to Lord Burghley in 1583 : 'But this I find among them and specially in the Marshalsea that those wretched priests which by her Majesty's lenity live there as it were in a college of caitiffs, do commonly say Mass within the prison, entice the youth of London unto them, and to my great grief and as far as I can learn, do daily reconcile them.'[20] The bishop had good reason to complain, for forty-eight men and women were arrested while listening to a sermon preached in the Marshalsea by a Franciscan friar. When Thomas Bell, a former minister in the State Church, reached England after his ordination he secured entry to the prison at York castle, saying Mass and preaching there for some days. A Welsh priest entered the prison at Chester and dressed 'in a white surplice did say service . . . and the service was in Latin and there was bread such as was used in the papist time'.[21]

The early seminary priests and Jesuits had radiated optimism and had looked forward to the reconversion of England, but by the end of the century such hopes had long faded. The Jesuit Richard Holtby had a remarkably long career as a missionary and was never captured, beginning his ministry as a secular priest in 1577 at the age of 27 and ending it with his death in 1640. Towards the end of 1594 he sent Henry Garnet a long and extremely pessimistic report on the state of Catholicism in the North, in which he expressed his fear that 'the little sparkle of the Catholic religion, as yet reserved among us, shall be quite extinguished'.[22] This was a result of the drive against recusancy conducted by Huntingdon, and it was something that Garnet could appreciate from his own experience in London, for not long before he had written to his superior in Rome : 'It is not worth while sending any more over to us for a while yet, unless they are willing to run straight into the direst poverty and the most atrocious brigandage : so desperate has our state become, so close, unless God intervenes, to utter ruin.'[23] Pessimism was understandable, but was it justified? Aveling has shown that in spite of the persecution recusancy was actually increasing among the Yorkshire gentry. His analysis of the families in Gilling West shows a remarkable degree of endurance with ten families of the twelve or thirteen local squires affected by

Catholicism and small congregations forming round the households of seven of them. In Gilling East sixteen out of forty landowners were more or less Catholic and by the end of the reign some heads of families who had conformed or remained non-communicant emerged as full recusants.[24]

The Catholic clergy included men drawn from all social classes including about 50 per cent drawn from the gentry class during Elizabeth's reign. Recusants indeed tended to pride themselves on the thought that their clergy by birth and education were superior to those of Elizabeth's Church. During the seventeenth century the proportion of gentry among their number steadily increased until by the Restoration the Catholic clergy were overwhelmingly drawn from the landowning class.[25] In 1591 a royal proclamation denounced them in fierce language as a multitude of 'dissolute young men' whose vocation was a result of 'lack of living' and of 'crimes committed'.[26] The charge drew a number of replies, notably from Robert Persons in his exile and from the young Jesuit Robert Southwell. Persons' work was intended for European circulation, it was written in Latin and published in Italy, Germany, France, Spain and the Netherlands. His attack on the queen and her ministers was not welcomed by Catholics in England, who felt that violent language from the safety of exile made their own lot much worse. Persons defended the clergy from the aspersions of the proclamation :

> Youths nobly born and wealthy for the most part, who could live quietly and comfortably at home, and who solely for zeal for the faith have left parents and friends, and all that is dear to them in this life in order to go into voluntary exile . . . They are not descended from the dregs of mankind like your ministers of the word, but frequently from noble families and wealthy parents, and I venture to say that in the three seminaries of Rome, Rheims, and Valladolid, there are more flowers of nobility than among all your clergy at home.[27]

The Elizabethans were greatly preoccupied with the question of social status, and both Persons, whose origins were humble, and Southwell, who was a member of the gentry, were concerned to rebut this attack on the social background of the Catholic clergy. Burghley too in former days had been sensitive about his family origins, and we are reminded of Richard Bertie's complaint in reply to the Earl of Arundel's comment that he was no gentleman : 'I am sure I can reach as far back as FitzAlan.' More important motives, however, lay behind the Catholic reaction than mere snobbishness. Very few of the common people of England were likely to meet the Catholic clergy, so it was important that they should not receive a false picture of them; moreover, an impression gained from the proclamation might alienate important sympathisers on the continent.

Southwell took up the same theme in an address to the Queen, which was not published until some time later :

> And for the baseness of their birth . . . the thing neither importeth any offence to God nor crime against your Majesty . . . The Cardinal's grace is of as good and ancient a house and in every way as worshipfully allied as some of the highest Councillors . . . As for other priests, how many of them are Knights' and Esquires' sons, and otherwise allied to both worshipful and noble houses, and heirs to fair revenues, let their own friends and parents dispersed throughout the Realm bear witness.[28]

Southwell was himself an uncle of Speaker Lenthall and a cousin of the Cecils. Lord Burghley, who drew up a genealogical chart of the Shelley family noting their recusancy, was well aware of the connection.

Late in the reign the Council complained to the Vice-Chancellor of Oxford University about the number of Oxford men among these 'dissolute' seminary priests. Perhaps some 170 of them spent time at Oxford, and another forty-five at Cambridge; many spent a period at the Inns of Court. A fall in the number of university men was noticeable in the latter part of the reign as it became increasingly difficult for Catholic students to avoid religious tests. John Gerard and his brother were sent up to Oxford in 1576, but they were forced to withdraw after a year in order to avoid compulsory communion in the State Church.

Both seminary priests and Jesuits came under strong Protestant attack for their supposed moral teaching that the end justified the means and that it was lawful to lie in support of a good cause. The puritan William Perkins expressed a common opinion in his *Reformed Catholike* (1598): 'In their doctrine they maintain perjury : because they teach with one consent that a Papist examined may answer doubtfully against the direct intention of the examiner : framing another meaning to himself in the ambiguity of his words'.[29] He was referring to a branch of moral theology termed 'casuistry', concerned with the circumstances that might make permissible an otherwise forbidden action. This line of reasoning had developed as a result of new problems brought about by the Reformation, and one aspect of it had particular relevance to English conditions. If a Catholic priest in England admitted to his priesthood under questioning he automatically became liable to the death penalty after the passing of the 1585 Act. Was he bound to incriminate himself by a truthful answer? Did this apply to answers to the Bloody questions? Common sense would answer that he was not so bound, but there were many who scrupled to give evasive answers as departing from the truth. The Catholic casuist condemned the direct lie but permitted the use of equivocation or mental reservation, on the ground that not everyone has a right to know the truth, especially if he intends to use that knowledge to compass the destruction of his informant. Casuistry was an answer to persecution, and its Protestant opponents were gradually driven to develop a similar system when the Anglican Church, in its turn, suffered persecution during the puritan revolution.

A number of the Catholic clergy – and they included some of the best educated – shared with their brethren of the Elizabethan Church the very common contemporary belief in portents, political prophecies, witchcraft and diabolical possession.

> The spirit that I have seen
> May be the devil; and the devil hath power
> To assume a pleasing shape.

An Act of Parliament of 1563 made it a felony to invoke evil spirits, and it has been claimed that prosecutions for witchcraft during the reign of Elizabeth greatly exceeded the parallel persecution of the Catholic clergy. These years produced a number of crack-brained pseudo-Messiahs, so that Lord Burghley might not have been greatly surprised by Miles Fry who claimed, in 1587, to be a son of Elizabeth by God the Father. It has been claimed that the revival of a witchcraft craze in England at this time was due to pressure from the returned Marian exiles.[30] In visitation articles for Salisbury, Bishop Jewel found it necessary to inquire if any prebendary was in the habit of invoking the devil or engaging in divination. Both leaders of the Counter Reformation and some bishops of the Elizabethan Church tried, with moderate success, to check the excessive credulity of clergy and people. The recusant English clergy did not escape these failings, and just as a contemporary could describe clergy of the Elizabethan Church as 'Egyptian enchanters', so the term 'conjurer' could be used as a synonym for a recusant priest.[31] Sir John Harington indeed believed that recusants generally were charged 'to be more superstitious and credulous and to attribute more to old prophecies and traditions of men than either Protestants or puritans'. The retention of a service for exorcism, omitted from the *Book of Common Prayer*, might have influenced this opinion but church authorities were usually reluctant to permit its use, and superstition was officially frowned upon : the prophecies of Merlin were placed on the Index of Forbidden Books.

The absence of episcopal government might have given the English Catholic clergy greater freedom to make use of exorcism and a series of these services were held in leading recusant houses during 1585–6. A prominent figure in these proceedings was the Jesuit William Weston who seems to have been not only shrewd and devout but also exceedingly credulous. Protestant ministers also attempted to cast out devils and there was some rivalry; the minister George More claimed in 1600 that 'if the Church of England have this power to cast out devils then the Church of Rome is a false church'.[32] The reputed success of Catholic priests with their exorcisms attracted followers in cases where Protestant clergy failed. A contemporary writer in 1590 referred to the 'false miracles, lying powers and wonders of the Papists by which feats they have increased and grown into the greater number . . . the people forsook their faith and ran a-gadding from place to place to gaze upon signs and wonders'. Foxe noted the dramatic fall of a priest from his pupit after he had announced his absolution by Cardinal Pole, and similarly recusant writers saw the finger of providence in the calamities of their opponents. After Campion's trial a story circulated that Judge Ayloff had pulled off his glove during the proceedings and had found that his hand was all bloody 'without any wrong, pricking, or hurt'.

11 *Jesuit Invaders*

They must not take part in affairs of state nor write to
us from there news concerning state affairs.
                    Roman instructions to the first Jesuits

Distinguished by name from the seminary priests in government proclamations and statutes, the Jesuits attracted
remarkable attention and odium, to an extent indeed that was
out of all proportion to their numbers. At a time when a
single elderly Jesuit was at liberty but in hiding the Parliament
of 1584–5 solemnly discussed the 'hurt' dealt the nation by its
'home Jesuits'. This solitary member of the Society of Jesus
was Jasper Heywood, a former page at Court and an uncle
of John Donne. In 1597 Christopher Yelverton – who sur-
passed Mildmay and Hatton, Neale has told us, 'in elegance
and sweetness of language' – spoke in the Commons of 'the
desperate and devilish devices of the Romish crew and Jesuits
whose unnatural affections, bloody hands, and most cruel
hearts do too, to evidently betray their irreligion.'[1] The handful of men who caused such excitement were also articulate,
and the annual letters to their Roman superiors, the accounts
of their ministry, and the poems of Robert Southwell tell us
more of their activities and characters. The Jesuit superiors
did not set England high on their list of priorities, for even in
1563 there had been thirty or forty English members of the
Society. From 1581 to 1586 there was never more than one
Jesuit at large in England, and by 1593 the number had risen
to only eighteen, four of whom were in prison. Few of these
Elizabethan Jesuits had received any special training : a number had joined the Society as secular priests working in

England; others, like John Gerard, were technically only novices when they landed in England. Not until the early seventeenth century, when the number of English Jesuits reached 300, could they be considered as Jesuit-trained. Government hatred of them resulted from the political activities of some of their number abroad but also was a tribute to the undoubted distinction of some of those who worked in England.

The first Jesuit to suffer death was Edmund Campion, and the immense publicity that his fate attracted and the inspiration that it gave the Caholic community mark something of a watershed in the history of Elizabethan Catholicism.[2] As a very young Fellow of St John's College, a Marian foundation to which still clung something of the atmosphere of its origins, Campion had acquired a remarkable influence over the youth of Oxford, who flocked to his lectures. Like Newman in the Victorian university he possessed all the advantages of charm, intellect and character. By his part in a public disputation for the entertainment of the Queen Campion obtained the patronage of the Earl of Leicester, to whom he later dedicated his *History of Ireland* : 'how by letters, how by reports, you have not ceased to further with advice . . . the hope and expectation of me, a single student'. He was therefore well placed to climb the ladder of preferment; a younger contemporary, Toby Mathew, was to become Archbishop of York with the help of Cecil patronage despite the embarrassment of a well-known Catholic son. After taking the first step by ordination as a deacon in the State Church Campion turned his back on a promising future, was reconciled as a Catholic and eventually entered the Society of Jesus. This brilliant recruit was then buried away, to his own satisfaction, in a new school that the Society had founded at Prague, where in 1576 Sir Philip Sidney came to visit him.

His return to England with Robert Persons in 1580 was not the result of Jesuit planning but was due to the importunity of Dr Allen, and within a year a legend had been born. Campion arranged that a copy of his *Decem Rationes*, a challenge to a public disputation, should be placed in every seat of St Mary's Church before the Oxford Convocation of 1581. This work was described later by Thomas Fuller as 'so purely for Latin, so plainly and pithily penned that they were very taking and fetched many (neuter before) to his persuasion'. Another *Challenge* or *Brag*[3] circulated through the indiscretion of a friend, and a copy soon reached the Council. This was a defiant manifesto of a kind not hitherto circulated in England, which set on foot an intense search for the author. Campion's younger Jesuit contemporary, John Gerard, was to survive through a ministry of eighteen years, but Campion himself was arrested after a single year's ministry through the folly of devout Catholic women. He had spent one night at a well-known Catholic house in Berkshire where a Mrs Yate lived with two chaplains and some Bridgettine nuns, while the son of the house was in prison for religion. After he left some visitors called at the house and, hearing of his visit, were distressed to have missed him. A messenger was sent to recall him, and on the Sunday morning over forty persons attended his Mass, among them an informer who was to secure his arrest.

This seizure of Campion was a great triumph for the government. He was lodged in the Tower in the dreaded cell called Little Ease, where a prisoner could neither stand upright nor lie at full length. One account claims that he was taken to Leicester House for confrontation with his former patron and the Queen and was offered preferment if he would return to the State Church. There followed four public disputations with ministers chosen by the Bishop of London, in one of which he was denounced as 'an unnatural man to his country, degenerate for an Englishman, an apostate in religion, a fugitive from this realm, unloyal to his Prince', whose object was 'to plant secretly the blasphemous Mass'. In August 1581 the Spanish ambassador reported that he had been tortured by iron spikes driven behind his nails, and the Venetian ambassador reported the same, adding that the fingernails had been torn off. Campion, in company with seventeen others, was charged under the Treasons Act of 1351 with conspiracy to murder the Queen, a conspiracy allegedly planned on specific dates at Rome and Rheims at a time when at least one of the accused was held in an English prison. Another indictment charged that on 30 July 1580 'in a certain room within the mansion house at Great Coxwell being vested in alb and other vestments according to papistical rites and ceremonies, did say and celebrate one private and detestable Mass in the Latin Tongue, derogatory to the blood of Christ and contrary to his due allegiance'.[4]

The execution of Edmund Campion had an affect comparable to the account written by Sir John Eliot of the death of Raleigh: 'Such was his unmoved courage and placid temper that, while it changed the affection of the enemies who had come to witness it and turned their joy to sorrow, it filled all men else with emotion and admiration.' One gay and careless Elizabethan, the young Henry Walpole, secured a front place to witness the execution; a drop of blood that splashed from the scaffold onto his coat began a process that led to his conversion and a similar death thirteen years later. Philip, Earl of Arundel, had attended one of Campion's disputations in the Tower, and this proved a first step that led him to conversion and life imprisonment. By 1590 some thirty pamphlets on the trial had been published, and the story of Campion's death had been cried in the streets of Paris. Even fifty years later a memory of his sermons survived in the North of England. Queen Mary had provided Protestants with their martyrs and a lasting reproach to Catholics; now Elizabeth provided Catholics with theirs, and the result was much the same : a strengthening of conviction and endurance. Before long the Oxford professor of divinity was writing to Leicester complaining that 'the ghost of the dead Campion has given me more trouble than the *Rationes* of the living . . . in place of one single Campion champion upon champions have swarmed to keep us engaged'.

When a revised edition of Holinshed's famous *Chronicle* was published in 1586–7 it included a description of Ireland based on Campion's history, edited by a former pupil. Richard Stanihurst included a tribute to his former teacher :

'so rare a clerk, who was so upright in conscience, so deep in judgement, so ripe in eloquence'. It is unexpected to find praise of Campion in a work of patriotic history published so soon after his execution, especially in a book that, as Dr Rowse has commented, 'was part of the march of English Protestantism'.[5] To balance this came the adoption of his fellow Jesuit's *Christian Directory* as a Protestant devotional work. Here was an unexpected windfall of the Jesuit 'invasion' of 1580.

The language of the Elizabethan establishment that saw a Jesuit under every bed was absurd but understandable, and the Jesuits' audacity and versatility were infuriating to their enemies. Richard Blount landed in England as a returned prisoner of war from Spain and was received with sympathy by the Lord High Admiral; Oswald Tesimond visited his brethren in prison, pretending to be curious to see what a Jesuit looked like, and after the Gunpowder Plot escaped by boat with a cargo of pigs. When John Bennett was arrested he gave an unexpected reply to the magistrates who asked him what he thought of the Queen : 'I am her subject and, as my duty is, I pray to God for her and have done this very day before you were out of your beds.' Not all English Jesuits worked in England : In 1577 William Good, a former Fellow of an Oxford college, was in Sweden; John Yates became a missionary in Brazil; and Thomas Stevens spent much of his life in India, one of the first Englishmen to visit that country. The account he sent to his father, a well-known London merchant aroused interest in the possibility of trade with the East Indies.

As the number of Jesuits increased and an organisation developed it became possible in the 1590s to hold six-monthly meetings for a spiritual retreat and the renewal of vows. These meetings were not without their danger, however. In 1591 the pursuivants arrived when many of the Jesuits were assembled at a house in Warwickshire, but they failed to find the hiding place.[6] Their capture would have been an important coup had it succeeded, but their escape was perhaps less exciting than that of Richard Blount when Scotney castle was

raided at night in 1598.[7] He managed to reach the hide with
his servant carrying the Mass vestments, but such was their
haste that a girdle was caught in a sliding panel and hung
outside until one of the Darrell family arrived and cut it off.
The hide was almost discovered when the searchers decided to
rest from their labours. The justices retired to bed and the
others settled by a fire in the hall to await the dawn, giving
priest and servant opportunity to escape. They climbed over
two walls and hence to a dilapidated tower some sixteen feet
above a wide moat. Blount dived into the moat but had to
return for his servant who could not swim. They then walked
fourteen miles to shelter in another house. Blount survived
the ordeal and was never caught during a ministry of forty
years. In the seventeenth century he became provincial
superior of the English Jesuits, was friendly with James I and
his Queen, and won the friendship of Henrietta Maria. The
Scotney episode was blamed for his rheumatism : 'Ever after
he had aches in his thighs from the cold taken in the stone
wall.' The Darrell son who wrote an account of the raid did
not fail to point a moral : the chief actors in the search subsequently decayed in their estates, and a servant who had betrayed the family 'being a young man soon after died among
them, his limbs rotting and falling from him'.

John Gerard was another Jesuit who figured in a long series of
such escapes, and he had the temperament to endure the
stresses of a hunted life over a long period, from 1588 until
he left in the suite of the ambassadors who had come to con-
gratulate James I on his escape from the Gunpowder plot.
Gerard was the second son of Sir Thomas Gerard, a former
sheriff of Lancashire who was twice imprisoned on suspicion
of plotting against the government. John Gerard first
encountered the Jesuits while studying in France. Returning
to England when he was 20 years old he was imprisoned for
religion in the Marshalsea and sent for an interview to the
Bishop of London, who treated him with 'nothing but kind-
ness' but failed to shake his Catholic faith. This was a prelude
to the years he spent in England as a Jesuit priest, which he

recalled in the autobiography written in 1609.[8] He told us that his dress in England was always that of a gentleman of modest means, an account given for the benefit of the Jesuit novices, but a spy described him as dressed more elaborately : 'for the most part attired costly and defencibly in buff leather, garnished with gold or silver lace, satin doublets, and velvet hose of all colours . . . and rapiers and daggers gilt or silvered'. In the house he wore a cassock, and he travelled with one in his baggage. He was described as 'tall in stature, black haired and dark complexion, hawk nosed and high templed'.

Gerard was helped by an ability to mix easily with his social equals, often adopting the role of a young man keenly interested in field sports. Not for him was the 'private life' of the priest hidden away; he would join in a hunt in order to meet a likely convert and was an expert in the terms of falconry. As he moved on to a new Catholic house he would leave behind a small Catholic community with a resident chaplain, and he described how this was a result of the conversion of Sir Everard Digby, then a Gentleman Pensioner at Court. The Digbys set up a house chapel and secured a chaplain : 'What this family did others did too. Many Catholic gentlemen when they visited this house and saw the arrangements there took it as a model. They founded congregations centred round their own homes, furnished their chapels . . . accommodation suited to a priest's needs.'[9] Escape from danger and arrest was almost a matter of routine. In 1594 he spent four days without food in a hide contrived 'in a thick wall of the chimney', and when the searchers lit a fire in the hearth above the hide Gerard was forced 'to move a little to one side to avoid hot embers falling on my head'. Betrayed in London by an informer he spent three months in chains in the Counter prison. He was then moved to easier confinement in the Clink, where a locksmith prisoner had made keys to all the cells, giving the prisoners freedom of movement at night. From there he was moved to the Tower and severely tortured until he lost consciousness. Gerard described the journey to the torture room 'in a kind of solemn procession, the attendants walking ahead with lighted candles'.

With his usual resource Gerard planned a successful escape from the Tower and became the most wanted priest on the government list, but this did not deter him from renting a house in London, also raided in due course, and establishing relations with members of the Court. To this period belonged the conversion of Sir Oliver Manners, son of the fourth Earl of Rutland and Clerk of the Privy Council. In the government proclamation after the Gunpowder plot Gerard was named as one of the three Jesuits whose apprehension was sought, although throughout his ministry he had kept clear of politics. So it became impossible for him to remain in England. He was in fact remarkably unlike the Jesuit of official government propaganda, being a straightforward uncomplicated character. Although his Jesuit training had been minimal his great success as a Retreat giver and spiritual director was based on Jesuit spirituality, and he brought the teaching of the Spiritual Exercises of St Ignatius Loyola to many of the Catholic laity.[10] He is believed to have influenced some thirty young men to enter the seminaries abroad. All was not sweetness and light, however, and the enthusiasm of some of his converts for Jesuit spirituality aroused misgiving and envy among some members of the secular clergy. This long and successful ministry showed, however, that the challenge of repression could be faced, and when John Gerard died in 1637 there were more Jesuits working in England than at any previous time.

12 Dissension

How the gold has grown dim
How the pure gold is changed.
Lamentations of Jeremias

When Cardinal Allen died in 1594 the Society of Jesus had
survived less than sixty years of corporate life but they had
been years of remarkable success: the society had spread
throughout Europe, the New World, and the Far East, and
attracting men of the highest quality; their work as missionaries, writers, theologians and educators had proved an out-
standing feature of the Counter Reformation. This brilliant
success was not achieved without arousing opposition and
even in Catholic countries the Jesuits had provoked envy as
well as admiration. The University of Paris was one example
of an implacable adversary. The number of Jesuits who
worked in England during Elizabeth's reign was small but
the distinction and devotion of Campion, Southwell and
Gerard did not preserve them from the enmities incurred elsewhere. By comparison the English secular clergy worked at
a disadvantage. For most of the reign they had no central
authority to guide them and they lacked the *esprit de corps*
that Jesuit life fostered. Inevitably the Jesuit superior in
England tended to influence and assist the secular priests,
while leading laymen in their turn deferred to the Jesuits who,
it was sometimes believed, received greater ecclesiastical
powers or faculties from their foreign superiors than those of
the secular clergy. As time passed envy and suspicion
developed. The Jesuits were accused by a few of concentrat-
ing on the wealthy, of securing the best chaplaincies in

Catholic houses, and of attracting able young men as recruits to the detriment of the secular clergy. Complaints of this nature were unfortunate but not in themselves important. They were well answered by the Jesuit superior, Henry Garnet. Behind, however, lay something more profound : two differing conceptions of the nature of English Catholicism. There were members of the secular clergy who claimed to represent the secular clergy of the medieval Church and were concerned to re-establish episcopal government and the rule of canon law. The Jesuits regarded England as a missionary country and themselves as active evangelists, but their secular opponents believed that the proper place for members of a Religious Order was the cloister and were prepared to do without the services of the Jesuits. The restoration of a hierarchy would bring them to heel.

The extent to which individual Jesuits were identified with the pro-Spanish party abroad did not help them with the secular clergy, and suspicion concentrated especially on Robert Persons, whose policies and influence in high places were believed to work to the detriment of the real interests of Catholics at home. During the last years of the reign the quarrel became increasingly bitter, and the government played a hand in fomenting it. The golden age of Catholicism under penal law was for the time at an end, while the Roman authorities allowed the quarrel to drag on for several years before bringing it to an end. The importance of this dispute for the individual priest or layman must not be exaggerated but it left an atmosphere of bitterness which remained well into the next century.[1]

The first troubles or 'broyles' appeared in the English College at Rome. More than twenty years after its foundation Robert Persons had referred to it as 'this college of Rome which seemeth from the beginning to have had a certain infelicity following it above other colleges of the English nation'. The college was under Jesuit direction and although not the largest of the colleges tended to attract more attention than the others. The restlessness that affected its students had a number of causes : the appointment of Italians to the staff who

did not understand the English character; the greater age of
the students; and the rigidity of the discipline. By contrast
Dr Allen's college had a more peaceful history. By the 1590s
the Roman students had become anti-Spanish and anti-Jesuit
and in 1596 the Italian Rector wrote to Robert Persons:
'They have such a hatred against the Society that I fear they
would be ready to join hands with the heretics in order to be
delivered.' The appointment of Persons as Rector in 1597 was
therefore unwelcome but it gave him the opportunity to dis-
play another facet of his remarkable personality: by his
charm and common sense he soon won over the students and
restored peace. The English Jesuits now controlled three
colleges, in Rome and Spain, for the training of the secular
clergy and when Dr Richard Barret became Rector of Dr
Allen's foundation they found in him a devoted supporter.

This extension of Jesuit influence did not go unnoticed in
England where a dispute had broken out between some secular
priests and Jesuits. They were prisoners in the concentration
camp which the government had established at Wisbech, in
Tresham's 'filthy and fennish country'. As time passed the
gaolers relaxed the harsh conditions, visitors were permitted,
Mass was celebrated, and funds for the maintenance of the
prisoners were received from the Catholic laity. Gradually
Wisbech became something of a Catholic centre and by 1594
the torturer Topcliffe had complained of the laxity of its
administration: 'the seminary of Wisbech did more damage
to England than half the seminaries in Christendom'. The
easing of conditions in time lowered morale among the
inmates, some of whom had been deprived of liberty for more
than twenty years, and friction developed with the arrival in
1588 of a Jesuit, William Weston.

Weston had been arrested in 1588 after a ministry of two
years. He spent a year in the Clink prison before his removal
to Wisbech and remained a prisoner, with a five-year stint
in the Tower, until released in 1603. He was an Oxford
convert and had spent many years in Rome and Spain: a
man of undoubted goodness, a genuine ascetic, but by no
means an easy character. The easy-going way of life at

Wisbech did not meet with his approval and soon he emerged
as leader of a group who wished to follow a stricter régime.
There were others who considered this ascetic movement as
a condemnation of themselves. Their leader was Dr
Christopher Bagshaw, a former Fellow of Balliol College who
had resigned his Oxford appointments in 1581. He had later
been dismissed from the English College at Rome and therefore had no happy memories of the Jesuits. He had also a
strong dislike of Persons dating back to their time at Balliol.
A second member of the anti-Jesuit group at Wisbech was
Thomas Bluet, a former Protestant minister.[2] Feeling between
the two parties at Wisbech ran high and by 1595 news of
these disputes had reached the Catholic community outside
the prison.

These Wisbech 'stirs' and the 'broyles' of the English College
were also exploited by an anti-Jesuit party among the exiles.
Such troubles were in part a result of the disillusionment and
uncertainty among Catholics that followed the defeat of the
Armada. At a time when the Jesuits were coming under
criticism the publication of Doleman's *Conference on the
Next Succession* was therefore thought inopportune, and it was
soon identified as a product of Robert Persons and his pro-
Spanish group among the exiles. Then in September 1596 a
student of the Roman college, Robert Fisher, visited Wisbech
and spent some months in England mobilising opinion against
the Jesuits before he returned to Flanders.[3] There with exile
help he composed a *Memorial*, which expressed the hope that
an English government might grant liberty of conscience to
Catholics provided the Jesuits were withdrawn. This
Memorial was forwarded to Rome but was not received with
any favour.

At this point a further source of conflict arose. In March
1598 the Roman authorities promulgated a scheme for the
organisation of English Catholics. The secular clergy were
placed under the jurisdiction of the papal nuncio in Brussels,
but his authority was to be delegated to an archpriest in
England who was to work with twelve assistants. The archpriest was instructed to consult the Jesuit superior on all

matters of importance.[4] When this decision became known in
England it did not inspire confidence : the office of archpriest
lacked tradition, and many believed that the whole scheme
was a result of Jesuit influence at Rome. The man selected for
this office was George Blackwell, a former Fellow of Trinity
College, Oxford, who had been reconciled to Catholicism
and had entered Allen's seminary in 1574. He was described
by John Gerard : a man 'of comely stature, not very low,
gray haired and about the age of 58 or 60; he is lean faced,
a little hollow eyed and well spoken'. Blackwell was known
to have a great admiration for the Jesuits, and this was no
commendation to the faction that followed Christopher
Bagshaw. More serious, however, was the lack of the qualities
needed for an exacting office. A temperate and intelligent
priest was later to sum up his rule unfavourably : 'He showeth
neither quietness, modesty, or learning, but rather hautiness,
severity and much indiscretion, tossing the censures of the
Church like tennis balls for every default, threatening the
taking away of faculties, suspension, interdiction, or excommunication.'[5]

The archpriest's authority was soon in question, and in the
event two appeals were made to Rome against him. The first
appeal was carried by two priests and asked for the appointment of a bishop and for the removal of the Jesuits from
control of the English College at Rome. The priests were soon
put under a form of house arrest and not permitted to see the
Pope. The failure of this mission was attributed by many to
the influence of Robert Persons, but the papal confirmation
of Blackwell's appointment seemed to have re-established peace
by the summer of 1599. At this point Blackwell's assertion
of his authority against his late opponents stirred up fresh
controversy and a number of publications, including
Bagshaw's *True Relation of the Faction Begun at Wisbech*,
in which he described the archpriest as 'a puppy to dance
after the Jesuit's pipe'.[6] Blackwell's opponents now decided on
a second appeal to Rome, and the government was drawn
into the conflict when one of the imprisoned priests, Thomas
Bluet, was permitted to visit London. His visit to London in

1601, his first for twenty-four years, became memorable when he was received almost as an honoured guest into the care of Bishop Bancroft. The authorities already knew of the first unsuccessful appeal and of the Wisbech 'stirs'. They had already received a lengthy denunciation of the Jesuits from an eccentric priest named William Watson, and when informed of the second appeal they appreciated that advantage might be obtained from this division within the Catholic body.[7] Government assistance was given for the printing of the appellant's writings, and it was decided to release four priests and facilitate their journey to Rome. The four were Dr Bagshaw, Barnaby, Champney and Bluet himself. They were provided with passports stating that they were travelling on business known to the English government, but for the sake of appearances they were to be officially 'banished' from the realm. In July 1601 Bluet wrote an account of these negotiations :

> I have by opening the case unto their honours and to Caesar obtained that four principal men shall be banished after a sort to follow the appeal . . . They shall be here with me on Wednesday next. A month they shall have within the realm to ride abroad for money amongst their friends, and then choose the port to be gone with some countenance. I hope no man will be offended with this plot of mine, but with their purses assist us . . . I have in some sort pacified the wrath of our prince against us and her council, and have laid the fault where it ought to be and proved that the secular priests are innocent for the most part.[8]

During the absence of the appellants a fresh paper warfare broke out in England after the publication of an *Apologie* by Robert Persons in January 1602, which attacked the anti-Jesuit party in strong language.[9] The second appellants, however, were more successful than those who had carried the first appeal. France under the rule of Henry IV was formulating a foreign policy that was welcome to Pope Clement VIII as a counterbalance to the influence of Spain. Since the appellants were anti-Spanish as well as anti-Jesuit they were received by the French Foreign Minister, provided with French passports and promised the assistance of the ambassador in Rome.[10] The deputation therefore arrived in far better shape than the first appellants, and with French government aid they had nothing to fear. It was agreed that they had just cause for complaint. The archpriest was forbidden in future to consult the Jesuits and ordered to deal with Rome on matters affecting the English secular clergy; he was also ordered to take three members of the appellant party as assistants when vacancies occurred. To balance these points in favour of the appellants, their negotiations with the Bishop of London and the English government were entirely condemned.[11] The decision on this second appeal was therefore a triumph, but in part only, for the opponents of the archpriest and the Jesuits. They had not secured either episcopal government or the withdrawal of the Jesuits from their work in England.

A further aim of the appeal made no progress. The hope that some form of toleration might be granted received a cold blast from both Pope and Queen. Clement VIII condemned the idea of freedom of conscience and was reported as having stated that 'for a toleration or liberty of conscience in England – it would do harm, and make Catholics become heretics, that persecution was profitable to the Church'.[12] The Queen asked the French ambassador in London to thank his colleague in Rome on her behalf for the services he had rendered to the deputation, but when the ambassador, as instructed by his government, pressed for toleration she made it clear that this was out of the question. Her last royal proclamation was intended to reassure Protestant opinion and repeated the standard government position : seminary priests and Jesuits had invited the Spaniards to invade while almost all the former 'have in effect subjected themselves to be wholly directed by the Jesuits men altogether alienated from their true allegiance to us and devoted with all their might to the King of Spain'. The proclamation also attacked those who claimed

. . . that we have some purpose to grant toleration of two
religions within our realm, where God . . . doth not only
know our own innocence from such imagination, but how
far it hath been from any about us, once to offer to our
ears the persuasion of such a course as would not only
disturb the peace of the Church but bring this our State
into confusion.[13]

Jesuit priests were ordered to depart at once; seminary priests
opposed to them might remain in England until January
1603; and those who presented themselves to the authorities
'acknowledging their allegiance' would have taken in their
regard 'such further order as shall be thought by us most
meet and convenient'.

Whereas the Jesuit superior had ordered all his priests to
obey the papal decision, urging peace and unity with their
opponents, some of the leading appellants ignored the Pope's
ruling and continued to negotiate with the government. They
were asked if they would abandon their ministry and refused
to do so. They were also asked if they would take an oath
of allegiance and, refusing the formula produced by Bishop
Bancroft, offered one of their own. This made no reference
to the papal deposing power, firmly stated their acceptance of
papal supremacy in spiritual matters, but said that the clergy
would maintain their allegiance to the Queen in any conflict
even under threat of excommunication.[14] Three priests took
this declaration with thirteen signatures to Bishop Bancroft,
but they were told that its wording was unacceptable and
sent to the Clink prison.

Viewed simply as an internal quarrel among the English
Catholics, the archpriest or appellant controversy must appear
as a rather squalid episode in the traditional rivalries of the
secular and regular clergy. It is sad that Robert Persons and
others on both sides could not avoid the intrigue and personalities that disfigured the quarrel. Yet it had a more than
local importance. It made clear the growing opposition to the
pro-Spanish policies of a group among the exiles and also
the belief of many Catholics that their loyalty to the Crown

gave them a claim to some form of toleration, which they were prepared to claim at the expense of the Jesuits. It marked the first attempt at negotiation between the Catholic clergy and the government, although the latter was motivated more by the desire to profit from Catholic divisions than by a wish to reach an understanding. For the first time also the new France of Henry IV began to intervene in English Catholic affairs and to compete with Spain for influence. On the papal side, Clement VIII had reiterated the traditional view that truth and heresy could not have equal rights and that freedom of conscience could not have papal approval. At the close of the controversy the Jesuits might seem to have lost ground, yet their school at St Omer, so important for the future of English Catholic education, was flourishing and never lost the confidence of the Catholic gentry. Vocations from England continued to flow to the Society, and the number of Jesuits working in England continued to increase.

The importance of the declaration of allegiance signed by the thirteen priests in January 1603 has been variously estimated. It has been considered as 'a show of disobeying the Pope' that might logically have ended in membership of the State Church, a view more recently endorsed by Hurstfield: 'Had all Catholics accepted terms with the State they might have come to terms with the English Church.'[15] The signatures of thirteen priests out of the 300 or so then working in England was not perhaps widely known at the time, and in denying the right of the Pope to compel subjects to rise against an excommunicated sovereign the thirteen were advocating an opinion held by reputable theologians in other countries. More significant is the fact that no action was taken against the thirteen by the Roman authorities, and when at last in 1623 a bishop was appointed for England it was from their group that the choice was made.

13 At the End of the Reign

An ill quarter to look for righteousness, at the hands of
a miserable Scot.

Hugh Owen

When the sixteenth century reached its end the high hopes
of the early Catholic exiles for the recovery of their country
had long faded, and so far as concerned England the Counter
Reformation had failed. Yet after forty years of Elizabeth's
religious settlement Catholicism survived as a minority religion,
chiefly where social institutions existed to sustain it and therefore
in the households of members of the nobility and gentry, in spite
of the slow but steady transfer of social power to the new
Protestant aristocracy that had taken the régime so long to
achieve. So late as 1596 it was found that in Lady Montague's
sphere of influence at Battle the dean of that town had long
ceased to enforce religious conformity or to minister according
to the *Prayer Book*, and that the local commissioners of the
peace were reluctant to enforce the laws against recusants,
led by a presiding justice who had a Catholic wife and was
described as 'chief of my Lady Montague's counsel'.[1] Across
the country similar pockets of Catholicism existed in greater
or less degree, although the ordinary gentry could not count
on the virtual immunity of some members of the peerage.
The transfer of social power from the Catholic aristocracy,
however, was achieved at a price that would be paid by
Elizabeth's successors : the inability of the bishops and church
courts to cope with recusancy led to government dependence
on commissioners chosen mostly from gentry of puritan

sympathies, and the increase of lay power that resulted tended ultimately to weaken royal control of the Church. The obstinacy of a section of the nobility and gentry in clinging to Catholicism made it a matter of concern to the government, for this was the class that mattered. Catholics were never allowed to feel immune from penalty and when the second Lord Burghley was appointed President of the Council of the North in 1599 he at once opened a forceful campaign against recusants in a part of the country that still gave the government some cause for anxiety. Although on the whole the government showed a flexible pragmatism in its treatment of Catholics it put eight members of the laity to death for religion between 1600 and 1603, and a priest was executed in the last weeks of the Queen's life, a reminder that the Catholic minority existed on sufferance and was still regarded as a potentially disloyal faction. Informers continued to feed the Councillors with absurd information, and in 1602 the Bishop of Limerick told Sir Robert Cecil that the spy William Udall had provided information of a secret gold mine supposedly worked by Catholics in Lancashire.[2] This type of rumour found fertile ground among the ordinary people, and the Jesuit Robert Southwell mentioned in a letter to his Roman superiors how the London mob blamed Catholics for every mischief : for the casual fires that broke out in London, for the uproars between gentlemen and apprentices. He even wrote : 'The puritan Hacket has been posted over to us as a papist and is so named to the vulgar sort.'[3] Hacket was a puritan fanatic who had planned to kill the Queen. On a more sophisticated level we see the same attitude at work in Sir Robert Cecil's interjection at the trial of the Earl of Essex : 'God be thanked now we know you; for indeed your religion appears by Blount, Davis, and Tresham, your chief counsellors, and your promising liberty of conscience hereafter.'[4] It is not surprising that this attitude persisted in spite of the decline of English Catholicism, for the Counter Reformation was constantly gaining fresh ground abroad. Ten years after Elizabeth's death a Protestant found little hope in the religious situation, reflecting a doubt as to the staying power of Protestantism in England that, it has been claimed, persisted down to 1640 :[5] 'To what purpose serves it to muster the names of protestants or to vaunt them to be ten to one of the Roman faction as if bare figures of numeration could prevail against a united party, resolved and advised beforehand how to turn their faces with assurance unto all dangers.'[6]

Yet it is doubtful if all members of the younger generation held apocalyptic views about their Catholic neighbours. Many lacked the religious interests of their seniors, and comment has been made on the 'sadly attenuated, definitely cool, even expedient attitude towards Christianity' of the younger Elizabethan generation.[7] Charges of atheism were not uncommon : Sir Walter Raleigh was made the subject of an investigation on this score by the High Commission; Francis Ket, tutor of Christopher Marlowe, was burnt at the stake in 1589 for supposed atheism; and Marlowe himself was summoned before the Council on the same charge. Elizabethan 'atheism' did not necessarily carry its modern meaning, but there is much evidence that many Elizabethans counted religion as but 'a childish toy'. There were also worshippers in the State Church who would have been willing to see their Catholic neighbours left in peace. Elizabeth's favourite godson, Sir John Harington, held that it was unwise to drive Catholics to despair by harsh legislation : 'Is this for the Queen's safety? I cannot dissemble my conscience : I do verily think nothing hath been a greater enemy to her safety.'[8] The son of Sir Nicholas Throckmorton occasionally visited with both the Catholic and the puritan branches of his family, and in the course of a grand tour abroad he called at the Jesuit house in Prague and lodged in a priest's house in Florence, noting also in his diary a city of the Empire where members of all religions lived in amity. As a Justice of the Peace he was pressed after the Gunpowder Plot to certify the names of recusants who refused the oath of allegience and was sent a list of local Catholics for this purpose. He considered it unneighbourly to do anything of the kind and entered a terse comment in his diary : 'I refused to set my hand.'[9]

If Elizabeth had retained the ancient services with moderate changes, as she had originally hoped to do, it is doubtful whether a Catholic survival would have presented any problem to her government. It was the Mass and the whole apparatus of Catholic devotional practice to which men were attached, and it is doubtful if many would have struggled simply to maintain the papal primacy. Paradoxically it was the opposition of the government that strengthened attachment to Rome, and the reign that had opened with Archbishop Heath's admission that Pope Paul IV had been but a stern father ended with one of the appellant priests referring to Pope Clement VIII as 'the good old man'. For the first time in any reign a number of the Catholic clergy had actually made their ecclesiastical studies in Rome and were familiar with its personalities and traditions, while the Jesuits were linked in a brotherhood with a broad international outlook. No doubt as they followed their hole-and-corner ministry in England these priests looked back with a certain nostalgia to the great baroque churches of Rome and their congregations. No doubt too as John Cornelius cared for the Catholics on the Arundell estates he recalled the memorable day when, as a young man, he had preached before the papal Court in the Sistine Chapel, newly decorated by the great Michelangelo. Not many of the recusant Catholics could remember a Catholic England and the peaceful days of Mass attendance with their fellows in the familiar parish church. The aged author of the *Rites of Durham* was possibly one of them, looking back in 1593 with regret to the days when the cathedral bells, now silent, called the townsfolk on Sundays to a sermon preached by one of the monks. By 1603 few Englishmen under middle age could have known any services but the hurried Masses and sermons with everyone alert to dismantle and hide the altar furnishings at the first knocking of the justices. Theirs must have been, in its external manifestations, an austere and puritan worship.

It has been noted that the list of names of the Bridgettine nuns of Syon on the eve of the Dissolution formed, 'a strangely complete epitome' of the more distinguished recusant families of a later age.[10] Syon was a house of rigid observance with a profound spirit of prayer, and here we can possibly see a bridge between the pre-Reformation Catholicism and Counter Reformation piety. But on the whole the secret that kept the rustic recusant squire, with no such family tradition, proud to be reckoned as a papist eludes us, for what in fact had the papacy achieved for the English Catholic body? During the crucial first ten years of the reign it had given practically no guidance, and the breaking of its silence by the Bull of Deposition roused innumerable problems and divisions. But for the genius of William Allen the Catholic priesthood would have died out in England as it did in the Scandinavian countries. Moreover, it was not until seven years after Allen's foundation of the Douai college that the Pope gave financial support, and in later years the Roman authorities preferred to limit the college's entrants rather than to increase its subsidy. The traditional lack of urgency in the Roman Curia allowed the unhappy quarrel between some Jesuits and secular priests to drag on far too long, and when at length – five years before the Queen's death – a form of government was established for the clergy the solution of that particular problem was not a happy one. When we consider the endurance of clergy and laity the words of Clement VIII condemning the idea of toleration fall coldly on the ear : 'Persecution is profitable to the Church.' Yet the link with Rome held and was strengthened and continued to be a source of anxiety to the English government.

It may well be questioned whether the Catholic minority deserved this attention in 1603. Estimates of its numbers vary considerably. It has been suggested that a large percentage of the population were indifferent to the religion and that Catholics numbered perhaps 750 000. Most estimates are far lower, and figures put forward for one county, Yorkshire, suggest that Catholics numbered little more than 2 per cent of the total population but a far higher proportion of the gentry.[11] During the years 1580–2 some 20 per cent of the Yorkshire gentry were charged with recusancy or noncommunicating, but by 1603–4 this figure had risen to almost 33 per cent.[12] Convicted recusants were certainly few in number, but there was a large number of occasional conformists and of those who would have subscribed to Catholicism had the law permitted or the Catholic clergy been free to proselytise. The survival of Catholicism owed a great deal to the occasional conformist, and it is difficult to accept the view that, whatever the theory might be, he was in fact regarded as a lost soul by the Catholic clergy.[13] Huntingdon regarded the Ingleby family of Ripley as among the strongest supporters of Catholicism in Yorkshire: Sir William, who died in 1579, was outwardly a conformist, but his wife and ten children, again with the exception of the eldest son, were strongly recusant. The same pattern was repeated in other families where the occasional conformity of the head made possible the existence of a strong Catholic centre.[14]

It is also impossible to be accurate about the numbers of the clergy, estimates being from 300 to 500 secular priests, some twenty Jesuits and a few Benedictines. In 1608 the archpriest reported to Rome that 500 priests were at work on the English mission. The hunted circumstances of their lives, however, restricted their ministry mainly to recusant Catholics, and at any given time a number of them were to be found in prison. In the familiar phrase of John Donne they were indeed 'men of suppressed and aflicted religion, accustomed to the despite of death'. By contrast it has been estimated that there were some 9 000 members of the State clergy working in 9 244 parishes.[15]

The constant inquiries into the numbers of recusants and their financial standing made by the bishops and local officials at the request of the Council, and the raids and searches of recusant homes, must by 1600 have afforded the government a fairly accurate picture of the minority religion. Lord Burghley had long possessed a map marked with the estates of Lancashire recusants,[16] and the links between the appellant priests, Bishop Bancroft and Sir Robert Cecil gave further detailed information from within the Catholic body. It has been said that the Catholic movement was both invincible to the Queen in terms of religion and invincible to her enemies in terms of politics, but the government did not draw any favourable conclusions from this fact.[17] A Spanish visitor towards the end of the reign wrote home ironically that 'the head of the Church of England and Ireland was to be seen in her old age dancing three or four galliards', but the Queen's dancing days were drawing to an end and she was conscious of being, in the words of a special prayer composed in 1598, 'an old mother in Israel'. It is unlikely that she had any regrets about her religious policy, but she had never shared the crusading zeal of Drake and others of her Protestant subjects, and at one time she had told the disgruntled Netherlanders that the religion of Philip II was good enough for them. In 1591 Elizabeth had invoked the aid of the King of Poland to secure from the Danzig authorities permission for a group of Protestant refugees to have freedom of religious assembly, not a class of people, she added, who were likely to overturn the lawful government.[18] It was never her intention to grant a similar toleration to the English Catholics, and the proclamation of 1602 was her final word.

The eyes of Catholics were now turned to the North, and it was hoped that a new king who had never been excommunicated might grant a modest form of toleration, possibly permitting the private practice of their faith. For five years the Edict of Nantes had shown that freedom of religion, under due safeguards, need not endanger the State, and in Poland two devout Catholic kings had granted toleration to the nobility. More interesting perhaps was the position of religion in the United Provinces of the Netherlands. There a newly established country, still like England at war with Spain, was under greater pressure with a Spanish army at its frontiers. Leaders of a large Catholic minority looked to the Archduke Albert and his wife at Brussels as their sovereign *de iure*, yet although the Dutch government prohibited public Catholic worship penalties for breaches of its religious laws were far milder than in England. Both the Northern and Southern provinces had abandoned the death penalty for religion, and Geyl has considered that the Catholic Church was tacitly

permitted to survive so long as it remained underground.[19]
Expectation of an easing of their burden was shown by
English Catholics during the new monarch's progress to
London, and the second Lord Burghley complained of the
great concourse of Catholic gentlewomen who came to greet
the new Queen at York. So numerous were the petitions that
a Yorkshire recusant's travel permit was issued in 1603 with
a clause that made it conditional on his not joining in any
petition for liberty of conscience or for repeal of the penal
laws.[20] Soon after his arrival in London King James held out
hopes that recusant fines would no longer be levied, and the
Jesuit Henry Garnet, destined to lose his life in the aftermath
of the Gunpowder Plot, wrote of 'a golden time of unexpected
freedom' that was accompanied by the release from prison of
a number of priests. But the golden time was brief, and it was
not long before one of the exiles expressed a different view :
'I perceive there is no hope of amendment in this stinking
king of ours. An ill quarter to look for righteousness at the
hands of a miserable Scot.'[21] Recusant fines were again
exacted, and two priests involved in the Bye Plot were
executed after the plot had been denounced to the government
by loyal Catholic clergy. King James might declare himself
to be averse from persecution, but he had to conciliate a
Protestant Parliament. This strengthened the existing legislation against Catholics, and in a drive to enforce the laws the
death sentence was again carried out. The disillusionment
resulting from this defeat of so many hopes led a small band
of comparatively young men into the disastrous Gunpowder
Plot with its permanent setback to the Catholic cause. Of that
conspiracy the Earl of Northampton commented in 1605 : 'if
any one green leaf for Catholics could have been visibly dis-
cerned they could neither have entered into practice . . . nor
missions and combinations'. The tree remained barren, and
the new reign brought still harsher laws.

Notes and References

CRS = Catholic Record Society; HMC = Historical Manuscripts Commission; CSP = Calendar of State Papers

CHAPTER 1

1 M. M. Knappen, *Tudor Puritanism* (Chicago, 1963), pp. 159–62.
2 R. H. Pogson, 'Cardinal Pole: papal legate to England in Mary Tudor's reign', unpublished PhD thesis (Cambridge, 1973), p. 15. See also: W. Schenk, *Reginald Pole* (London, 1950); D. M. Loades, 'The enforcement of reaction 1553–1558', *Journal of Ecclesiastical History*, vol. 16 (1965); R. H. Pogson, 'Revival and reform in the Marian Church', *Journal of Ecclesiastical History*, vol. 25 (1974).
3 A. G. Dickens, 'Robert Parkyn's narrative of the Reformation', *English Historical Review* (1947), p. 58.
4 J. H. Crehan, 'St Ignatious and Cardinal Pole', *Archivum Historicum SJ*, vol. 25 (1956), p. 72, and 'The return to obedience: new judgement on Cardinal Pole', *The Month* (1955).
5 For the monastic restoration see D. Knowles, *The Religious Orders in England*, vol. 3 (Cambridge, 1959), pp. 421–43.
6 Pogson, op. cit., p. 302.
7 D. M. Loades, *Two Tudor Conspiracies* (Cambridge, 1965), pp. 88, 244; A. Fletcher, *Tudor Rebellions*, 2nd edn (London, 1973), p. 78.
8 C. H. Garrett, *The Marian Exiles: A Study of the Origins of Elizabethan Puritanism* (Cambridge, 1938).
9 W. H. Haller, *Foxe's Book of Martyrs and the Elect Nation* (London, 1963), p. 201; D. M. Loades, *The Oxford Martyrs* (London, 1970); P. Hughes, *The Reformation in England*, vol. 2 (London, 1954).
10 D. Fenlon, *Heresy and Obedience: Cardinal Pole and the Counter Reformation* (Cambridge, 1972), p. 284.
11 See C. Haigh, *Reformation and Resistance in Tudor Lancashire* (Cambridge, 1975).
12 W. R. Trimble, *The Catholic Laity in Elizabethan England* (Cambridge, Mass., 1964), p. 52.
13 Quoted in J. E. Neale, *Essays in Elizabethan History* (London, 1958), p. 142.
14 L. Hicks (ed.), *The Letters and Memorials of Father Robert Persons SJ. 1578–88*, CRS 39 (1942), p. 46.

CHAPTER 2

1 SP Venetian 1558–80, February 1559, p. 26.
2 SP Venetian 1556–7, p. 1075.

3   W. P. Haugaard, 'The coronation of Elizabeth I', *Journal of Ecclesiastical History*, vol. 19 (1968), p. 161.

4   H. Robinson (ed.), *The Zurich Letters*, 1st series (Cambridge, Parker Society, 1842), p. 9.

5   J. E. Neale, *Elizabeth and Her Parliaments*, vol. 1 (London, 1953), pp. 51–84. See also: W. T. McCaffrey, *The Shaping of the Elizabethan Regime* (Princeton, NJ, 1968); M. C. Cross, *The Royal Supremacy in the Elizabethan Church* (London, 1969).

6   G. R. Elton, *England under the Tudors* (London, 1962), p. 275.

7   Robinson, op. cit., 1st series, p. 100

8   W. P. Haugaard, *Elizabeth and the English Reformation* (Cambridge, 1968), p. 36.

9   Haugaard, *Elizabeth and the English Reformation*, p. 321; G. de C. Parmiter, 'Bishop Bonner and the oath', *Recusant History*, vol. 11, no. 5 (1972).

10 H. R. Trevor-Roper, *Historical Essays* (London, 1957), p. 127; A. L. Rowse, *The England of Elizabeth* (London, 1950), p. 389.

11 P. Collinson, *The Elizabethan Puritan Movement* (London, 1967), p. 61.

12 S. E. Lehmberg, *Sir Walter Mildmay and Tudor Government* (University of Texas, 1964), pp. 200–5.

13 R. B. Manning, *Religion and Society in Elizabethan Sussex* (Leicester, 1969), p. 95.

14 F. W. Brooks, *Council of the North* (Historical Association, 1953), p. 24; Manning, op. cit., p. 205; J. S. Leatherbarrow, *Lancashire Elizabethan Recusants* (Chetham Society, 1947), p. 124.

15 A. L. Rowse, *The Expansion of Elizabethan England* (London, 1955), p. 79.

16 Robinson, op. cit., 1st series, p. 87.

17 Haugaard, op. cit., p. 202. In 1573 the same was true of Norwich, and Parker wrote to Cecil during a vacancy in the deanery: 'The church is miserable and hath but six prebendaries, and but one of them at home both needy and poor . . . An hungry, scraping and convetous man as Dean should not do well in that so decayed a church' (quoted in V. J. K. Brook, *A Life of Archbishop Parker* (Oxford, 1962), p. 325).

18 P. H. Hembry, *The Bishops of Bath and Wells 1540–1640* (London, 1967), pp. 154–81.

19 C. Hill, *Economic Problems of the Church* (Oxford, 1956), p. 32. Haugaard criticises this judgement (op. cit., p. 169). For evidence of one courtier's spoliation see E. St J. Brook, *Sir Christopher Hatton* (London, 1946), ch. 15.

20 M. R. O'Day, 'Thomas Bentham: a case study in the problems of the early Elizabethan episcopate', *Journal of Ecclesiastical History*, vol. 23 (1972), p. 155.

21 M. C. Cross, *The Puritan Earl: The Life of Henry Hastings, Third Earl of Huntingdon* (London, 1966), pp. 240, 250.

22 Hill, op. cit., pp. 214, 217.

23 Quoted in M. R. O'Connell, *Thomas Stapleton and the Counter Reformation* (Yale, 1964), p. 137.

24 M. L. Zell, 'Personnel of the clergy in Kent in the Reformation

period', *English Historical Review*, vol. 89 (July 1974); M. Bowker, *The Secular Clergy in the Diocese of Lincoln 1495–1520* (Cambridge, 1968), p. 44.

25 R. Hooker, *Laws of Ecclesiastical Polity*, Everyman edn (London, 1922), vol. 2, bk 5, p. 476; Hill, op. cit., p. 28.

26 Robinson, op. cit., 2nd series, p. 248.

27 J. Booty (ed.), *An Apology of the Church of England* by John Jewel (Cornell, 1963).

28 See P. Hughes, *The Reformation in England*, vol. 3 (1954), pp. 96–101.

29 V. J. K. Brook, op. cit., p. 162.

30 Robinson, op. cit., 1st series, p. 286.

31 Collinson, op. cit., p. 352.

32 K. Thomas, *Religion and the Decline of Magic* (London, 1971), pp. 164, 169.

33 For Greenham see: H. C. Porter, *Reformation and Reaction in Tudor Cambridge* (Cambridge, 1958); M. M. Knappen, *Tudor Puritanism* (Chicago, 1963).

34 H. R. Trevor-Roper, *Historical Essays* 'James I and his bishops', p. 130.

35 C. V. Wedgwood, *The King's Peace* (London, 1955), p. 95. For a harsh judgement on Elizabeth's church policy see R. G. Usher, *The Reconstruction of the English Church*, vol. 1 (London, 1910), p. 6.

CHAPTER 3

1 On this see J. Bossy, 'The character of Elizabethan Catholicism', *Past and Present*, vol. 21 (1962).

2 H. Robinson (ed.), *The Zurich Letters*, 1st series (Cambridge, Parker Society, 1842), p. 39.

3 L. Stone, *Crisis of the Aristocracy 1558–1641* (Oxford, 1965), p. 739. When Lord Vaux was presented for recusancy in 1581 he claimed 'his house to be a parish in itself' (G. Anstruther, *Vaux of Harrowden: A Recusant Family* (Newport, 1953), p. 113). For similar Protestant attitudes see C. Russell, 'Arguments for religious unity in England 1530–1650', *Journal of Ecclesiastical History*, vol. 18 (1967).

4 The 12-penny fine could be levied on more than seventy days in the year. One parishioner warned his churchwardens that 'he cared not if they did present him for it is but a matter of xiid' (R. B. Manning, *Religion and Society in Elizabethan Sussex* (Leicester, 1969), p. 25).

5 A. G. Dickens, 'The extent and character of recusancy in Yorkshire in 1604', *Yorkshire Archaeological Journal*, vol. 37 (1948).

6 M. Bateson (ed.), *A Collection of Original Letters from the Bishop to the Privy Council*, Camden Miscellany 9 (1893).

7 Manning, op. cit., p. 68.

8 J. H. Pollen (ed.), *Unpublished Documents Relating to the English Martyrs 1584–1603*, CRS 5 (1908), p. 72.

9 C. Haigh, *Reformation and Resistance in Tudor Lancashire* (Cambridge, 1975), p. 218.

10 Haigh, op. cit., p. 249; H. Aveling, *Northern Catholics: The Catholic Recusants of the North Riding of Yorkshire 1558–1790* (London, 1966), p. 34.

11 Printed in T. G. Law (ed.), *A Catechisme of Christian Doctrine necessarie for Children and ignorante People* by Laurence Vaux (Chetham Society, vol. 4, new series, 1885), pp. xxxii–ix.

12 J. E. Neale, *Elizabeth and Her Parliaments*, vol. 1 (London, 1953), pp. 118, 120.

13 J. S. Leatherbarrow, *Lancashire Elizabethan Recusants* (Chetham Society, 3rd series, no. 19, 1947), p. 24; K. R. Wark, *Elizabethan Recusancy in Cheshire* (Manchester, 1971), p. 8.

14 Aveling, op. cit., p. 12.

15 J. S. Cockburn, *A History of English Assize 1558–1714* (Cambridge, 1972), p. 193.

16 J. B. Black, *The Reign of Elizabeth*, Oxford History of England series (Oxford, 1959), p. 1.

17 Witness the case of the minister who permitted a Catholic to attempt his conversion and was loath to displease him 'for that he had a living at his commandment' (A. Davidson, 'The recusancy of Ralph Sheldon', *Worcestershire Recusant*, vol. 12 (December, 1968), p. 7).

18 A. Davidson, 'A further note on judges', *Worcestershire Recusant*, vol. 20 (December, 1972), p. 80.

19 R. Marchant, *The Church under the Law* (Cambridge, 1960), p. 227. By the 1590s about 1,000 Lancastrians were being excommunicated at each visitation (Haigh, op. cit., p. 235).

20 C. Hill, *Society and Puritanism in Pre-Revolutionary England* (London, 1964), p. 371.

21 Manning, op. cit., p. 55; H. Aveling, 'The Catholic recusants of the West Riding of Yorkshire 1558–1790', *Proceedings of the Leeds Philosophical and Literary Society*, vol. 10, pt 6 (1963), p. 203.

22 D. Mathew, *The Celtic Peoples and Renaissance Europe* (London, 1933), p. 21.

23 Quoted in A. J. Loomie, *The Spanish Elizabethans: The English Exiles at the Court of Philip II* (New York, 1963), p. 38.

24 For the Northern rising see: A. Fletcher, *Tudor Rebellions*, 2nd edn (London, 1973); M. E. James, 'The concept of order and the northern rising of 1569', *Past and Present*, vol. 60 (1973), and *Change and Continuity in the Tudor North* (York, 1965). In later years Dr Allen in his *Defence* and the Jesuit Southwell in his *Supplication* both referred to the rising as a religious rebellion.

25 Aveling, 'Catholic recusants of the West Riding', p. 207.

26 W. R. Trimble, *The Catholic Laity in Elizabethan England* (Cambridge, Mass., 1964), pp. 49–60.

27 Papal attempts at negotiations are detailed in C. G. Bayne, *Anglo-Roman Relations 1558–1565* (Oxford, 1913).

28 Bayne, op. cit., p. 110.

29 The Latin text of the Bull with a translation is printed in G. R. Elton, *The Tudor Constitution* (Cambridge, 1960), pp. 414–18.

30 J. E. Paul, 'Hampshire recusants in the time of Elizabeth I, with special reference to Winchester', *Proceedings of the Hampshire Field Club*, vol. 21, pt 2 (1959).

31 See C. Z. Weiner, 'The beleaguered isle: a study of Elizabethan and early Jacobean anti-Catholicism', *Past and Present*, vol. 51 (May, 1971).
32 L. von Pastor, *The History of the Popes*, trans. R. F. Ker, vol. 18 (London, 1928), pp. 219–21.

CHAPTER 4

1 Star Chamber, 15 June 1570; J. E. Neale, *Elizabeth and Her Parliaments*, vol. 1 (London, 1953), pp. 191–2.
2 Neale, op. cit., vol. 1, p. 225. Legislation printed by G. R. Elton, *The Tudor Constitution* (Cambridge, 1960).
3 See R. B. Manning, *Religion and Society in Elizabethan Sussex* (Leicester, 1969), p. 135.
4 Neale, op. cit., vol. 1, p. 286.
5 J. S. Leatherbarrow, *Lancashire Elizabethan Recusants* (Chetham Society, 1947), pp. 90–2.
6 Manning, op. cit., pp. 78–9.
7 W. R. Trimble, *The Catholic Laity in Elizabethan England* (Cambridge, Mass., 1964), p. 76.
8 F. A. Youngs, 'Definitions of treason in an Elizabethan proclamation', *Historical Journal*, vol. 14 (1971), p. 675.
9 Neale, op. cit., vol. 1, p. 383.
10 Neale, op. cit., vol. 1, pp. 388–9.
11 Neale, op. cit., vol. 2 (1957), p. 29.
12 R. B. Manning, 'Richard Shelley of Warminghurst and the Catholic petition for toleration of 1585', *Recusant History*, vol. 6 (1962), p. 265.
13 J. E. Paul, 'Hampshire recusants in the time of Elizabeth I, with special reference to Winchester', *Proceedings of the Hampshire Field Club*, vol. 21, pt 2 (1959).
14 Cal. SP Dom. 1547–80, p. 549.
15 See: H. Bowler (ed.), *Recusant Roll No. 2, 1593–4*, CRS 57 (1965), introduction; F. X. Walker, 'The implementation of the Elizabethan statutes against recusants 1581–1603', unpublished PhD thesis (London, 1961).
16 R. C. Bald (ed.), *An Humble Supplication to Her Maiestie* by Robert Southwell (Cambridge, 1953), p. 43.
17 Trimble, op. cit., pp. 246–8.
18 Bowler, op. cit., p. cxi.
19 R. B. Manning, 'Elizabethan recusancy commissions', *Historical Journal*, vol. 15 (1972), p. 23.
20 Neale, op. cit., vol. 2. p. 281.
21 P. L. Hughes and J. F. Larkin, *Tudor Proclamations*, vol. 3 (New Haven, 1964–9), p. 86.
22 Printed in Elton, op. cit., p. 427.
23 Neale, op. cit., vol. 2, pp. 396, 399.
24 K. R. Wark, *Elizabethan Recusancy in Cheshire* (Manchester, 1971), p. 115.
25 H. Aveling, *Northern Catholics: The Catholic Recusants of the*

North Riding of Yorkshire 1558–1790 (London, 1966), p. 129. Information on the fining system will be found in Walker, op. cit.

26 M. O'Dwyer, 'Catholic recusants in Essex *c.* 1580–1600', unpublished MA thesis (London, 1960), and 'Recusants' fines in Essex', *The Month* (July 1958).

27 Manning, *Religion and Society*, pp. 138–40.

28 Wark, op. cit., p. 59.

29 Manning, *Religion and Society*, p. 141.

30 Leatherbarrow, op. cit., pp. 99, 140.

31 Trimble, op. cit., pp. 207–8.

32 Trimble, op. cit., pp. 245–6.

33 Aveling, op. cit., p. 125; Bowler, op. cit.

CHAPTER 5

1 See R. B. Wernham, *Before the Armada* (London, 1966).

2 G. Mattingley, *The Defeat of the Spanish Armada* (London, 1959), p. 27.

3 J. E. Neale, *Queen Elizabeth* (London, 1934), p. 247; C. Read, *Mr Secretary Walsingham and the Policy of Queen Elizabeth*, vol. 3 (Oxford, 1925), p. 217.

4 J. Lynch, 'Philip II and the papacy', *Transactions of the Royal Historical Society*, 5th series, vol. XI (1961), pp. 23–42.

5 A. J. Loomie, 'Philip II's Armada proclamation of 1597', *Recusant History*, vol. 12, no. 5 (1974), p. 217.

6 The Ridolfi and other plots are described in detail by C. Read, op. cit., 3 vols. See also J. H. Pollen, *The English Catholics in the Reign of Elizabeth* (London, 1920).

7 A. C. Southern, *Elizabethan Recusant Prose 1559–1582* (London, 1950), p. 544.

8 15 July 1580. P. L. Hughes and J. F. Larkin, *Tudor Proclamations*, vol. 2 (New Haven, 1964–9), p. 469.

9 Neale, *Elizabeth and Her Parliaments*, vol. 1 (London, 1953), p. 313.

10 P. Hughes, *Rome and the Counter Reformation in England* (London, 1942), pp. 210–26.

11 C. Read, *Lord Burghley and Queen Elizabeth* (London, 1960), p. 499.

12 L. Hicks, 'The strange case of Dr William Parry: the career of an agent-provocateur', *Studies* (1948); Read, *Walsingham*, vol. 2, pp. 399–405.

13 H. Mss. C., *Various Collections*, vol. 3, p. 125.

14 J. Ayre (ed.), *The Sermons of Edwin Sandys* (Cambridge, Parker Society, 1841), p. 72.

15 W. K. Clay, *Liturgies and Occasional Forms of Prayer Set Forth in the Reign of Queen Elizabeth* (Parker Society, 1847), pp. 505, 688.

16 C. Hill, *Anti-Christ in the Seventeenth Century* (London, 1971), pp. 1–19.

17 S. E. Lehmberg, *Sir Walter Mildmay and Tudor Government* (University of Texas, 1964), p. 158.

18 W. H. Haller, *Foxe's Book of Martyrs and the Elect Nation* (London, 1963).

19 C. Z. Weiner, 'The beleaguered isle: a study of Elizabethan and early Jacobean anti-Catholicism', *Past and Present*, vol. 51 (May 1971), p. 27.

20 Hughes and Larkin, op. cit., vol. 2, p. 489.

21 R. B. Kingdon (ed.), *A True, Sincere and Modest Defense of English Catholics* by William Allen (New York, 1965), p. 72.

22 K. R. Wark, *Elizabethan Recusancy in Cheshire* (Manchester, 1971), p. 89.

23 J. H. Pollen (ed.), *Unpublished Documents Relating to the English Martyrs 1584–1603*, CRS 5 (1908), p. 325.

24 Hughes and Larkin, op. cit., vol. 2, pp. 518–20.

25 Printed in P. Caraman, *The Other Face: Catholic Life under Elizabeth I* (London, 1960), pp. 258–60; R. Lacey, *Sir Walter Ralegh* (London, 1973), p. 113.

26 J. Lecler, *Toleration and the Reformation*, trans. by T. L. Westow, vol. 2 (London, 1960), p. 114.

27 R. B. Kingdon (ed.), *The Execution of Justice in England* by William Cecil (New York, 1965).

28 Kingdon (ed.), *The Execution of Justice in England*, pp. 37–9.

29 R. C. Bald (ed.), *An Humble Supplication to Her Maiestie* by Robert Southwell (Cambridge, 1953), p. 34.

30 Kingdon (ed.), *A True, Sincere and Modest Defense . . .*, pp. 121–2.

31 L. Hicks (ed.), *The Letters and Memorials of Father Robert Persons SJ. 1578–88*, CRS 39 (1942), p. 147.

32 CSP Venetian 1603–7, p. 230.

33 T. H. Clancy, 'English Catholics and the papal deposing power', *Recusant History*, vol. 6 (1961–2), p. 115.

34 Pollen, *English Catholics*, op. cit., p. 294.

35 Hughes, op cit., p. 189; L. von Pastor, *The History of the Popes*, trans. R. F. Ker, vol. 18 (London, 1928), pp. 219–21.

36 W. R. Trimble, *The Catholic Laity in Elizabethan England* (Cambridge, Mass., 1964), p. 63.

37 J. Brodrick, *Robert Bellarmine*, vol. 1 (London, 1928), pp. 270 ff.

38 J. Bossy, 'The character of Elizabethan Catholicism', *Past and Present*, vol. 21 (1962).

39 Clancy, art. cit., p. 206.

40 Clancy, art. cit., p. 132.

41 HMC, *Various Collections*, vol. 3, p. 38.

42 Read, op. cit., p. 431; J. H. Pollen, 'An anti-Catholic forgery', *The Month* (1911).

43 HMC, *Various Collections*, vol. 3, p. 51.

44 CSP Dom. Addenda 1580–1625, pp. 297, 411.

CHAPTER 6

1 T. H. Clancy, *Papist Pamphleteers* (Chicago, 1964), p. 8.

2 R. Lechat, *Les Réfugiés anglais dans les Pays-Bas Espagnols 1558–1603* (Louvain, 1914), p. 24; P. Guilday, *The English Catholic Refugees on the Continent 1558–1795* (London, 1914), p. 5.

3 W. R. Trimble, *The Catholic Laity in Elizabethan England* (Cambridge, Mass., 1964), pp. 18, 39.

4   A. J. Loomie, *The Spanish Elizabethans: The English Exiles at the Court of Philip II* (New York, 1963), p. 30.

5   Lechat, op. cit., p. 107; Guilday, op. cit., p. 12.

6   A. C. Southern, *Elizabethan Recusant Prose 1559–1582* (London, 1950), p. 22.

7   R. B. Manning, *Religion and Society in Elizabethan Sussex* (Leicester, 1969), p. 44. See also J. McConica, *English Humanists and Reformation Politics* (Oxford, 1965), p. 292.

8   Southern, op. cit., pp. 60–6.

9   T. G. Law (ed.), *A Catechisme of Christian Doctrine necessarie for Children and ignorante People* by Laurence Vaux (Chetham Society, vol. 4, new series, 1885). For the practice of catechising children see J. Bossy, 'The Counter Reformation and the people of Europe,' *Past and Present*, vol. 47 (1970).

10 Southern, op. cit., pp. 231–54; P. Hughes, *The Reformation in England*, vol. 3 (London, 1954), pp. 299–302.

11 J. H. Pollen (ed.), *Unpublished Documents Relating to the English Martyrs 1584–1603*, CRS 5 (1908), pp. 35–6.

12 On Munday see C. Turner, *Anthony Munday: An Elizabethan Man of Letters* (University of California, 1928), p. 58.

13 P. L. Hughes and J. F. Larkin, *Tudor Proclamations*, vol. 2 (New Haven, 1964–9), p. 489.

14 Southern, op. cit., p. 276; J. Gillow, *Biographical Dictionary of the English Catholics*, vol. 5 (London, 1885–1903), p. 277.

15 T. F. Knox (ed.), *The Letters and Memorials of William, Cardinal Allen* (London, 1882), p. 25.

16 L. Rostenberg, *The Minority Press and the English Crown 1558–1625: A Study in Repression* (1971), p. 49.

17 Rostenberg, op. cit., p. 23.

18 The only biography of Allen is by M. Haile, *An Elizabethan Cardinal* (London, 1914).

19 T. F. Knox (ed.), *The First and Second Diaries of the English College, Douay* (London, 1878), p. xxiii.

20 For Owen Lewis see: D. Mathew, *The Celtic Peoples and Renaissance Europe* (London, 1933), p. 76; G. Anstruther, *The Venerabile* (Rome, 1962).

21 For the early days of the Douai college see: Guilday, op. cit., pp. 63–120; A. C. F. Beales, *Education under Penalty* (London, 1963), pp. 39–42.

22 E. Rose, *Cases of Conscience* (Cambridge, 1975); Hughes, op. cit., p. 292.

23 Allen to Richard Hopkins 1579: Knox, *Letters and Memorials*, p. 76.

24 Beales, op. cit., pp. 117–19.

25 For Barrett and Worthington see: Guilday, op. cit., p. 106; G. Anstruther, *Elizabethan Seminary Priests 1558–1603* (Ushaw, 1966).

26 The list of foundations is given by Beales, op. cit., p. 273.

27 For the Roman college see: A. O. Meyer, *England and the Catholic Church under Queen Elizabeth*, trans. by J. R. McKee, 2nd edn (London, 1967). pp. 99–114; Beales, op. cit., pp. 39–45.

28 L. Hicks (ed.), *The Letters and Memorials of Father Robert Persons SJ. 1578–88*, CRS 39 (1942), pp. 3, 5, 10.

29 Meyer, op. cit., p. 117.
30 For the colleges in Spain see: L. Hicks, 'Father Persons and the seminaries in Spain', *The Month* (July 1931); Beales, op. cit., pp. 45–8, 123–5; Loomie, op. cit., p. 187.
31 For Creswell see Loomie, op. cit., p. 183.
32 H. Chadwick, *St Omers to Stonyhurst* (London, 1962); Beales, op. cit., p. 64.
33 Quoted in Beales, op. cit., p. 70.
34 Dom. Cal. Eliz. 1598–1601, 13 November 1599; quoted in Guilday, op. cit., p. 258, n. 1.
35 D. M. Lunn, 'Benedictine reform movements in the later Middle Ages', *Downside Review* (October 1973).
36 J. McCann and H. Connolly (eds), *Memorials of Fr Augustine Baker (1575–1641)*, CRS 33 (1933); D. M. Lunn, 'The origins and early development of the revived English Benedictine congregation 1558–1647', unpublished PhD thesis (Cambridge, 1970); D. Knowles, *The Religious Orders in England*, vol. 3 (Cambridge, 1959), pp. 445–55.
37 D. Rogers, 'An English Friar Minim in France', *Recusant History*, vol. 10, no. 5 (1970).
38 H. Bremond, *Histoire du sentiment religieux en France*, vol. 2 (Paris, 1920), pp. 152–68.

CHAPTER 7

1 T. N. Veech, *Dr Nicholas Sander and the English Reformation 1530–1581* (Louvain, 1935).
2 A. L. Rowse, *Raleigh and the Throckmortons* (London, 1962), p. 148.
3 C. Read, *Lord Burghley and Queen Elizabeth* (London, 1960), p. 242.
4 For Englefield see the essay by A. J. Loomie in his *The Spanish Elizabethans: The English Exiles at the Court of Philip II* (New York, 1963).
5 L. Hicks (ed.), *The Letters and Memorials of Father Robert Persons SJ. 1578–88*, CRS 39 (1942); J. H. Pollen (ed.), *Miscellanea*, Memoirs of Robert Persons SJ (continued vol. 4), CRS 2 (1905).
6 Pollen, op. cit., pp. 21–2; J. H. Pollen (ed.), *Miscellanea*, Memoirs of Robert Persons SJ (cont. and concl.), CRS 4 (London, 1907).
7 For Dr Lewis and the Pagets see: D. Mathew, *The Celtic Peoples and Renaissance Europe* (London, 1933), pp. 76–86, 87–91; G. Anstruther, *The Venerabile* (Rome, 1962).
8 Hicks, op. cit., p. 246. Persons, however, further tells the queen that he has received a 'new order and commandment . . . to renew or rather continue our suit to the Prince of Parma'.
9 Hicks, op. cit., pp. 292–4, 306–9.
10 T. F. Knox (ed.), *The Letters and Memorials of William, Cardinal Allen* (London, 1882).
11 L. Hicks, *An Elizabethan Problem: Some Aspects of the Careers of Two Exile Adventurers* (London, 1964), p. 73, which is largely concerned with Morgan's career.

12 For Wright see A. O. Meyer, *England and the Catholic Church under Queen Elizabeth*, trans. J. R. McKee, 2nd edn (London, 1967), p. 355.
13 L. Hicks, 'Father Robert Persons and the Book of Succession', *Recusant History*, vol. 4, no. 3 (1957), p. 104; T. H. Clancy, *Papist Pamphleteers* (Chicago, 1964), p. 57.
14 C. H. McIlwain (ed.), *The Political Works of James I* (Cambridge, Mass., 1918), p. li.
15 For the layman's view of political priests see J. Bossy, 'The character of Elizabethan Catholicism', *Past and Present*, vol. 21 (1962).
16 T. H. Clancy, 'Notes on Persons' Memorial for the Reformation of England (1596)', *Recusant History*, vol. 5, no. 1 (1959), p. 17; J. E. Parish, 'Robert Parsons, English Jesuit', unpublished PhD thesis (Columbia University, 1951).
17 J. J. Scarisbrick, 'Robert Persons' plans for the True Reformation of England', in N. McKendrick (ed.), *Historical Perspectives: Studies in English Thought and Society* (1974).
18 Pollen, op. cit., p. 213.
19 J. P. Driscoll, 'The supposed sources of Persons' Christian Directory', *Recusant History*, vol. 5, no. 6 (1960), p. 236.
20 See Loomie's essay on Stanley, op. cit.
21 D. M. Lunn, 'Chaplains to the English regiment in Spanish Flanders 1605–6', *Recusant History*, vol. 11, no. 3 (1971).
22 See A. C. F. Beales, *Education under Penalty* (London, 1963), p. 53.
23 Hicks, *Elizabethan Problem*, pp. 215–16.
24 J. E. Neale, *Essays in Elizabethan History* (London, 1958), p. 164.
25 Loomie, op. cit., p. 73.
26 A. G. R. Petti, *The Letters and Despatches of Richard Verstegen, 1550–1640*, CRS 52 (1959).
27 For Hugh Owen see: Loomie, op. cit.; H. Dodd, 'The Spanish treason, the Gunpowder plot and the Catholic refugees', *English Historical Review* (1938).
28 Loomie, op. cit., p. 89.

CHAPTER 8

1 *Thomas Bels Motives* (1593), quoted in C. Z. Weiner, 'The beleaguered isle: a study of Elizabethan and early Jacobean anti-Catholicism', *Past and Present*, vol. 51 (May 1971).
2 L. Stone, *Crisis of the Aristocracy 1558–1641* (Oxford, 1965), p. 741.
3 J. Bossy, 'The English Catholics and the French marriage 1577–81', *Recusant History*, vol. 5, no. 1 (1959), p. 2; L. Hotson, *I, William Shakespeare* (London, 1937), p. 170.
4 J. S. Cockburn, *A History of the English Assizes 1558–1714* (Cambridge, 1972), p. 215.
5 K. R. Wark, *Elizabethan Recusancy in Cheshire* (Manchester, 1971), pp. 33, 116.
6 H. Aveling, *Northern Catholics: The Catholic Recusants of the North Riding of Yorkshire 1558–1790* (London, 1966), p. 141.

7   C. Read, *Mr Secretary Walsingham and the Polity of Queen Elizabeth*, vol. 3 (Oxford, 1925), p. 410.
8   A. H. Smith, *County and Court: Government and Politics in Norfolk 1558–1603* (Oxford, 1974), p. 214; *Worcestershire Recusant*, vol. 14 (December, 1969), p. 44.
9   Aveling, op. cit., p. 134.
10   Cockburn, op. cit., p. 207.
11   R. B. Manning, *Religion and Society in Elizabethan Sussex* (Leicester, 1969), p. 245.
12   HMC, *Various Collections*, vol. 3, p. 98.
13   Cockburn, op. cit., p. 214.
14   H. Aveling, 'The Catholic recusants of the West Riding of Yorkshire 1558–1790', *Proceedings of the Leeds Philosophical and Literary Society*, vol. 10, pt 6 (1963), p. 230.
15   J. Wake, *The Brudenells of Dene*, 2nd edn (London, 1954), p. 78.
16   G. Anstruther, *Vaux of Harrowden: A Recusant Family* (Newport, 1953), p. 219.
17   J. E. Neale, *The Elizabethan House of Commons* (London, 1949), pp. 185–8.
18   Neale, op. cit., p. 135.
19   E. A. Barnard, *The Sheldons* (Cambridge, 1936), p. 35.
20   Aveling, *Northern Catholics*, pp. 140–1.
21   H. Aveling (ed.), *Miscellanea*, Recusancy Papers of the Meynell Family, CRS 56 (1964), p. xxviii.
22   G. H. Ryan and L. J. Redstone, *Timperley of Hintlesham* (1931), p. 52.
23   A. Davidson, 'The recusancy of Ralph Sheldon', *Worcestershire Recusant* vol. 12 (December, 1968), p. 1; Hotson, op. cit., p. 30.
24   J. H. Pollen (ed.), *Miscellanea*, Memoirs of Robert Persons SJ, CRS 2 (1905), pp. 71–3.
25   H. C. Porter, *Reformation and Reaction in Tudor Cambridge* (Cambridge, 1958), p. 236.
26   E. Walsh and A. Forster, 'The recusancy of the Brandlings', *Recusant History*, vol. 10, no. 1 (1969), p. 35.
27   Aveling, *Northern Catholics*, p. 191.
28   A. C. F. Beales, *Education under Penalty* (London, 1963), p. 79, and 'A biographical catalogue of Catholic schoolmasters 1558–1603', *Recusant History*, vol. 7, no. 6 (1964).
29   See N. Birt, *The Elizabethan Settlement: A Study of Contemporary Documents* (London, 1907), p. 385.
30   Beales, op. cit., p. 58.
31   Stone, op. cit., p. 739.
32   Aveling, *Northern Catholics*, p. 203.
33   Wark, op. cit., pp. 108–14.
34   J. H. Pollen (ed.), *Unpublished Documents Relating to the English Martyrs 1584–1603*, CRS 5 (1908), p. 126.
35   Beales, op. cit., p. 86.
36   See: M. H. Curtis, *Oxford and Cambridge in Transition 1558–1642* (Oxford, 1959), p. 170.
37   Aveling, *Northern Catholics*, p. 77.

38 A. C. Southern (ed.), *An Elizabethan Recusant House* (1627) by Richard Smith (London, 1954), p. 20.

39 Aveling, *Northern Catholics*, p. 254.

40 G. Anstruther, *Elizabethan Seminary Priests 1558–1603* (Ushaw, 1966), p. 88; A. L. Rowse, *Raleigh and the Throckmortons* (London, 1962), p. 181; L. Hicks (ed.), *The Letters and Memorials of Father Robert Persons SJ. 1578–88*, CRS 39 (1942), p. 77.

41 Wark, op. cit., pp. 124–5.

42 D. Mathew, 'The library at Naworth', in D. Woodruff (ed.), *Essays for Hilaire Belloc* (London, 1942), H. S. Reinmuth Jr, 'Lord William Howard (1563–1640) and his Catholic associations', *Recusant History*, vol. 12, no. 5 (1974); A. L. Rowse, 'Nicholas Roscarrock and his lives of the saints', in N. McKendrick (ed.), *Historical Perspectives: Studies in English Thought and Society* (London, 1974); J. H. Pollen (ed.), *The Venerable Philip Howard, Earl of Arundel 1557–1595*, CRS 21 (1919).

43 H. Aveling, 'Marriages of Catholic recusants', *Journal of Ecclesiastical History*, vol. 14 (1963).

44 Wark, op. cit., pp. 168–9.

45 Wark, op. cit., pp. 6, 98. A prison was reserved for recusant women at Hull; see J. H. Hirst, *Blockhouses of Kingston-upon-Hull* (Hull, 1913).

46 H. Bowler (ed.), *Recusant Roll No. 2, 1593–4*, CRS 57 (1965), introduction, p. xxxiv.

47 Manning, op. cit., p. 260; M. Finch, *The Wealth of Five Northamptonshire Families 1540–1640* (Northamptonshire Record Society 19, 1956); Aveling, 'Catholic recusants of the West Riding', pp. 223, 225.

48 M. Hodgetts, 'Elizabethan recusancy in Worcestershire', *Transactions of the Worcestershire Archaeological Society*, 3rd series, vol. 1 (1965–7), p. 73; Cockburn, op. cit., p. 74.

49 Aveling, 'Catholic recusants of the West Riding', p. 214.

50 D. J. Steel and E. Samuel, *Sources for Roman Catholic and Jewish Genealogy and Family History* (London, 1974), p. 878.

51 R. Mathias, *The Whitsun Riot* (London, 1963); J. S. Leatherbarrow, *Lancashire Elizabethan Recusants* (Chetham Society, 1947), pp. 131–5, 145–6, C. Haigh, *Reformation and Resistance in Tudor Lancashire* (Cambridge, 1975), p. 328.

CHAPTER 9

1 H. Aveling, *Northern Catholics: The Catholic Recusants of the North Riding of Yorkshire 1558–1790* (London, 1966), p. 181.

2 K. R. Wark, *Elizabethan Recusantcy in Cheshire* (Manchester, 1971), p. 65.

3 J. H. Pollen (ed.), *Unpublished Documents Relating to the English Martyrs 1584–1603*, CRS 5 (1908), pp. 231–2; P. Caraman (ed.), *William Weston: The Autobigraphy of an Elizabethan* (London, 1955), appendix C.

4 P. V. McGrath and J. Rowe, 'The recusancy of Sir Thomas Cornwallis', *Proceedings of the Suffolk Institute of Archaeology*,

vol. 28, pt 3 (1961); A. H. Smith, *County and Court: Government and Politics in Norfolk 1558–1603* (Oxford, 1974), ch. 10.

5　Correspondence of Tresham was discovered in 1828 walled in at Rushton, probably at the time of the Gunpowder Plot. It was printed in HMC, *Various Collections*, vol. 3 (1903–4).

6　M. E. Finch, *The Wealth of Five Northamptonshire Families 1540–1640* (Northamptonshire Record Society 19, 1956). See also J. H. Hexter, *Reappraisals in History* (London, 1961), appendix C, p. 160.

7　Finch, op. cit., p. 76 and appendix VII, p. 79.

8　G. Austruther, *Vaux of Harrowden: A Recusant Family* (Newport, 1953).

9　J. Morris, *The Troubles of our Catholic Forefathers*, 1st series (London, 1872) prints the life written probably by Tregian's son Charles; CRS 32 (London, 1932) prints the brief life written by his grandson. See also: P. A. Boyan and G. R. Lamb, *Francis Tregian: A Cornish Recusant* (London, 1954); A. L. Rowse, *Tudor Cornwall* (London, 1941), p. 350.

CHAPTER 10

1　H. Aveling, *Northern Catholics: The Catholic Recusants of the North Riding of Yorkshire 1558–1790* (London, 1966), pp. 34–5; J. Bossy, 'The character of Elizabethan Catholicism', *Past and Present*, vol. 21 (1962).

2　A. M. Hodgson, 'Note on Paul Spencer, seminary priest', *Worcestershire Recusant* (July 1964), p. 32.

3　C. Haigh, *Reformation and Resistance in Tudor Lancashire* (Cambridge, 1975), p. 277.

4　H. Aveling, *Post Reformation Catholicism in East Yorkshire* (East Yorkshire Local History Society, 1960), p. 11.

5　J. Pollen (ed.), *Unpublished Documents Relating to the English Martyrs 1584–1603*, CRS 5 (1908), p. 74.

6　C. W. Clarke, 'Simon Southern's early life', *Worcestershire Recusant* (June 1968), p. 1.

7　J. S. Leatherbarrow, *Lancashire Elizabethan Recusants* (Chetham Society, 1947), pp. 90–2.

8　A. C. Southern (ed.), *An Elizabethan Recusant House* (1627) by Richard Smith (London, 1954), p. 20.

9　A. L. Rowse, *The England of Elizabeth* (London, 1950), p. 423, n. 2.

10　*Miscellanea*, Lord Burghley's map of Lancashire 1590, annotated J. Gillow, CRS 4 (1907), p. 91.

11　On this see J. Bossy, 'Rome and the Elizabethan Catholics: a question of geography', *The Historical Journal*, vol. 7, no. 1 (1964).

12　L. Hicks (ed.), *The Letters and Memorials of Father Robert Persons SJ. 1578–88*, CRS 39 (1942), p. 216.

13　Pollen, op. cit., p. 30.

14　C. Devlin, *The Life of Robert Southwell* (London, 1956), p. 114. For Richard Bold see Leatherbarrow, op. cit., pp. 86–7.

15　P. Caraman (ed.), *William Weston: The Autobiography of an Elizabethan* (London, 1955), p. 45.

16 Devlin, op. cit., p. 181.

17 M. Hodgetts, 'Elizabethan priest holes', *Recusant History*, vol. 11, no. 6 (1972), p. 279; vol. 12, no. 3 (1973), p. 1 and no. 4 (1974), p. 171; vol. 13, no. 1 (1975), p. 99, vol. 13, no. 4 (1976), p. 254. G. Squiers, *Secret Hiding Places* (1934).

18 H. Foley (ed.), *Records of the English Province of the Society of Jesus*, vol. 2 (1877–83), pp. 3–6. See also B. Bassett, *The English Jesuits* (London, 1967), pp. 140–2.

19 Quoted in Devlin, op. cit., p. 159. For Tyrell see J. Morris, *The Troubles of our Catholic Forefathers*, vol. 2 (London, 1875), p. 287.

20 Pollen, op. cit., p. 47. An assistant gaoler admitted under examination that he had been a papist for the past three years: J. E. Paul, 'Hampshire recusants in the time of Elizabeth I, with special reference to Winchester', *Proceedings of the Hampshire Field Club*, vol. 21, pt 2 (1959), p. 74.

21 K. R. Wark, *Elizabethan Recusancy in Cheshire* (Manchester, 1971), p. 71.

22 C. Dodd, *The Church History of England*, with notes, additions and a continuation by M. A. Tierney, vol. 3 (London, 1839–43), pp. 75–148.

23 Quoted in Devlin, op. cit., p. 255.

24 Aveling, *Northern Catholics*, op. cit., pp. 170–4.

25 J. Bossy, *The English Catholic Community 1570–1850* (London, 1975), pp. 199, 415.

26 P. L. Hughes and J. F. Larkin, *Tudor Proclamations*, vol. 3 (New Haven, 1964–9), pp. 86–92.

27 Quoted in A. O. Meyer, *England and the Catholic Church under Queen Elizabeth*, trans. by J. R. McKee, 2nd edn (London, 1967), pp. 352–3. He comments: 'It spoke every language, and was at once an indictment and a justification.'

28 R. C. Bald (ed.), *An Humble Supplication to Her Maiestie* by Robert Southwell (Cambridge, 1953), p. 5.

29 W. Perkins, *A Reformed Catholike* (1598), p. 346, quoted in E. Rose, *Cases of Conscience* (Cambridge, 1975), p. 94.

30 H. R. Trevor-Roper, *Religion, the Reformation and Social Change*, 2nd edn (London, 1972), p. 138; A. L. Rowse, *The Elizabethan Renaissance* (London, 1971), vol. 1, ch. 9.

31 K. Thomas, *Religion and the Decline of Magic* (London, 1971), p. 68.

32 Thomas, op. cit., p. 484.

CHAPTER 11

1 J. E. Neale, *Elizabeth and Her Parliaments*, vol. 2 (London, 1957), p. 331.

2 The standard life of Campion is R. Simpson, *Edmund Campion* (London, 1896); short life also by E. Waugh, *Edmund Campion* (London, 1947).

3 The 'brag' is printed in Simpson, op. cit., and Waugh, op. cit.

4 Cited in G. Anstruther, *Vaux of Harrowden: A Recusant Family* (Newport, 1953), p. 115.

5 A. L. Rowse, *The England of Elizabeth* (London, 1950), p. 54.
6 See P. Caraman, *Henry Garnet 1555–1606* (London, 1964), ch. 13.
7 J. Morris, *The Troubles of our Catholic Forefathers*, 1st series (London, 1972), p. 207.
8 P. Caraman (ed.), *John Gerard: The Autobiography of an Elizabethan* (London, 1956).
9 Caraman, *John Gerard*, op. cit., p. 169.
10 For Jesuit spirituality and the *Exercises* see H. O. Evennett, *The Spirit of the Counter-Reformation* (Cambridge, 1968).

CHAPTER 12

1 T. G. Law, *A Historical Sketch of the Conflicts between Jesuits and Seculars in the Reign of Queen Elizabeth* (London, 1889); *The Archpriest Controversy* (Camden Society, 1898) 2 vols. J. H. Pollen, *The Institution of the Archpriest Blackwell* (London, 1920). J. Bossy, *The English Catholic Community 1570–1850* (London, 1975). P. Renold (ed.), *The Wisbech Stirs 1595–1598*, CRS 51 (1958).
2 For Bagshaw and Bluet see G. Anstruther, *Elizabethan Seminary Priests 1558–1603* (Ushaw, 1966).
3 Renold, op. cit., p. xvi.
4 The papal brief is printed in C. Dodd, *The Church History of England*, with notes, additions and a continuation by M. A. Tierney (5 vols, London, 1839–43), vol. 3, appendix xxi, p. cxix.
5 H. Ely, *Briefe Notes* (Paris, 1603), p. 104.
6 C. Bagshaw, *A True Relation of the Faction begun at Wisbech* (1601), printed in T. G. Law, *Conflicts between Jesuits and Seculars in the Reign of Queen Elizabeth* (London, 1889).
7 Law, op. cit., p. lxxix, and *The Archpriest Controversy*, vol. 1 (Camden Society, 1898), pp. 210–26.
8 Law, *Conflicts*, op. cit., p. lxxxvii; Bluet's report to the Roman curia is printed on p. 153. See also Dodd, op. cit., p. cxlvi.
9 For the main pamphlets see Law, *Conflicts*, p. cxxviii; G. Jenkins, 'The Archpriest Controversy and the Printers 1601–3', *The Library*, vol. 2, 5th series (1948).
10 J. Bossy, 'Henry IV, the Appellants, and the Jesuits', *Recusant History*, vol. 8, no. 2 (1965).
11 The brief of Pope Clement VIII, of October 1602, is printed in Dodd, op. cit., vol. 3, p. clxxxi.
12 Quoted in Law, *Conflicts*, op. cit., p. cvi.
13 P. L. Hughes and J. F. Larkin, *Tudor Proclamations*, vol. 3 (New Haven, 1964–9), p. 253.
14 Printed in Dodd, op. cit., vol. 3, p. clxxxviii. Summary in A. O. Meyer, *England and the Catholic Church under Queen Elizabeth*, trans. J. R. McKee, 2nd edn (London, 1967), p. 456.
15 J. Hurstfield, *Freedom, Corruption and Government in Elizabethan England* (London, 1973), p. 133.

CHAPTER 13

1 R. B. Manning, *Religion and Society in Elizabethan Sussex* (Leicester, 1969), p. 162.

2 P. R. Harris, 'The reports of William Udall, informer', *Recusant History*, vol. 8 (1965), p. 197.

3 Quoted in C. Devlin, *The Life of Robert Southwell* (London, 1956), p. 243.

4 L. Hotson, *I, William Shakespeare* (London, 1937), p. 170.

5 C. Hill, *Society and Puritanism in Pre-Revolutionary England* (London, 1964), p. 49.

6 Quoted in C. Z. Weiner, 'The beleaguered isle: a study of Elizabethan and early Jacobean anti-Catholicism', *Past and Present*, vol. 51 (May 1971), p. 30.

7 A. Esler, *The Aspiring Mind of the Elizabethan Younger Generation* (Durham, NC, 1966), p. 81.

8 Quoted in Hotson, op. cit., p. 53.

9 A. L. Rowse, *Raleigh and the Throckmortons* (London, 1962), p. 299.

10 D. Knowles, *The Religious Orders in England*, vol. 3 (Cambridge, 1959), p. 212.

11 R. G. Usher, *The Reconstruction of the English Church*, vol. 1 (London, 1910), p. 269; A. G. Dickens, 'The extent and character of recusancy in Yorkshire in 1604', *Yorkshire Archaeological Journal*, vol. 37 (1948).

12 H. Aveling, 'Some aspects of Yorkshire recusancy history', in G. J. Cuming (ed.), *Essays in Church History IV* (Leiden, 1967), p. 324.

13 See E. Rose, *Cases of Conscience* (Cambridge, 1975), p. 111.

14 H. Aveling, 'The Catholic recusants of the West Riding of Yorkshire 1558–1790', *Proceedings of the Leeds Philosophical and Literary Society*, vol. 10, pt 6 (1963), p. 223.

15 Usher, op. cit., p. 240.

16 *Miscellanea*, Lord Burghley's Map of Lancashire 1590, annotated J. Gillow, CRS 4 (1907), pp. 162–222.

17 J. Hurstfield, *Freedom, Corruption, and Government in Elizabethan England* (London, 1973), p. 118.

18 H. Robinson (ed.), *The Zurich Letters*, 2nd series (Cambridge, Parker Society, 1842), p. 321.

19 P. Geyl, *The Revolt of the Netherlands* (London, 1932), p. 227. See also J. Lecler, *Toleration and the Reformation*, trans. by T. L. Westow, vol. 2 (London, 1960), pp. 253–5.

20 H. Aveling, *Northern Catholics: The Catholic Recusants of the North Riding of Yorkshire 1558–1790* (London, 1966), p. 200.

21 A. J. Loomie, *The Spanish Elizabethans: The English Exiles at the Court of Philip II* (New York, 1963), p. 82.

Index

BX
1492
M57
1978

222118

DATE DUE

MAY 10 79			
MAY 18 79			
MAY 10 1984			
APR 18 1990			

WHEATON COLLEGE LIBRARY
NORTON, MASS. 02766

DEMCO